The 9/11 Novel

The 9/11 Novel
Trauma, Politics and Identity

ARIN KEEBLE

McFarland & Company, Inc., Publishers
Jefferson, North Carolina

A version of Chapter Three originally appeared in *Modern Language Review*, 106:2. A version of Chapter Six originally appeared in *European Journal of American Culture*, 31.1.

LIBRARY OF CONGRESS CATALOGUING-IN-PUBLICATION DATA

Keeble, Arin, 1977– author.
 The 9/11 Novel : Trauma, Politics and Identity / Arin Keeble.
  p.   cm.
 Includes bibliographical references and index.

  ISBN 978-0-7864-7834-7 (softcover : acid free paper) ∞
  ISBN 978-1-4766-1562-2 (ebook)

  1. American fiction—21st century—History and criticism.
 2. September 11 Terrorist Attacks, 2001, in literature.
 3. Terrorism in literature. 4. September 11 Terrorist Attacks, 2001—Influence. I. Title.
 PS374.S445K44 2014
 813'.6093587393—dc23   2014015855

BRITISH LIBRARY CATALOGUING DATA ARE AVAILABLE

© 2014 Arin Keeble. All rights reserved

No part of this book may be reproduced or transmitted in any form or by any means, electronic or mechanical, including photocopying or recording, or by any information storage and retrieval system, without permission in writing from the publisher.

On the cover: New York City Fire Department during the aftermath of the September 11th terrorist attack (unattributed 9/11 photograph collection, Library of Congress)

Printed in the United States of America

McFarland & Company, Inc., Publishers
 Box 611, Jefferson, North Carolina 28640
  www.mcfarlandpub.com

For Holli

Acknowledgments

I'd like to thank the School of English Literature, Languages and Linguistics and Faculty of Humanities and Social Sciences at Newcastle University and the English Department at Bishop Grosseteste University for their institutional support. I am also indebted to the *Modern Language Review* and *European Journal of American Cultures* for their permission to reprint parts of chapters three and six. I'd also like to thank several individuals who have inspired me during the writing of this book, people who research and write for all the right reasons, and who I've modeled my own work after: the poet and my dear friend Toby Martinez de las Rivas; my mentor James Annesley; and the outstanding scholars John Beck, John Batchelor, Sam Thomas, Craig Hankin, Simon James, Neelam Srivastava, Pablo Mukherjee, Jon Begley, David Holloway, Rebecca Gill, Ellen Turner and Ivan Stacy. I would also like to thank my colleagues at Changing Lives for the amazing work the organization does with homeless, vulnerable and socially excluded people, and for providing a much needed counterpoint to my academic work.

Table of Contents

Acknowledgments vi
Preface 1
Introduction: A Conflicted Homeland 3

ONE	"The New Normal" in Art Spiegelman's *In the Shadow of No Towers*	17
TWO	*Windows on the World* and *Extremely Loud and Incredibly Close*: A Crisis in Representation?	40
THREE	Marriage, Relationships and 9/11: The Seismographic Narratives of *Falling Man, The Good Life* and *The Emperor's Children*	69
FOUR	*The Road*: Disaster, Allegory and the Exhaustion of the Early 9/11 Novel	92
FIVE	First World National Allegory and Otherness in *The Reluctant Fundamentalist*	115
SIX	*Netherland* and 9/11 Meta-Fiction	139
SEVEN	The Multidirectional Memorialization of 9/11 in Amy Waldman's *The Submission*	165

Conclusion 188
Notes 195
Bibliography 197
Index 205

Preface

In 2001 I was studying literature at Newcastle, keeping homesickness at bay by immersing myself in the discovery of fiction and film and enjoying being a young man studying English in the UK, where I still live. As it did to many others, 9/11 disoriented me in more ways than one. Almost simultaneously I felt a stirring pang of patriotism, magnified, perhaps, by my position as an expatriate American, and an impending sense of fear at the possibility of war and retribution and the aggression of the George W. Bush administration. Reflecting on this time now, it is clear to me that 9/11 politicized me. As I developed a worldview and continued to study literature as a postgraduate, the way literature negotiates the intersection between the personal and political has made its way to the heart of my intellectual interests. This book represents years of research on the literary and cultural response to 9/11 and builds on an excellent body of existing work in 9/11 studies and the literary representation of 9/11.

The lively debates featured at three excellent conferences, *Before and After 9/11* (Leicester University, UK, 2009), *Screens of Terror* (University of East London, UK, 2010) and *The Depoliticization of 9/11,* which featured an inspiring keynote talk from David Holloway (Newcastle University, UK, 2010), were instrumental to the development of my research. I am also greatly indebted to Holloway's outstanding monograph *9/11 and the War on Terror* (2008), which provides an excellent outline of the way the attacks have been processed and represented in literature, cinema, television, media, politics and history, and to Amina Yaqin and Peter Morey's culmination of the Framing Muslims project, *Framing Muslims: Stereotyping and Representation After 9/11* (2011), which is another landmark in 9/11 studies and an important intervention. Excellent edited collections of essays, Ann Keniston and Jeanne Follansbee-Quinn's *Literature After 9/11* (2007) and Victoria Bragard, Chris Dony and Warren Rosenberg's *Portraying 9/11* (2011), have provided multifaceted approaches to the literary response to 9/11 that have enriched the field. Kristiaan Versluys has produced the definitive study of "trauma" in 9/11 literature, *Out of the Blue* (2009), and almost in opposition to this is Richard Gray's *After the Fall* (2011), a trenchant survey of literature after 9/11. In these and in many of the other articles on the literature of 9/11, from scholars such as Michael Rothberg, Bruce Marzec and Catherine Morley, an increasingly polarized debate has emerged between a body of work that has focused on the representation of trauma and the domestic, and another, which has been critical of the domestic turn in 9/11 fiction and called for literary engagement with a series of political or international imperatives.

Hopefully, my book distinguishes itself by turning this critical debate back on to the novels themselves and locating a complex and nuanced conflictedness that exists throughout the canon of 9/11 fiction. Additionally, while the work mentioned above has variously addressed "literature after 9/11" in all of its different forms, or focused on other particular areas of representation—trauma or "otherness," for example—this is the first monograph that provides a comprehensive account of the first decade of the "9/11 novel," and examines the conflicts, divisions and tensions within these novels chronologically. Lastly, this book locates Hurricane Katrina as a key cultural moment which alters the course of 9/11 fiction.

Introduction:
A Conflicted Homeland

Showtime's popular and critically acclaimed television program *Homeland* (2011–) has gone some way toward returning 9/11 to the center of popular debate and discussion about American foreign policy, surveillance, national security, the War on Terror and the wars in Afghanistan and Iraq. The lives of the program's two central protagonists (or antagonists) are and continue to be shaped by events set in motion by 9/11 throughout the narrative. Carrie, a CIA anti-terrorist operative, is haunted by her perceived failure to prevent the 9/11 attacks. Nicholas Brody, an American soldier who was presumed dead in Iraq in 2003, is found in an Al-Qaeda prison eight years later and returned to his family. The intersection of these two characters occurs immediately when Carrie begins to suspect that Brody may have been "turned" by Al-Qaeda. This conceit sets in motion what is essentially a political thriller, and in addition to being popular with audiences, reviewers have lauded the program's formal qualities and suspenseful narrative, which features some kind of "cliff-hanger" in nearly every episode. Critics have also been generally positive about the politics of *Homeland*, in particular its criticism of revanchist American military aggression. Lorrie Moore argues that it carries an even more specific rhetoric: "*Homeland* can be viewed as a criticism not just of cyclical revenge in general but of the American drone program in particular" (Moore 2013: n.p.). The drone program is certainly instrumental as a plot device, and *Homeland* deploys an impressive literary flourish in the tenth episode of the second season, "Broken Hearts," when Brody facilitates the killing of Vice President Walden by enabling a co-conspirator to remotely adjust his pacemaker. This echoes the remote killings of the drone program and evokes the critical event of the back-story, a drone strike ordered by the vice president, which hits a school in Lebanon and kills the child Issa, who Brody had become attached to during his time in captivity.

Another key area of critical discussion and debate around *Homeland* is its representation of Islam. Despite the program's criticism of American foreign policy, it has struggled to adequately represent Islam, frequently reverting to the practice of "framing" that Amina Yaqin and Peter Morey describe in *Framing Muslims: Stereotyping and Representation After 9/11* (2011) as "the restricted, limited ways that Muslims are stereotyped and 'framed' within the political, cultural and media discourses of the West" (Yaqin and Morey 2011: 2). In *Homeland*'s defense, many of its champions have pointed to the sympathetic portrayal of Brody's conversion to Islam, as well as, again, its explicitly critical portrayal of U.S. foreign policy. Nevertheless, there are no moderate Muslim characters, and critics like Laila Al Arian have argued that it is guilty of "conflating the goals and intentions of various Arab, Middle Eastern and Islamist groups from Al-Qaeda to Hezbollah, without providing any context about their backgrounds or motivations" (Al Arian 2012: n.p.).

However, while *Homeland* has been phenomenally popular with audiences in the U.S. and Europe, bringing 9/11 sharply back into the focus of the public imagination, and despite the generally favorable reviews and its prescience to contemporary debates about the representation of Islam, there is one central part of the program that has not been critically assessed in any detail. At the heart of *Homeland* is a stark and resonant conflictedness in the portrayal of the two central protagonists, who mirror and reflect each other in many ways. This conflictedness relates to Brody and Carrie's respective political orientations and identities, and in both cases it is traced back to the rupture of 9/11. The divided or fragmented identities of Brody and Carrie are integral to the wider appeal of the program as the fundamental tension of the narrative revolves around the audience's understanding of their motives and beliefs. Both characters experience great inner turmoil: Brody is caught in a complex web of emotions and loyalties between his love for his family, his love for his country, his growing affection for Carrie, his religious beliefs and his loyalty to the terrorist Abu Nazir, who is the father of the slain Issa. Carrie's inner conflicts and struggles parallel Brody's with the added dimension of her being clinically bipolar. Throughout the series she is torn between a quiet family life and her political imperatives, which are further complicated by her eventual romantic entanglement with "the enemy." Crucially, both characters are forced to articulate criticisms of the U.S. and its policies out of a fundamental patriotism and belief in core American values, and both struggle to reconcile traumatic memories with their political priorities. When Carrie reproaches Brody in the fifth episode of the second season, "Q &A," their interlinked internal struggles are evident:

> Because of you, I questioned my own sanity, I had myself admitted to a mental institution. I lost my job, too. I lost my place in the world. I lost everything.... It was hearing Dana's voice that changed your mind, wasn't it? Maybe because you suddenly understood that killing yourself and ruining Dana's life wouldn't bring Issa back. Maybe because you knew then how much you loved your own child. Maybe because you were just sick of death. That's the Brody I'm talking to. That's the Brody that knows the difference between warfare and terrorism.

This drama takes place within exceptional circumstances, but it is clear that Brody and Carrie's deeply divided selves reflect wider American or Western divisions, illuminated or brought to the surface by 9/11. Is this not what truly ties *Homeland* to its 9/11 context, this powerful portrayal of inner conflict in the realms of politics, domestic life and identity—including Western society and culture's continued struggle to understand the "other?" Furthermore, is *Homeland* not evidence that these concerns remain unresolved?

The 9/11 Novel

This sense of conflictedness that pervades *Homeland* finds its fullest expression in the growing and evolving corpus of what has come to be called the "9/11 novel" or "9/11 fiction." This is not to suggest that there is a selection of exceptional novels that are each uniquely able to articulate certain aspects of this conflictedness, but rather that the corpus of novels as artifacts have cumulatively much to say about the nuances and patterns of the wider Western response to 9/11. For instance, what does the early tendency to employ visual and typographical gimmickry or the preoccupation with marriage and relationships tell us? Similarly, what does the more recent trend toward meta-fiction reveal? These novels may have as much to say in their limitations or omissions as in the subjects that they cover. Nevertheless, it is the novel form that allows for in-depth textual analysis of this conflictedness. The importance of the formal qualities of the novel, in facilitating this representation of conflictedness, lay simply in its capacity for long-form narrative. Cinema, theater, and serial television programs such as *Homeland* also have the narrative space for more nuanced depictions of the attacks, and instances of these will be called upon in the coming chapters for comparative analysis; in particular we will look at Paul Greengrass' *United 93* (2006) and Oliver Stone's *World Trade Center* (2006) in Chapter Four, and Spike Lee's *25th Hour* (2002) in Chapter Five. It is undoubtedly the novel, however, that has the most capacity to attempt, at least, to both internalize and contextualize traumatic or catastrophic events.

What is equally important to this idea of narrative capacity, in establishing the significance of the 9/11 novel, is a consideration of the phenomenal anticipation that quickly built for the literary representation of 9/11: these novels were written under the pressure of an expectation that literature would provide answers and give meaning to a newly uncertain world. Much of this anticipation was built around a series of newspaper and magazine articles composed by some of the world's most celebrated literary authors in the first months after the attacks. One of these articles was Don DeLillo's "In the Ruins of the Future," an essay which first appeared in December 2001 in *Harper's* and the *Guardian*. DeLillo points explicitly to the 9/11 novels to come in describing how "the writer" begins to approach 9/11: "The writer begins in the towers, trying to imagine the moment, desperately. Before politics, before history and religion, there is the primal terror" (DeLillo 2001: n.p.). DeLillo's essay also evokes the popular idea of the individual "stories" of 9/11 (a conceit embodied by the *New York Times*' popular "Portraits of Grief" series) and steadily constructs the idea of a "counternarrative."[1]

> The Bush administration was feeling a nostalgia for the cold war. This is over now. Many things are over. The narrative ends in the rubble and it is left to us to create the counternarrative. There are 100,000 stories crisscrossing New York, Washington, and the world. Where we were, who we know, what we've seen or heard. There are the doctors' appointments that

saved lives, the cellphones that were used to report the hijackings. Stories generating others and people running north out of the rumbling smoke and ash. Men running in suits and ties, women who'd lost their shoes, cops running from the skydive of all that towering steel. People running for their lives are part of the story that is left to us [DeLillo 2001: n.p.].

The promise, pregnant in such passages, is that literary fiction will provide this "counternarrative" and tell these "stories." DeLillo's essay was one of the more high-profile instances of a widespread initial literary response, including short pieces in magazines like the *New Yorker* and multicontributor collections such as Ulrich Baer's *110 Stories* (2002), which seemed to point toward the long-form narratives to come. Looking retrospectively at this initial literary response, however, the difficulty of an appropriate register, style and tone in representing 9/11 is clear, and these short pieces anticipate the conflictedness of the novels. This is partly due to the fact that, as Alex Houen points out, fiction was not what these authors were producing or being asked to produce:

> Call in the novelists: This was the response of many newspapers in the immediate aftermath of September 11. Call in the novelists—experts at imagining the unimaginable, the masters of other worlds of possibility. What was remarkable about the novelists' newspaper articles, though, was that fiction is precisely what they were not being asked to produce [Houen 2004: 419].

So while this early wave of literary "responses" to 9/11 built anticipation for the novels to come, it also revealed a discomfort with the idea of "fiction," and much of this initial literary response was essayistic or narrative non-fiction. "Real life" stories or reflections on real events were the dominant mode and almost none of the initial writings could be classified as "fiction." John Updike's *New Yorker* piece is a typical example. Updike describes how he "watched from the Brooklyn building's roof as the south tower dropped from the screen of our viewing.... We knew we had just witnessed thousands of deaths; we clung to each other as if we ourselves were falling" (Updike 2001: n.p.). This poetic rendering of real experience certainly was preferred to "fiction," which was felt by many authors to be inappropriate. Jay McInerney was explicit about his post–9/11 discomfort with fiction, reflecting on the conception of *The Good Life* (2005):

Introduction

> Most novelists I know went through a period of intense self-examination and self-loathing after the terrorist attacks on the World Trade Center. I certainly did. For a while the idea of "invented characters" and alternate realities seemed trivial and frivolous and suddenly, horribly outdated [McInerney 2005: n.p.].

This uneasiness with the process of writing the 9/11 novel was widely noted and itself anticipates the conflictedness of the novels. The central argument of this book is that by examining a representative group of these 9/11 novels, a group of texts that both reflects and represents a divided response to the attacks, we can engage with and begin to unpack some of the complexities, conflicts and tensions that mainstream news media and the official government response attempted to unify and simplify; in this sense the first decade of 9/11 novels does truly provide a "counternarrative." Additionally, as it operates (for the most part) chronologically, we can see how this response evolves and develops over the first decade of 9/11 fiction, from Art Spiegelman's early graphic novel *In the Shadow of No Towers* (2003) to Amy Waldman's recent novel *The Submission* (2011).

One way in which we can begin to map out this conflictedness is through the paradigm of "continuity and discontinuity." This paradigm has been mistakenly characterized as an opposition of politics and trauma, and while this is a reductive binary, it is a useful starting point. Trauma and trauma theory were among the first frameworks deployed in trying to understand the attacks, and this has certainly been a dominant interpretive mode in examining 9/11 fiction. For example, in *Out of the Blue* (2009), Kristiaan Versluys states that "in the instantaneity of its horror and in its far-flung repercussions, 9/11 is unpossessable. It is a limit event that shatters the symbolic resources of the culture and defeats the normal processes of meaning making and semiosis" (Versluys 2009: 1). Versluys goes on to support this claim by citing numerous other theoreticians of trauma who have posited similar interpretations. But while Versluys sees complete rupture, in *9/11 and the War on Terror*, David Holloway sees narrative: "9/11 was long in the making, and the pre–9/11 and post–9/11 worlds were broadly continuous not discontinuous, however much it suited politicians to claim that the attacks came out of the blue" (Holloway 2008: 3–4). These two statements constitute a canny articulation of what has become an increasingly polarized debate between the perceived importance of honoring the trauma and rupture of the attacks, and a series of political imperatives, though this disorienting division has existed since the day of the attacks. President Bush himself delivered a conflicted message in the days and weeks after 9/11, stating, "All of this was brought upon us in a single day—and night fell on a different world, a world where freedom itself is under attack," while also repeatedly encouraging citizens to get on with normal life and to invest in the American economy, something that President Bush repeatedly urged Americans to do (Bush 2001: n.p.).[2]

As stated, the following chapters will work (loosely) chronologically, and it is tempting to try and locate a movement from discontinuity to continuity as the canon evolves. Ann Keniston and Jeanne Follansbee Quinn suggest precisely this in the introduction to their excellent edited collection *Literature After 9/11* (2007)—that there is a *"transition* from narratives of rupture to narratives of continuity" (Keniston and Quinn 2007: 5). This is qualified with the suggestion that earlier novels, such as Frédéric Beigbeder's *Windows on the World* (2004), simply "grapple with representing 9/11," while later novels, such as Don DeLillo's *Falling Man* (2007), "grapple with more complex representational challenges"—what they describe as "the reverberations of 9/11" (Keniston and Quinn 2008: 5). However, this notion of a transition can be reductive as earlier novels such as *Windows on the World* and Jonathan Safran Foer's *Extremely Loud and Incredibly Close* (2005) are not simply focused on rupture. While many criticisms have been leveled at both of these texts, they have also been repeatedly cited as operating "trans-national" narratives that at least gesture toward history and context (Birgit Däwes 2007: 517). *Falling Man*, on the other hand, as well as many of the novels that appeared after *Windows on the World* and *Extremely Loud and Incredibly Close*, have come under much scrutiny for their circumscribed domestic settings. This book defines the paradigm as a series of conflicts and tensions in the politics, representations of identity, and engagements with individual and collective trauma. These conflicts and tensions are manifest throughout the first decade of 9/11 fiction, and while I argue against the idea of a transition from "rupture to continuity," this book will demonstrate that there is a movement toward points of dialectical reconciliation in later texts that attempt to find narrative space to explore both rupture and continuity.

Introduction

As stated, this opposition between trauma and politics is a simplistic or reductive binary. Trauma itself is a conflicted or unstable phenomenon with its own binaries. Judith Herman establishes this in *Trauma and Recovery* (1992): "The conflict between the will to deny horrible events and the will to proclaim them aloud is the central dialectic of psychological trauma" (Herman 1992: 1). Extending from this, and despite usually being characterized as something that indicates complete rupture, Cathy Caruth identifies trauma as being fundamentally continuous while also being connected to a singular event: "The event is not assimilated or experienced fully at the time, but only belatedly, in its repeated possession of the one who experiences it" (Caruth 1995: 5). Furthermore, private or individual trauma is often distinct from or in dialogue with "collective trauma," and trauma isn't necessarily tied to ideas of rupture or discontinuity. Michael Rothberg's observation that "the structures of individual and collective memory are multidirectional" and "difficult to contain in the molds of exclusivist identities" is particularly resonant in regards to 9/11 as the official government response certainly tried to map America's grief on to a particular agenda (Rothberg 2009: 19). This book locates trauma in this corpus of 9/11 novels as an inherently unstable phenomenon that can relate to both a singular moment and a larger timespan.

The paradigm of continuity and discontinuity also extends to historical understandings of the attacks. The discursive lurch from 9/11 to the War on Terror, and wars in Afghanistan and Iraq, was justified and rationalized by the idea of complete rupture, that everything had changed. As Holloway notes, this notion was the "ideological lynchpin" for the "Bush Doctrine," the preemptive military aggression and intense national securitization introduced through policy, and particularly the National Security Strategy of 2002.[3] Bizarrely, though, the Bush Doctrine's aesthetic qualities were comprehensively nostalgic, explicitly evoking the past rather than breaking from it. As James Der Derian states, 9/11 was mostly presented in the "sepia tones of the Second World War" (Der Derian 2002: 178). This tension between nostalgia and the rhetoric of rupture became another key conflict in the aftermath of 9/11. There was a simultaneous declaration of a new world order and retreat into the past. Susan Faludi has offered one of the most comprehensive accounts of post–9/11 nostalgia, questioning the logic of this turn: "Why were our political and cultural stages suddenly packed with Lone Ranger leaders, Davy Crockett candidates, and John Wayne manly men ... why, in short, when confronted with an actual danger, did America call rewrite?" (Faludi 2008: 199).

The Cultural Politics of the 9/11 Novel

The "central dialectic of trauma," and the tension between nostalgia and the rhetoric of rupture, are just two of a series of binaries that characterized the political and social backdrop of the 9/11 novel. Nevertheless, the particular aspects of society that the 9/11 novel "ought" to be engaging with has become the key tenet of the criticism of these texts. Critical debates over the 9/11 novel have proliferated in recent years, and one of the distinctions of this book is that it aims to turn an increasingly polarized dialogue about what constitutes a "successful" rendering of 9/11 and its political and social aftermath back onto the texts themselves. Rather than delivering a series of value judgments about what is and is not acceptable for the 9/11 novel, or which texts have been "successful," the aim here is to demonstrate how this critical evaluation is actually a clear reflection of the conflicts and tensions evident in a larger corpus of 9/11 novels. With this in mind, it is necessary to examine the critical debate around the 9/11 novel before turning to the texts themselves.

One of the early fears regarding the artistic and critical emphasis on trauma after 9/11 was that it would depoliticize the attacks. Michael Rothberg addressed this concern as early as 2003 in his suggestion that trauma as an interpretive framework might lend itself to the conservative political and media strategies looking for manageable ways of explaining and understanding the attacks:

> Most disturbing would be the possibility that a focus on trauma solely as a structure of reception might ... actually end up unwittingly reinforcing the repressive liberal-conservative consensus in the United States that attempting to explain the events amounts to explaining them away or excusing them [Rothberg 2003: 151].

That 9/11 has in fact been depoliticized by its literary response and representation is an argument that has been repeatedly made and fiercely contested. There is no doubt, though, that some of the most high-profile examples of 9/11 fiction, particularly the novels that were released, conceived of, or written before Hurricane Katrina, focus on the American domestic and on traumatized individuals, families and couples. In one of the first overviews of 9/11 fiction, "The End of Innocence," Pankaj Mishra, actually discussing Ken Kalfus' 9/11 novel *A Disorder Peculiar to the Country* (2006), expresses his frustration at this trend: "Are we really meant to think of domestic discord, also deployed by DeLillo and McInerney, as a metaphor for post–9/11 America?" (Mishra 2007: 2). Mishra's argument was developed by both Richard Gray and Michael Rothberg in a special issue of *The Journal of American Literary History.* In "Open Doors, Closed Minds: American Prose Writing at a Time of Crisis," Gray cites Don DeLillo's *Falling Man* (2007), Jay McInerney's *The Good Life* (2005), Ken Kalfus' *A Disorder Peculiar to the Country* (2006), and Claire Messud's *The Emperor's Children* (2006) in his prognosis that the early 9/11 novel "simply assimilate[s] the unfamiliar into familiar structures. The crisis is in every sense of the word domesticated" (Gray 2009: 134). Gray goes on to develop his criticism of these texts in the first chapter of his subsequent book, *After the Fall: American Literature Since 9/11* (2011). Michael Rothberg, in responding to Gray's article, develops Gray's critical analysis of the early 9/11 novels and calls for a "fiction of international relations and extraterritorial citizenship" (Rothberg 2009: 150). Rothberg cites a more recent 9/11 novel, Joseph O'Neil's *Netherland* (2009), as a text that begins to undertake this project. As stated, the failures that Gray, Rothberg and Mishra perceive to be inherent in the domestication and depoliticization of 9/11 by its literary representation is a concept that is contested. John Duvall and Robert Marzec, in their introduction to a special issue of *Modern Fiction Studies,* take issue with this position: "Gray and Rothberg are both unwilling to look very closely at what 9/11 fiction sets out to do because they are both sure that they know what 9/11 fiction ought to be doing" (Duvall and Marzec 2011: 384). The key tenet of their argument, which Duvall further develops in his contribution to *The Cambridge Companion to American Literature After 1945* (2011), is that political traumas have historically been dealt with in domestic settings:

> If one retrospectively applied their [Gray, Rothberg and Mishra] perspective to fiction after World War I, one might be forced to say that Virginia Woolf's *Mrs. Dalloway* and Ernest Hemingway's *The Sun Also Rises* are

failures for their oblique treatment of the root cause of a historical trauma, since Woolf's Septimus Smith and Hemingway's Jake Barnes only imagine the private traumas of war veterans [Duvall and Marzec 2011: 384].

September 11 and World War I have vastly different social and political contexts, and this is surely a problematic comparison. What Duvall and Marzec do effectively here, though, is interrogate the suggestion that the 9/11 novel is obliged to employ some kind of international or political panorama. Catherine Morley has also raised explicit concerns regarding the expectations and demands issued by Mishra, Gray and Rothberg:

> Perhaps most troubling is the suggestion that fiction is no more than a political tool, through which writers can understand (and educate readers about) the United States' place in the world. Of course fiction certainly can play precisely this role, but one of the joys of fiction is that its power goes well beyond the narrowly political [Morley 2011: 721].

Mishra, Gray and Rothberg make valuable interventions into what is an undeniably insular body of work, while Duvall, Marzec and Morley balance their insistence on international or political imperatives by rightly reminding us that a work of fiction is not obliged to be political. The aim of this book, as stated, is to reflect back on the first decade of 9/11 fiction, projecting this polarized debate back onto the text themselves. It locates this tension between political, international or transnational agendas, and the rhetoric of trauma and rupture in the novels, and uses this as a starting point to map out a complex and nuanced conflictedness in this group of texts. Rather than diagnosing the problems of the 9/11 novel, this book aims to consider what these problems have to tell us about the way the West has responded to and absorbed 9/11, and the way this response has evolved.

An Evolving Canon

Another key facet of the argument presented here is that in the first decade of the 9/11 novel we can identify three distinct phases, and that Hurricane Katrina marks an important turning point in the politics of the 9/11 novel. The continuity in these three stages is provided by the thematic concerns for the idea of "rupture," the fraught relationship with the politics of 9/11 and the preoccupation with identity—particularly the location of individual grief or trauma within the larger collective or public trauma of 9/11. The first phase, explored here in chapters on Art Spiegelman's graphic novel *In the Shadow of No Towers* and another on Frédéric Beigbeder's *Windows on the World* and Jonathan Safran Foer's *Extremely Loud and Incredibly Close*, was marked by unorthodox formal qualities and strained efforts to balance references to history and individual trauma. Chapter One, "'The New Normal' in Art Spiegelman's *In the Shadow of No Towers*," argues that Spiegelman's graphic text remains the most dissenting and overtly political 9/11 text, but that its politicized rhetoric is muted and mitigated by a powerful visual and inter-textual emphasis on individual trauma. Chapter Two, "*Windows on the World* and *Extremely Loud and Incredibly Close*: A Crisis in Representation?" argues that rather than indicating a crisis in representation through their postmodern or meta-fictional aesthetics, the real crisis in these novels lies in a fundamental narrative tension between the transnational or historical components, which are prominent parts of the texts, and a rhetoric of rupture trauma.

The second section examines novels that appeared in the period 2005–2007, and discusses the texts that have been the primary focus of critics like Gray, Rothberg and Mishra. Chapter Three, "Marriage, Relationships and 9/11: The Seismographic Narratives of *Falling Man*, *The Good Life* and *The Emperor's Children*," argues that while these texts certainly do domesticate 9/11, there is an underlying, "seismographic" suggestion of a return to normality in the way the narratives conclude with a restoration of equilibrium. Chapter Four, "*The Road*: Disaster, Allegory and the Exhaustion of the Early 9/11 Novel," argues that Cormac McCarthy's post-apocalyptic novel is best understood as a conservative, messianic allegory that exhausts a cycle of novels that approach 9/11 indirectly. It locates Hurricane Katrina as a key context for the novel and argues that the vision of apocalypse in *The Road* simultaneously speaks to the images of a devastated, flood-wracked New Orleans, and exhausts the possibility of approaching crisis and disaster indirectly in the 9/11 novel. This chapter concludes with a reading of Dave Eggers' Hurricane Katrina narrative *Zeitoun* (2009) as a response to this aspect of *The Road* and to the 9/11 novel in general.

In the closing pages of *9/11 Culture* (2009), Jeffrey Melnick states, "It seems possible that the pivotal moment for our study of 9/11 art will turn out to have been the moment of the next American tragedy, Hurricane Katrina's devastation of New Orleans and other sites on the Gulf Coast and the abandonment of the region and its people by the United States federal government" (Melnick 2009: 157). This book takes precisely this position and demonstrates this in its final section, with chapters that examine the most directly political 9/11 novels, Mohsin Hamid's *The Reluctant Fundamentalist* (2007), Joseph O'Neil's *Netherland* (2008), and, more recently, Amy Waldman's *The Submission* (2011). One might rightly point out here that some of the novels discussed in previous chapters, particularly *Falling Man*, were published long after Hurricane Katrina and the flooding of New Orleans, and while this is undeniably true, according to DeLillo (in a rare interview for *Die Ziet*), *Falling Man* was begun in 2004, and its emphasis on relationships and private traumas anchors it to what I will identify as pre–Katrina themes and conceits. *The Reluctant Fundamentalist* and *Netherland* cultivate and capture the politicized mood of dissent that began with Hurricane Katrina and focus it back on 9/11. These final chapters continue to locate the tensions and conflictedness of the texts, but also begin to identify points of reconciliation where narrative strands of "continuity" and "discontinuity" coexist more comfortably. Chapter Five, "First World National Allegory and Otherness in *The Reluctant Fundamentalist*," argues that Hamid's novel constructs a complex and conflicted first-world national allegory that provocatively suggests that America's response to 9/11 reveals pre-existing, unresolved issues. Furthermore, it demonstrates that this national allegory only functions through the novel's unique "dual perspective." Chapter Six, "*Netherland* and 9/11 Meta-Fiction," identifies O'Neil's novel as the first "self-conscious" 9/11 novel and argues that this aspect of the text allows it to open up narrative space for a sector of American society that had previously not been represented in 9/11 fiction. More importantly, *Netherland* offers a powerful portrayal of the intersections of private and public traumas while remaining engaged politically. While *Netherland*'s meta-fiction comes in the way it is responding to and aware of tropes and trends of the 9/11 novel, Amy Waldman's *The Submission* deploys a different kind of meta-fiction. *The Submission*'s subject is the problematic process of memorializing 9/11, and so the reader is constantly aware that the novel's task (which is also to remember 9/11) is co-extensive with its subject. Chapter Seven, "The Multidirectional Memorialization of 9/11 in Amy Waldman's *The Submission*," argues that Waldman's novel works against the unilateralism of the Bush Doctrine, and attempts to reanimate some of the nuance, complexity and conflictedness that was overshadowed by Manichaeism and clash-of-civilizations discourse.

ONE

"The New Normal" in Art Spiegelman's *In the Shadow of No Towers*

"The new normal" is one of many memorable and often-quoted coinages in *In the Shadow of No Towers* that suggests a changed cultural condition in the wake of rupture or trauma. Indeed, out of the growing corpus of 9/11 literary texts, Spiegelman's early graphic novel is unique in the way that it explicitly discusses the traumatic experience of 9/11, exhibits an awareness of trauma theory, and features a narrator/protagonist who self-diagnoses PTSD. Consequently, *In the Shadow of No Towers* has accrued a substantial amount of critical attention centering on the narrator/protagonist's experience of trauma and the ways in which the unique form and presentation of the text handles this aspect of the narrative. For example, trauma and trauma theory are the primary rubrics used in Kristiaan Versluys's "Art Spiegelman's *In The Shadow of No Towers* and the Representation of Trauma" (2006), Karen Esperitu's "'Putting Grief into Boxes': Trauma and the Crisis of Democracy in Art Spiegelman's *In the Shadow of No Towers*" (2004), Richard Glejzer's "Art Spiegelman and the Persistence of Trauma" (2007), Mitchum Huehls's "Foer, Spiegelman, and 9/11's Timely Traumas"(2007) and also Jordan Rendell Smith's "9/11 Tragicomix: Allegories of National Trauma in Art Spiegelman's *In the Shadow of No Towers*" (2008). These essays all explore ways in which Spiegelman's representation of personal trauma coexists with a narrative of political dissent and satire; though the emphasis remains rooted in discussions of personal trauma, and the political aspect of the text is generally characterized as either a mechanism for the "working through" of this trauma or something that is arrived at through the experience of trauma. For example, Versluys describes the way *In the Shadow of No Towers* shows us how "mourning leaves the strictly private realm and acquires a public dimension," charting a journey from private trauma to public dissent (Versluys 2006: 982). This actually follows the lead of Spiegelman's introduction, in which he describes the experience of "reeling on the fault line where World History and Personal History collide" (Spiegelman 2004: n.p.). This chapter, however, argues that rather than representing an awakening or the working-through of trauma, the politics of Spiegelman's text are most usefully identified as part of a larger paradigmatic tension that sees the rhetoric of rupture and discontinuity pressing against a historicist impulse and political imperative. For Spiegelman, I argue, the "new normal" is not simply a state of individual or collective trauma, but a state of conflictedness where political discourse and traumatic memory do not sit comfortably together, creating the sense of disorientation that is at the heart of the text.

Spiegelman's graphic narrative has three strands, one telling the story of his and his family's frantic experience of 9/11 in Lower Manhattan, another telling the story of the narrator/protagonist's experience of making the graphic plates (which were originally published serially one plate at a time) in the months and years after the attacks, and a final strand that tells a story of unilateral American politics and foreign policy before and after 9/11. Rather than isolating these strands, or attempting to identify a transformation from trauma to dissent, what follows will show how these elements of the narrative are entangled, how Spiegelman's personal trauma is itself rooted in a politicized continuity narrative, and how the socially conscious and politicized narrative doesn't simply emerge from the personal trauma of 9/11 but corresponds to it throughout the text. The "new normal," as dramatized in *In the Shadow of No Towers,* is both an individual and collective social condition characterized by the disorienting need to mourn and work-through while thinking and acting politically. The narrator/protagonist's struggle to reconcile this collision between "world history and personal history" in *In the Shadow of No Towers* remains one of the most vivid representations of post–9/11 disorientation. This chapter will interrogate the meanings and implications of "the new normal," mapping out the tensions and conflicts that operate within its three entangled narrative strands.

Spiegelman and the Dialectics of Trauma

In the dominant paradigm of 9/11 fiction, the dialectical tension between narratives of "continuity" and "discontinuity," trauma generally relates to discontinuity. Nevertheless, the dialectical conflict within the discourse of trauma itself can be mapped onto this larger paradigm. As we have seen, Judith Herman characterizes this as a tension between the need for articulation and the inexpressible: "The conflict between the will to deny horrible events and the will to proclaim them aloud is the central dialectic of psychological trauma" (Herman 1992: 1). This can be extended, though, from the problems of the articulation or expression of trauma to the representation. Trauma is usually understood to involve a "limit event" or violent rupture which changes the lives of the victims irrevocably, an experience so unhinging that it is unknowable and therefore un-representable. Also, though, trauma is understood as an event which possesses or haunts an individual, recurring psychologically over months or years in aggregate, reigniting previous traumas or bringing to the surface repressed emotions. As Huehls states, "Trauma is thus not of a moment, but instead spans an individual's temporal continuum, constituting her past, present, and future" (Huehls 2008: 42). The "central dialectic of trauma," which we can identify in both the experience and representation of trauma, is certainly evident in *In the Shadow of No Towers* and constitutes an important layer of the text's conflictedness.

From the first plates, Spiegelman repeatedly displays an awareness not only of the discourses of trauma and trauma studies, which have surrounded his Pulitzer-winning *Maus* narratives *My Father Bleeds History* (1986) and *And Here My Troubles Began* (1991), both celebrated Holocaust narratives, but also of the variations and limits of this discourse. The top panel of the second plate directly illustrates this, offering one of many examples of the text's dramatization of the relationship between personal and public in its account of post–9/11. The narrator/protagonist is drawn with a bald eagle in an "Uncle Sam" hat hung in a noose around his neck, suggesting enforced nationalism or patriotism. He states: "I insist the sky is falling; they roll their eyes and tell me it's only my Post-Traumatic Stress Disorder. That's when Time stands still at the moment of trauma ... which strikes me as a totally reasonable response to current events!" (Spiegelman 2004: 2). Simultaneously, however, while the narrator/protagonist agonizes over a sensation which is at once a compulsion to "retell the calamities of September 11 to anyone who will listen" and also a "moment when time stands still," the eagle squawks expressions which illustrate the nature of much of the post–9/11 media and government rhetoric. In one frame the eagle exclaims, "Everything's changed! Awk!" and in another, "Go out and shop! Awk!" (Spiegelman 2004: 2). In this single frame Spiegelman shows the conflictedness of trauma and also the paradoxical aspect of the political messages emanating from the White House after 9/11.[4] Not only is Spiegelman lampooning the conflicted nature of the Bush administration's rhetoric of rupture, which warned citizens of a changed world while insisting that they keep shopping, but he is also highlighting the fluidity and limitations of personal trauma as a term in engaging with a subject that clearly carries such a political and public aspect. This is a central concern of Spiegelman's narrative: the difficulty of working through the trauma of the experience while simultaneously remaining politically engaged, especially when unilateral politics is stifling objective analysis. Essentially what we see in this segment is not a simple division between the political and the traumatic, but fractures distilled within each discourse: the trauma of the attacks represents both continuity and discontinuity, while the politics of 9/11 demand that we acknowledge epoch and then resume the normal currents of capitalism. These smaller fissures work to complicate the already fraught dynamic.

While Spiegelman is eager to make the reader aware that he understands the potential limitations of focusing on trauma, it is through the discourse of trauma that the reader enters into the text. This is, as previously suggested, partly due to intertextualities with the *Maus* books. Spiegelman makes explicit references in the introduction and throughout the text to his parents being Auschwitz concentration camp survivors, to the mice characters in *Maus* who appear periodically in the text, and to the fact of his own Jewishness, relating these elements to his and his immediate family's own traumatic experiences of 9/11. This personal or autobiographical aspect of the text, despite the narrator/protagonist's repeated emphasis on it being strictly personal, works in two significant ways in corresponding to a public, political narrative.

Firstly, Spiegelman's persistent emphasis on his 9/11 trauma being individual ironically suggests a wider plurality of experience within collective trauma, effectively demonstrating that individuals experience trauma through different filters. The diversity and individuality of the victims of the attacks was a popular conceit in the wake of 9/11, and one which was perpetuated by the popular *New York Times* "Portraits of Grief" section, which ran until December 31, 2001, where over 1800 victims were remembered (these short pieces were also eventually compiled in a book collection). As editor Janny Scott attests, the daily pieces were designed "to give a snapshot of each victim's personality, of a life lived. And they were democratic; executive vice presidents and battalion chiefs appeared alongside food handlers and janitors" (Scott 2001: n.p.). Spiegelman's emphasis on the narrator protagonist's individuality evokes this sense of diversity and plurality throughout the text: for the narrator/protagonist it is his family history, his Jewishness and his occupation as a maker of comics that are emphasized.

Secondly, Spiegelman's Jewishness and the experience of his parents as Holocaust survivors gives the text both a historical reference point, contributing to what becomes a genuine vision of larger historical cycles, and an entrance into post–9/11 identity politics. We will come to Spiegelman's evocation of the Holocaust in the coming pages, but first it is important to analyze the way the narrator protagonist's professional identity consolidates his individuality while also evoking a multitudinous and diverse New York. Indeed, *In the Shadow of No Towers* has a unique capacity to dramatize individual and collective experience; as Esperitu states, "individual grief translates to a tapestry of collective concerns and responsibilities" (Esperitu 2006: 189).

The narrator/protagonist's role as a cartoonist and the inclusion of "The Comic Supplement" section of the book, as well as the insertion, in many of the plates, of characters from these old turn-of-the-century comics, emphasizes the individualized nature of his response. Spiegelman eloquently states his reasons for the inclusion of the "supplement" and why he believes it to be important and relevant, but the very fact of its presence, the comics within a comic, within the autobiographical context of the narrative, is a clear facet of the narrator/protagonist's individuality. This is played out in the central scene of the second plate, which shows him as he "looks over some ancient comics pages instead of working," and then in the next part of this panel depicts him and his wife in caricature as Rudolph Dirk's The Katzenjammer Kids (Spiegelman 2004: 2). The personal aspect of this vision is clear, though the individualization of the narrator/protagonist's experience is set against the backdrop of what is clearly rendered as a collective experience. This is exemplified in the fourth plate, which also features the Spiegelmans as The Katzenjammer Kids. This plate offers an unevenly scattered collection of drawings of tourists, civilians and school children, as well as the Spiegelmans, in the first frantic hours after the attacks: the Spiegelmans are individuals in a multitude of individuals. The effect of this is, as stated, to suggest a massive plurality in collective trauma, and this helps sustain an important tenet of public discourse from the beginning of the text. This is supported by the last panel in the plate, which finds Spiegelman declaring his affinity for New York: "Y'know how I've called myself a 'rootless cosmopolitan,' equally homeless anywhere on the planet? I was wrong.... I finally understand why some Jews didn't leave Berlin right after Kristallnacht!" (Spiegelman 2004: 4). The cosmopolitanism of New York is an exemplary location for what Michael Hardt and Antonio Negri have termed "the multitude": "The multitude is composed of innumerable internal differences that can never be reduced to a unity or a single identity-different cultures, races, ethnicities, genders, and sexual orientations" (Hardt and Negri 2004: xiv). This is the New York of *In the Shadow of No Towers*, a backdrop which features diverse languages, races and ethnicities, and the narrator/protagonist is individualized within this "multitude." Consequently, the personal witness story of this idiosyncratic individual carries a palimpsestic public dimension, even when the witness is immersed in his personal trauma.

The depiction of personal trauma in *In the Shadow of No Towers* evokes ideas from Irene Kacandes' essay "9/11/01 = 1/27/01: The Changed Post-Traumatic Self," which explores the idea of trauma in aggregate. Kacandes' essay describes the seemingly inexplicable relationship between her experience of a strictly personally traumatic event and her experience of 9/11. Kacandes narrates the resurfacing of the trauma of losing loved ones in a violent homicide some months before 9/11: "For me, much of how I experienced September 11 was determined by events that had taken place months earlier" (Kacandes 2003: 168). The filtered response she describes resembles the way the narrator/protagonist in *In the Shadow of No Towers* is immediately consumed by thoughts of his parents' experience of Auschwitz. This is clearly very different to Kacandes' loss, but this difference is precisely the point: trauma is individual and particularly so in aggregate. As Kacandes states:

> My aim here can only be to offer clarification about a few features of the phenomenon of trauma in the hope that this analysis might allow some readers to become more compassionate towards themselves and others by better understanding what they might otherwise have considered inappropriate responses [Kacandes 2003: 169].

The narrator/protagonist's self-deprecation, and the text's characterization of him as "paranoid" and "traumatized," occasionally seems to individualize him against a greater homogenous public, but predominantly his individuality is defined by the same kind of humility that Kacandes describes, and works to evoke sympathy and to depict a logic in the way he comes to terms with a unique and powerful response.

9/11 in History

As stated, the historical strand of *In the Shadow of No Towers* correlates to personal trauma throughout the text, and this is facilitated by the aggregation of trauma. Ann Kaplan also describes the sensation of previous traumatic experience shaping her experience of 9/11 and, like Spiegelman, harks back to World War II. In "9/11 and Disturbing Remains," Kaplan states, "Ever since experiencing World War II as a small child in war-torn England, I have been ready to jump at any unexpected sound. Every time I hear a police siren it recalls the warnings of an impending air-raid attack.... When the Towers were struck some of these muted symptoms returned" (Kaplan 2005: 3). While the narrator/protagonist in *In the Shadow of No Towers* did not experience World War II or the Holocaust himself, his immediate response is similar to Kacandes' and Kaplan's. In the third plate the narrator/protagonist, in his *Maus* guise, muses, "I remember my father trying to describe what the smoke in Auschwitz smelled like.... The closest he got was telling me it was 'indescribable.' ... That's exactly what the air in Lower Manhattan smelled like after September 11" (Spiegelman 2004: 4). While ostensibly the narrator/protagonist's reaction is part of his individual experience of 9/11, as in Kaplan's essay account, this specific historical reference point also begins to locate 9/11 temporally in terms of historical events. Ironically, then, these aspects of personal trauma are part of what pushes the text into the realms of public and political spheres. Spiegelman is not trying to draw any direct comparisons to 9/11 in his references to the Holocaust, and any suggestion that this is the case is quashed by this persistent personalization. Indeed, in some ways the opposite is the case, as the constant reminders of the Holocaust work against the "end of the world" rhetoric that the Bush administration, in Spiegelman's estimation, is trying to sell to the public. The evocation of the Holocaust actually reminds the reader that history has seen far greater calamities. Principally, though, the effect here is to make wider suggestions about history. Versluys makes an astute observation about this aspect of the text by pointing to the title page, which features an image of the front page of former New York newspaper *The World* from September 11, 1901, which describes how President William McKinley's bullet wound was re-opened. Versluys points to how this "indicates how Spiegelman interprets history as a concatenation of shocks, as a never-ending series of wounds that will not heal and keep festering" (Versluys 2006: 982). Many other instances in the text support this claim, from Spiegelman's description of his parents' lesson to "always keep my bags packed" in the Introduction, to some of the historical allusions made by the turn-of-the-century comics from the "Comic Supplement." These comics invariably depict some kind of threat to New York or some kind of reference to violence in American history. As Esperitu states, "The samples from classic comic strips Spiegelman includes in *In the Shadow of No Towers* employ the New York city skyline as the backdrop or target of chaotic rampages and large-scale destruction. Moreover, buildings of colossal proportions topple spectacularly, and representations of American identity and independence are either problemitized or blatantly undermined" (Esperitu 2006: 181). In any case, it is clear that they all support this idea of history as violent and cyclical. However, returning to Spiegelman's own aggregation of traumas and the comparison to Kaplan's example, it is important to see here how this phenomenon explicitly bridges into the public strand of the text. This broad model of history as a succession of "shocks" or violent events is the wider, abstract historical continuum into which Spiegelman inserts a contemporary, more condensed and politicized narrative strand.

The smaller, more focused narrative of pre- and post-9/11 politics also correlates to trauma. Indeed, a crucial moment comes in the fifth plate where the narrator/protagonist describes another instance of the aggregation of trauma: "Trauma piles on trauma! Over half the country was already doubled over in pain after the coup d'etat in 2000" (Spiegelman 2004: 5). This is an overtly partisan statement, a direct connection between the trauma of 9/11 and the despair the narrator/protagonist felt (and suggests many felt) after the controversial election of G.W. Bush in 2000. If the references to the Holocaust amount to both a personal connection between 9/11 and the Holocaust, and an evocation of the cyclical nature of history, then this is a directly politicizing statement which establishes an explicit and direct prehistory for 9/11. This is already alluded to in the third plate when, discussing government negligence after 9/11, the narrator/protagonist exclaims, "It's back to business as usual" (Spiegelman 2004: 3). This rhetoric is also clearly expressed in the Introduction:

> When the government began to move into full dystopian Big Brother mode and hurtle America into a colonialist venture in Iraq—while doing very little to make America genuinely safer beyond confiscating nail clippers at airports—all the rage I'd suppressed after the 2000 Election, all the paranoia I'd barely managed to squelch immediately after 9/11, returned with a vengeance [Spiegelman 2004: n.p.].

This narrative arc, which contextualizes 9/11, beginning with the controversial and contested election of George Bush in 2000 through to the attacks and the subsequent wars in Afghanistan and Iraq that were so fervently advocated by President Bush, as well as the securitization and nationalism that characterized national politics, is also used by Michael Moore, whose documentary *Fahrenheit 9/11* (2004) begins with scenes of the "stolen election." Moore's film opens with a voiceover commentary which is strongly reminiscent of the passage above: "Was it all just a dream? Did the last four years really happen?" This four-year period of history that Moore's film discusses contains roughly the same sequence of events that this strand of *In the Shadow of No Towers* focuses on. Moreover, the same basic narrative arc is featured in *In the Shadow of No Towers*, and as the political aspect of the text clearly goes beyond the confines of trauma discourse, the important nuances in meaning in the placing of 9/11 and its immediate prehistory and aftermath on a larger historical continuum are missed in readings that suggest the political commitment is a way of working through trauma. Versluys states:

> Since trauma is that for which there is no language, no discursive practice can ever be adequate in rendering it. Trauma is not transmissible through words or images, except if the representation has a built-in reference to its own inadequacy, self-reflexively meditates on its own problematic status, and/or incorporates traumatic experience not so much thematically (on the surface) as stylistically (deep down in the tensions of style and texture) [Versluys 2006: 988].

It is clear that there are "reference[s] to its own inadequacy" and self-reflexivity present throughout *In the Shadow of No Towers*. However, this succession of allusion to pre–9/11 politics quoted above, and the political commitment that characterizes the text throughout, amount to more than representational tactics and can be read as an act of defiance against the limitations of discourse around personal trauma. *In the Shadow of No Towers* astutely dramatizes the entanglements of personal traumas and public, political discourse, and sustains its engagement with both throughout.

One example of this which also illustrates the importance the text places on moving beyond discussion of personal trauma and into political and social spheres is the preoccupation with "wakefulness" identified by Esperitu. In the latter part of her essay, Esperitu focuses on three panels in the penultimate plate which are spliced with other images and panels centering on the scene that finds the narrator/protagonist in bed with several other men. In the first panel he is in his usual fatigued and red-eyed condition while the others are all asleep. He exclaims, "How can they be so complacent? How can they sleep??!" (Spiegelman 2004: 9). In the next panel in the sequence he screams, "The Sky is Falling," and the men around him are all woken up. In the final panel he is the only one sleeping while the others assume his wide-eyed terror, and a speech bubble states, "Whew! Sometimes complaining is the only solace left! … zzzzzzzzzzzzzzzzz" (Spiegelman 2004: 9). Esperitu's argument is that the wakefulness and compulsion to rouse his bedfellows, given the political element of the text, represents a paranoia that has "evolved into a more sophisticated form of wariness—that is, one that falls in line with educated vigilance, *rather* than paranoia" (Esperitu 2006: 179). Esperitu makes a convincing case for this, but what is integral to the argument here is that this "wakefulness" that is repeatedly identified as a symptom of trauma is evident in the visual appearance of the narrator/protagonist throughout the text and not just in the later stages. Furthermore, there is no evidence of a transition or political awakening; the narrator/protagonist clearly exhibits his frayed "wakefulness" and obsessive political thinking throughout the text. There is undoubtedly, though, a connection between the two, as evident in the "bed" panels. It is a logical aspect of his trauma but also another clever way that the text simultaneously sustains its political engagement. This is also another example of crossover between the personal and public that can be understood more fluidly within the wider paradigm of continuity and discontinuity. Spiegelman has created a narrative that has a capacity for the very individual experience of trauma to coexist with a response to the post–9/11 rhetoric of U.S. and international political and media institutions. *In the Shadow of No Towers* is able to powerfully illustrate that there were and are extremely disorienting and problematically polarized compulsions to simultaneously feel that the world has changed fundamentally (and to the point of incomprehension), while simultaneously sensing that there is a narrative and context available that might provide answers and explanations.

Dissent and Polemic

While the thematic drive of *In the Shadow of No Towers* dramatizes the disorienting rhetoric of the discontinuity and continuity paradigm, it also builds a strong argument for understanding 9/11 strictly in a political and historical framework. Ultimately, and ironically, it is the unique form of the text that actually mutes its political dimension in the way it draws an almost overbearing emphasis on traumatic repetition, and we will come to a discussion of the text's form in the coming pages. It is essential here, though, to firstly come to terms with its political dimension. The instances discussed above, where the text points explicitly to a pre–9/11 political reality, begin to establish the primary rhetorical position of the text, which is that 9/11 mobilized an already corrupt and isolationist U.S. government's political and military agenda. The strength of its indictment should not be underestimated, particularly considering that the plates were created and serially published between 2002 and 2003, arguably the height of the American government's post-9/11 patriotic bombast. It also explains why the plates were first published in Germany in *Die Zeit* and Great Britain in *The Independent* (what Spiegelman calls his "coalition of the willing") before American publishers commissioned the book version in 2004. It is important to note, though, that this rhetoric of dissent is supported by the text's continued references to the narrator/protagonist's Holocaust survivor heritage, and this chapter will now examine the way this works to add weight and substance to the political polemic. It is useful again to compare the text to *Fahrenheit 9/11*, which, as stated, utilizes a similar narrative arc. Geoffrey O'Brien, in the *New York Review of Books*, describes the style of Moore's film as a "first-person polemic, or expressionist bulletin board, or theatricalised Op-Ed piece" (O'Brien 2004: 56). Obviously, the styles and forms of the two texts are very different, but in terms of narrative, it is primarily the personal history of the narrator protagonist—his position as a survivor/witness to 9/11 and secondary witness to the Holocaust—that gives *In the Shadow of No Towers* an extra dimension and legitimizes the polemic. Both texts make important references to the perceived injustice of the 2000 presidential election of George W. Bush and again argue, using cutting political satire, that the shocking and tragic events of 9/11 were used to advance military aggression on targets that were not related to the 9/11 attacks. However, while Michael Moore's film received favorable reviews, it also has generally been regarded, as O'Brien does, as a highly stylized polemic; and despite a certain amount of visual "evidence," it is seen as limited to being simply one man's opinion or a singular version of events. While Spiegelman's narrative is also very consciously personal, it is precisely this that elevates and substantiates his argument, giving depth to an equally stylized surface. In their critical account of "new atheist" polemics, Arthur Bradley and Andrew Tate point out that the polemical texts they discuss, which targeted religion as a whole, but largely the kind of Christian fundamentalism exemplified by President

Bush, gained traction in 2004–5, the same years that *Fahrenheit 9/11* and the book version of *In the Shadow of No Towers* first appeared. Bradley and Tate are heavily critical of the new atheist polemics on the grounds of their "intellectual crudity," which, they argue, are masked by their fundamental "ability to tell a good story" (Bradley and Tate 2010: 10). This criticism could and has been extended to *Fahrenheit 9/11*, which features a comparable flamboyancy and aggression. *In the Shadow of No Towers*, however, despite its unique stylistics, cannot be assailed for "intellectual crudity," and, crucially, it has a kind of emotional and intellectual authenticity that these kind of polemics often lack.

Spiegelman has the authority of not only being a first-hand witness to the attacks but also of experiencing the frantic search for a loved on the morning of 9/11. This may have been the catalyst for the narrative, but what political or social authority does he have? In the introduction to the text, Spiegelman expresses his discomfort with handling politics:

> I'd never wanted to be a political cartoonist. I work too slowly to respond to transient events while they're happening. (It took me 13 years to grapple with World War II in *Maus!*) Besides, nothing has a shorter shelf-life than angry caricatures of politicians, and I'd often harbored notions of working for posterity—notions that seemed absurd after being reminded how ephemeral even skyscrapers and democratic institutions are [Spiegelman 2004: n.p.].

This bears some resemblance to Oliver Stone insisting that he is "not a political filmmaker" in defense of *World Trade Center* (2006), though Stone's film supports this notion in its essentially apolitical aspect (Stone 2006: n.p.). The passage above illustrates two things: firstly, Spiegelman's reluctance to be overtly political and how ill-equipped he felt he was to handle politics, but also in positing these as abandoned pretenses, the affirmation that there will indeed be political engagement from the beginning of *In the Shadow of Towers*. Unlike Stone, who is defending an apolitical film about an intrinsically political subject, Spiegelman is stating the impossibility of excluding a political aspect from his narrative. That he happens to be the author of a (Pulitzer-winning) Holocaust narrative is an aside, but it is also an important aspect of his authority as a witness. Spiegelman displays much humility in the introduction and throughout the text, and isn't necessarily claiming his credentials here, though there is a clear suggestion that someone who has spent 13 years working on representing the Holocaust, and who witnessed 9/11, might be as well-placed as anyone to create this narrative. These are the key autobiographical elements that work to legitimize his polemic, elements that *Fahrenheit 9/11* does not have—his proximity to the 9/11 attacks, his personal connection to the Holocaust, and his history as a chronicler of the Holocaust. Furthermore, the passage again also subtly betrays the author's intention to engage with both the personal trauma and the politics of 9/11 from the beginning of the narrative, as he explicitly evokes the "ephemeral" nature of both "skyscrapers and democratic institutions," which, I would suggest, symbolize the trauma and politics of the narrative respectively. The narrator/protagonist's position as not only a witness to the attacks, but as a parent desperately attempting to locate his children while the towers burned clearly gives some amount of authority in describing the attacks, and this is stated from the outset. In the first plate, in the first panel of the middle strip, the narrator/protagonist says, "Those crumbling towers burned their way into every brain, but I live on the outskirts of Ground Zero and first saw it all live—unmediated" (Spiegelman 2004: 1). This first-hand witnessing is quickly made distinct from media representations, which were burned into "every brain" in the next two panels:

> Maybe it's just a question of scale. Even on a large TV, the towers aren't much bigger than, say Dan Rather's head.... Logos on the other hand, look *enormous* on television; it's a medium almost as well suited as comics for dealing in abstractions [Spiegelman 2004: 1].

The drawing in the middle panel is a caricature of the television broadcasting of the first few days following the attacks, and the third shows the screen completely covered by the American Flag. In this way, Spiegelman is not only distinguishing himself as a first-hand witness, but in pointing out the patriotic bombast of mainstream American 9/11 coverage he is already directly alluding to what in later plates he will call the "hi-jacking" of 9/11 (Spiegelman 2004: 2). In this allusion the narrator/protagonist is also registering what will be an important trope throughout the text, which is supported by his position as a "secondary witness" to the Holocaust—that from the beginning, the human tragedy of 9/11 is not being honored appropriately.

Spiegelman establishes his position as a secondary witness to the

Holocaust in the introduction to the text, and it is manifest powerfully in the third plate, when the narrator/protagonist appears in all of the panels in his *Maus* guise, evoking his father's Holocaust experience. One could argue that the casual reader may not recognize the significance of the *Maus* guise, though it is so striking that it is difficult to imagine that it would not inspire the small amount of research required to acknowledge the reference. Spiegelman's aggregation of traumas is important here in a legitimizing capacity. While the text in no way attempts to suggest that 9/11 and the Holocaust are analogous, the narrator/protagonist is shown to have experience of trauma and the violence of history. As he was in *Maus*, Spiegelman is, as Versluys asserts, "the indirect or secondary witness of the Holocaust" (Versluys 2006: 981). Therefore, when the narrator/protagonist suggests, as he does in nearly every plate, that the tragedy of 9/11 is being dishonored by the Bush administration, it isn't simply polemic but polemic with the support of personal experience; and even though, like *Fahrenheit 9/11*, the text features an abundance of caricature and satire, it is constantly backed by references to what is now consensus: the unimaginable horror of the Holocaust. But, as stated, it is the narrator/protagonist's Jewishness as well as his status as "secondary witness" that supports his account of 9/11, particularly in the frequent accounts of post–9/11 identity politics. The vast majority of the sixth plate is devoted to an account of the narrator/protagonist walking through his neighborhood on 9/11 and passing a Russian homeless woman who he has passed on his daily walk to work for years. He is accustomed to her "hurling anti–Semitic epithets" in Russian but is surprised when she exclaims in English, "You Damn Kikes—You did it! Dirty Jew! We'll hang you from the lamp posts, one by one!" (Spiegelman 2004: 6). This evokes a continuity narrative of 9/11 in the sense that it is an example of a latent, preexisting issue rising to the surface, and the racist rant is reminiscent of the character Monty who delivers a disturbing and memorable racist rant in Spike Lee's compelling 9/11 allegory *25th Hour* (2002). This shocking episode is echoed in the eighth plate when a television report states, "An Arab American spokesman claims that no Jews were in the towers that morning" (Spiegelman 2004: 8). The narrator/protagonist's Jewishness is most important, though, in relation to his parents and their experience of the Holocaust, and nowhere is this more evident than the powerful central image of the second plate, where the narrator/protagonist, in his *Maus* guise, is "equally terrorized by Al-Qaeda and his own government" (Spiegelman 2004: 3). While it is one thing for Michael Moore to draw conspiratorial connections between Osama Bin Laden and George Bush, and proclaim their equal criminality, it is quite another for the narrator/protagonist to appear in his *Maus* guise, beleaguered by the weight of history, between the two figures who face each other in caricatured scenes of violence. In *Maus*, the Jews were all depicted as mice, while the Germans were cats and the Polish pigs. It is clear then, as the narrator/protagonist sits resigned, head down between the caricatured Osama Bin Laden and George Bush, as a mouse, he is evoking his parents' Holocaust survivor heritage. As Versluys notes, he is also positioning himself in a larger Jewish tradition. "His meekness is a token of ineffectuality and disorientation, but it is obvious from the confrontations with the perpetrators of violence and counter-violence that his innocence is also a form of sainthood" (Versluys 2006: 985). What is central in this plate, though, is the sadness and resignation of the narrator/protagonist in his *Maus* guise. It is the notion of history repeating itself that causes the "violence and counter-violence" to upset him so much—the confrontation with evidence that despite the atrocities of the past, humans are still quick to turn to violence. Interestingly, though, there is no correlative logic in this particular sense, as of course there was no "counter-violence" from the Jews during World War II or the Holocaust. In one memorable scene in *Maus*, when Artie asks his father why "didn't the Jews at least try and resist," his father alludes to the idea of the larger Jewish tradition: "The Jews lived always with hope" (Spiegelman 1991: 73).

It is this persistence of hope that leads the narrator/protagonist of *In the Shadow of No Towers* to be so dismayed by the political maneuverings of the Bush administration after 9/11. In the introduction he describes the sense of possibility, peace and goodwill that pervaded the first few days after the attacks: "Idealistic peace signs and flower shrines briefly flourished in Union Square, the checkpoint between lower Manhattan and the rest of the city. That was all washed away by the rains and police as the world hustled forward into our 'New Normal'" (Spiegelman 2004: n.p.). The political aspect of *In the Shadow of No Towers* can thus be perceived as authentic and more legitimate in the following way: the underlying conceit beneath the narrator/protagonist's outrage at the

Bush administration is that 9/11 is not being honored properly, and this assertion is underpinned by Spiegelman's intense personal connection to the Holocaust and his position of authority on what it means to honor large-scale political violence. The polemic, which does exist separately and, as stated, contextualizes with references to pre–9/11 politics, is repeatedly bolstered by this. The point of connection comes as Spiegelman illustrates the way the government used the patriotic sentiment it stirred up in the aftermath of 9/11 to garner support for the War on Terror and wars in Afghanistan and eventually Iraq. In the fifth plate the narrator/protagonist states:

> I'm just trying to comfortably relive my September 11 trauma but you keep interrupting—Like that mind-numbing 2002 anniversary event, when you tried to wrap a flag around my head and suffocate me! You rob from the poor and give to your pals like a parody of Robin Hood while distracting me with your damn oil war! [Spiegelman 2004: 5].

For Spiegelman, the dishonoring of 9/11 is two-fold: not only is the tragedy being abused in its use as a political fulcrum, but this push toward counter-violence, in the eyes of the narrator/protagonist, defies the solemnity with which moments of political violence or catastrophe should be dealt, and ignores the lessons of history. One caption on the eighth plate summarizes this: "The killer apes learned nothing from the twin towers of Auschwitz and Hiroshima ... and nothing changed on 9/11" (Spiegelman 2004: 8). This is a more far-reaching evocation of these atrocities of World War II then the referencing of Hiroshima and parallel story of the Dresden fire-bombings in Jonathan Safran Foer's *Extremely Loud and Incredibly Close* (2005), which I will examine in the next chapter. While the extent of these historical reference points in Foer's novel stops with the notion that there is equality in suffering (a point implied here), Spiegelman explicitly emphasizes our inability to learn from and understand violent episodes of the past by situating them next to his politicized discussion of the post–9/11 foreign policy of the Bush administration. Spiegelman's referencing of the Holocaust and Hiroshima rhetorically advocate the kind of memory theorized by Michael Rothberg in *Multidirectional Memory: Remembering the Holocaust in the Age of Decolonization* (2009). Rothberg's theory of multidirectional memory is posited as an alternative to "competitive" memory: "I suggest that we consider memory as multidirectional: as subject to ongoing negotiation, cross-referencing, and borrowing; as productive and not privative" (Rothberg 2009: 4). In *In the Shadow of No Towers*, Spiegelman mourns our inability to remember 9/11 in this way and implicitly advocates a multidirectional memory of 9/11 in his statements about the U.S. government's failure to learn from "the twin towers of Auschwitz and Hiroshima." As an aside, it is interesting that Rothberg only mentions Spiegelman in passing in *Multidirectional Memory*, though he has written extensively on the literary response to 9/11 in other volumes, including Judith Greenberg's *Trauma at Home* (2003), and Ann Keniston and Jeanne Follansbee Quinn's *Literature After 9/11* (2008), and also extensively on the *Maus* books in his own *Traumatic Realism* (2000). In any case, Spiegelman's heritage leaves him yearning for diplomacy, peace and global condemnation of violence. In the seventh plate the narrator/protagonist asks, "Why did those provincial American flags have to sprout out of the embers of Ground Zero? Why not ... a globe" (Spiegelman 2004: 7). As he takes cover under an American flag, he states, "I should feel safer under here, but—damn it—I can't see a thing," illustrating the blinding capacity of the patriotism propagated all around him (Spiegelman 2004: 7). The most powerful evocation of the duality of the dishonoring of 9/11 comes in the final panel of the final plate, which refers back to the first plate. The first plate features the "Etymological Vaudeville" sequence, the first appearance of the 19 and early 20 century Comic Supplement appropriations, which are used to present the "21 Century's dominant metaphor: waiting for the other shoe to drop." This suggests, as does the first use of the "new normal," a kind of post-9/11 paranoia. In the tenth and final plate, though, the other shoes do drop in the form of cowboy boots as the Spiegelmans stand in the crowded streets in their *Maus* guises. Firstly, this image offers a final and explicit statement on the dishonoring of 9/11 by the Bush administration: "And September, '04? Cowboy boots drop on Ground Zero as New York is transformed into a stage set for the Republican Presidential Convention, and Tragedy is transformed to Travesty" (Spiegelman 2004: 10). Not only has the Bush administration dishonored the tragedy by using it as a fulcrum for war, but it continues to dishonor the attacks in using their memory for political capital. Also this scene embodies the text's representation of 9/11 as defined by the policies of the first four years of the Bush administration, and provides a final illustration of the text's narrative tension between continuity and discontinuity. The quotation from Auden at the top of the panel, "the unmentionable odor of death offends the September night," references the underpinning idea of violent historical cycles (Spiegelman 2004: 10). The *Maus* characters do the same while also emphasizing the narrator/protagonist's experience of personal trauma; and the setting of the 2004 Republican Convention completes the narrative arc, which is shown to define the narrator/protagonist's experience of the attacks. Finally, in the final panels the central image of the text, the burning towers, is shown to fade, providing a final statement that not only does 9/11 have a pre-history but a post-history as well.

Before concluding, the form of Spiegelman's text, and particularly the way it is effective at rendering trauma, must be discussed. The book is not a conventional graphic text but is presented as an oversized book with seventeen thick cardboard pages, ten of which comprise the main plates and seven the "Comic Supplement." While this is the version of the text under consideration here, it is worth considering the fact that it was originally published serially. The plates were first published between 2002 and 2003, so the chronology of the text has an intense correlation to the escalating political climate of the time, particularly the first stages of the wars in Afghanistan and Iraq. The fact that the plates were only published in Germany in *Die Zeit* and in the UK in *The Independent* shows how challenging the politics of the plates were to American publishers. Scott Thill notes that the serial versions were conspicuously avoided by U.S. publishers in 2002 and 2003, even by "the supposedly liberal New York publications," which "avoided Spiegelman's post–9/11 rants like they were undocumented Arab immigrants" (Thill 2004: n.p.). Considering the condemnation Susan Sontag's early *New Yorker* piece, which dared to allude to American imperialism, received in the weeks after 9/11, this is perhaps unsurprising.[5] But what is compelling about the medium of the text is that it has become integral to the way in which it has been interpreted, predominantly in terms of trauma. Much has been made of the way graphic texts in general are suited to address the temporal concerns of trauma. Esperitu highlights this in *In the Shadow of No Towers*, describing the way "one must always repeatedly go back to the interplay between the text and images," as one does in any graphic text. This process of repetition is linked with the processes of repetition that define the experience of psychological trauma. She also suggests that the collage-style narrative of *In the Shadow of No Towers*, which deviates markedly from the traditional panels of the *Maus* books, to some extent distinguishes Spiegelman's 9/11 trauma:

> Rather than prescribing "ready-made" assumptions and specific narratives about 9/11 and its aftermaths, Spiegelman's intentionally scatter-shot style of addressing—within and in between each plate—the immediate and subsequent trauma he experienced, effectively demonstrates the extent to which traumatic experience necessitates a breakdown not only of linguistic mastery, but also of "conceptual continuity" [Esperitu 2006: 287].

Undoubtedly, certain features of the text lend themselves to the discourse of trauma, particularly what is often referred to as the central image of the text, what Spiegelman calls the "Glowing Bones" of the towers. This image appears dozens of times throughout the text in several variations, which suggests that it signifies a vivid but unstable memory imposing itself onto the story. As Versluys states, "This image of the incandescent tower, moments before its collapse, figures on each and every plate and therefore serves as the leitmotif of the series. As such it can easily be identified as an essential part of the protagonist's posttraumatic stress disorder" (Versluys 2006: 993). Indeed, the narrator/protagonist identifies this image as relating to his experience of trauma in several places, notably in the introduction: "The pivotal image of my 9/11 morning—one that didn't get videotaped into public memory but still remains burned onto the inside of my eyelids several years later—was the image of the looming north tower's glowing bones just before it vaporized" (Spiegelman 2004: n.p.). There are other important repetitious features that reinforce this effect of frozen time: the "Comic Supplement" stars are repeated and also require cross referencing back and forth from the supplement to the main plates; the characters in their *Maus* guises are repeated intermittently as well as being fundamentally inter-textual. This experience of traumatic repetition in the text has, as evidenced above, been emphasized repeatedly in critical accounts of this text.

However, there is also clearly a teleological narrative and chronology in the entangled socio-political and traumatic strands of *In the*

Shadow of No Towers. As we have seen, Esperitu and others have suggested that this comes in the form of a movement from trauma to political commitment or a narrative of working through. Richard Glejzer suggests that the narrator/protagonist's destabilizing trauma supersedes any understanding or historicizing of 9/11, negating any possibility for narrative or context: "Spiegelman's text offers up a witness without such grounding, a witness who consciously does not know what he has seen, who only knows that he has seen" (Glejzer 2008: 118). Huehls, who also focuses on the unique format of the text and its function in representing trauma, is slightly more in tune with the argument here when he suggests the allusions to history, particularly the "Comic Supplement," allow a kind of reconciliation between personal trauma and politics: "Spiegelman incorporates historical cartoon characters into his own work to represent safe temporality in which personal and public times are reconciled" (Huehls 2008: 56). However, it is evident here that the private/personal and public/political aspects of the texts are correspondent and coextensive rather than reconciliatory. That there is a clear relationship between the narrator's personal experience of 9/11 and the public, political narrative has, hopefully, been clearly demonstrated in the previous pages. It is worth noting, though, that individually the narrative markers are clear, from the framed opening and closing of the "waiting for the other shoe to drop" metaphor, to the frequent references to the election of 2000 as a point of origin, to the many allusions to the slow process of making the plates, to the many references to the process of working through trauma. Furthermore, the passing of time is constantly monitored. Each plate is dated at the bottom, and there are many references to the passage of time: in the first plate he states, "okay! Let's say it's not September anymore"; in the fifth plate he references the "mind-numbing 2002 'anniversary event'"; in the eighth plate he states that "time passes"; in the ninth plate he mentions that "it's almost two years later"; and plate ten is partially set at the next year's Republican Convention, 2004. Returning to the idea of the central image, and my argument here that it represents more than traumatic repetition (though it certainly relates to this in part), there is a crucial line in the introduction where Spiegelman describes how working for posterity seemed absurd after being reminded how ephemeral even "skyscrapers" and "democratic institutions" are. Those "glowing bones" that feature on every page do not just represent traumatic repetition and the vaporizing of the towers but also the destruction, in the narrator/protagonist's view, of "democratic institutions" (Spiegelman 2004: n.p.). This is a plain manifesto to correlate trauma, politics and history on every plate, and the text consistently explores 9/11 and its aftermath as a phenomenon and situation well described by Jenny Edkins as an instance when "trauma time collided with the time of the state, the time of capitalism, the time of routine" (Edkins 2003: 233). Moreover, rather than the suggested trajectory of the political commitment stemming from personal trauma, we could consider the traumatic image as being inserted into scenes of political satire—the constant reminder of what is being dishonored by the militarization and "the hijacking" of 9/11 by the government. Crucially, in either of these equally plausible readings, the framework of trauma or trauma theory as a tool in itself for understanding the text is reductive and limiting.

The ephemeral nature of both "skyscrapers and democratic institutions" is one of many dualities that comprise the complex and multifaceted narrative dialectic of *In the Shadow of No Towers*. The narrator/protagonist is "equally terrorised by Al-Qaeda and his own government." There are two hijackings (the planes that attacked the U.S. and the hijacking of 9/11 by "brigands suffering from war fever"), and there is the constant presence of the trauma dialectic—the will to proclaim against the idea of the inexpressible. Like many people, Spiegelman's immediate response to 9/11 is a sense of disorientation—the disorientation of feeling like the world has changed fundamentally, coupled with the simultaneous need for context and understanding. This is the achievement of the text in capturing a predominant sensibility, and also a platform that it uses to grapple with the larger question of whether or not "everything's changed." The difficulty in trying to reconcile private trauma and public events and politics results in the pervading disorientation that forms the true meaning of the "new normal." As Spiegelman writes in the introduction, immediately after 9/11

> the world hustled forward into our "New Normal." When the government began to move into full dystopian Big Brother mode and hurtle America into a colonialist adventure in Iraq—while doing very little to make America genuinely safer beyond confiscating nail clippers at airports ... [Spiegelman 2004: n.p.].

This articulates the difficulty that agonizes the narrator/protagonist, the problem of simultaneously coming to terms with a genuinely perspective-shifting tragedy while also dealing with the equally profound changes caused by the dishonoring and use as political capital of the tragedy. Ultimately, the fact that the text's bold politics are muted by its formal qualities and intertextualities, which dictate an emphasis on private trauma, doesn't necessarily signal a dramatic failure. In fact, this only consolidates the portrayal of "the new normal" as a multifaceted condition of conflictedness.

Two

Windows on the World and *Extremely Loud and Incredibly Close*: A Crisis in Representation?

Frédéric Beigbeder's *Windows on the World* (2003) and Jonathan Safran Foer's *Extremely Loud and Incredibly Close* (2005) follow on from *In the Shadow of No Towers* in several ways. For example, they both rely on important visual elements in their respective narratives, and they are also both deeply preoccupied with their protagonist's experiences of trauma. Ostensibly, as novels, they are also, like Spiegelman's outsized graphic novel, unconventional or experimental examples of their form. However, while Spiegelman's graphic plates were genuinely innovative and challenging, both formally and thematically, neither Beigbeder or Foer push the boundaries of the contemporary novel. While these texts are conspicuously playful and self-reflexive, most of the reviews and initial critical analyses of the novels have been quick to point out that their meta-fictional or postmodernist aesthetics are part of a well-established tradition that originated in the 1960s. Keith Gessen writes in his review of *Extremely Loud and Incredibly Close* that "Foer's use of so many techniques of the 'postmodern' novel of the 1960s and 1970s would suggest he is dealing with phenomena like the ones faced by its writers.... Rather, he has dressed a commonplace and sentimental response to his times in what are now our parent's clothes" (Gessen 2005: 72). Similarly, Holloway describes *Windows on the World* as "old fashioned meta-fiction" (Holloway 2008: 120). While the degree of genuine "experimentalism" in these texts, in the sense of newness or the probing of existing boundaries of representation is seriously questionable, there is no doubt that stylistically and structurally they are very different from the novel representations of 9/11 that would follow them, and indeed to no small extent, from most contemporary fiction in general (even if this is simply in the utilizing of a tried formula that was out of fashion at the time of publication). Therefore, while many of both novels' reviewers and critics have made comments such as Walter Kirn's, who states that the novels "can't really be called experimental, since their signature high jinks, distortions and addenda first came to market many decades back," are essentially correct to point out that these are not new or unique forms or ideas, they do not always register the awareness within the texts that this is the case (Kirn 2005: n.p.). Rather than attempting to push the boundaries of the contemporary novel, these texts engage in an explicit struggle to find appropriate tools or forms to represent 9/11, and a self-consciousness of this enterprise is evident in their aesthetics. This chapter will explore the various ways in which the aesthetic qualities of each text betray an uncertainty and tentativeness at the heart of each text in their relationships to history, tradition and the new. Nearly all of the existing critical work on these texts focuses on some aspect of their postmodernist or meta-fictional aesthetics. For example, Scott M. Powers' article "Postmodern Narratives of Evil and 9–11: The Case of Frédéric Beigbeder" looks explicitly at *Windows on the World* as a postmodern novel, and Mitchum Huehls focuses on *Extremely Loud and Incredibly Close* as "meta-fiction." These articles probe the stylistics of the novels, examining the relationship between their aesthetic conceits and trauma or ideas of the un-representable. However, Beigbeder's and Foer's aesthetic conceits betray a tension at the core of the narratives: while the aesthetic strategies of the texts are designed to engage with ideas of traumatic rupture or epoch, as we have seen, the experimental qualities of the texts are equally associated with tradition, convention and history. This chapter will map this surface tension onto a deeper conflictedness that courses through both texts.

This evident aesthetic "conflictedness" relates to the way both novels attempt to construct what Birgit Däwes calls "transnational" narratives of 9/11 (Däwes 2007: 518). It is in this aspect that they depart from the preoccupations of *In the Shadow of No Towers* most significantly: where Spiegelman's text built in a narrative of political commitment and polemic, it is the transnational compulsion in both texts that pushes against their dramatizations of trauma. The two novels are very similar in the respect that they both alternate chapters between an American narrator and a European narrator, though the ways in which this conceit relates to their stylistic qualities depart fairly significantly. Nevertheless, while the meta-fictionality of these novels operates in different ways, it is structurally enmeshed in the transnational aspects of both.

Metafictions of Crisis

Windows on the World is as explicit as possible in this aspect, as the novel operates a dual narrative: chapters alternate between those narrated by the fictional American character Carthew Yorston and those narrated by the novel's French author or a slightly embellished version of the author we can refer to as "Beigbeder" (with the exception of four short chapters near the end, which are narrated by Carthew's son). Beigbeder refers to this narrative style as "autosatire," a reference to the popular "auto-fiction" genre and Beigbeder's playful tone (Beigbeder 2004: 219). The author-character continually interrupts and comments on the fictional narrative of Carthew Yorston, and the fact that the two "characters" are so similar ironically comments on the limits of distance between author and protagonist. It is as if to say that the rhetoric of the text is ultimately the opinion of one man with very particular predilections and perspectives. This conspicuous limitation is a part of a larger frustration the author explicitly reveals in trying to engage with the subject of 9/11. An important continuing trope that the Beigbeder character meditates on is the difficulty of orchestrating the fiction:

> Writing this hyperrealist novel is made more difficult by reality itself. Since September 11, 2001, reality has not only outstripped fiction, it's destroying it. It's impossible to write about this subject, and yet impossible to write about anything else. Nothing else touches us [Beigbeder 2004: 8].

Like many aspects of both of these novels, this passage is clearly referential; Beigbeder here is echoing Don DeLillo's character Bill Gray's often quoted statement in *Mao II* (1991): "Years ago I used to think it was possible for a novelist to alter the inner life of the culture. Now bomb-makers and gunmen have taken that territory. They make raids on human consciousness. What writers used to do before we were all incorporated" (DeLillo 1991: 41). What is important, though, and evident in Beigbeder's digressions, is not simply the unconventional narrative conceit but the apparent sense of struggle to find a way to narrate 9/11 and to connect what is clearly a personal emotional or traumatic response to wider political and international concerns, which are frequently manifest in the form of comparisons between French and American perspectives (as similar as these may be in the particular instance of Carthew and Beigbeder).

A similar sense of struggle is evident in *Extremely Loud and Incredibly Close*. The text contains three narrators, also from different countries: the nine-year-old American boy, Oskar, who has lost his father in the attacks, and his German grandparents, traumatized survivors of the Dresden fire-bombings of World War II. Foer's novel contains a myriad of visual devices that relate to the narrative in various ways. There are forty-eight photographs or graphics, not including the fifteen-page photographic "flipbook" at the end. There are also several blank pages or pages with single phrases, three pages with nothing but numbers, several pages with certain words circled in red, and a section where the words gradually get closer and closer together until they are printed on top of each other and are eventually just black. Ostensibly this may be to facilitate a more three-dimensional experience or, ironically, a kind of deeper realism or impressionism in that it literally shows you what the protagonists see or experience. In certain instances it undoubtedly works to create what Holloway calls an "aggregation of prose and visual imagery for a doubling of emotional effect" (Holloway 2008: 121). In these instances the visuals are usually reflecting the traumatized condition of the narrator, and, as some commentators have pointed out, the use of still photographs is particularly related to what is seen as the unique ability of still photography to engage with the temporality of trauma; the way a disturbing or violent image can haunt an individual. Marianne Hirsch, for example, has stated that "still photography has emerged as the most responsive medium in our attempts to deal with the aftermath of September 11," describing how it "captures the trauma and loss ... the sense of monumental, irrevocable change that we feel we have experienced," in its temporality (Hirsch 2003: 71).

In *Extremely Loud and Incredibly Close*, though, the visuals are also occasionally disruptive to the emotional or sentimental core of the text. This, as Mitchum Heuhls states, is one of the objects of meta-fiction—to "rupture readers from rather than enmesh them in time's measured passage" (Huehls 2009: 84). For example, at one point, after experiencing severe disappointment, the young narrator states, "I sat back down and started to cry in the lobby of an apartment," but rather than looking to the next page to read on about Oskar's disappointment, the reader is presented with a photograph of the Brooklyn Bridge, which Oskar had crossed before arriving at his present emotional state and which urges the reader to look back (Foer 2005: 89). This kind of interruption to the narrative flow is reinforced by the alternating of narrators, as in *Windows on the World*. Crucially, though, as this is a quest narrative or a detective narrative—Oskar is trying to find a keyhole for a key he found that belonged to his father who died in the World Trade Center—the reader cannot help but interpret this plethora of visual aids as a way of assisting with this quest, which for the reader is also a quest for meaning and insight into the trauma of 9/11. This stifling combination of the interruption of the visuals and the compulsion to attempt to reconnect them to sections of the prose is reflective of the author's frustration with the limitations of prose or, as Gessen states, "impatience with the written word as a marker or describer of reality" (Gessen 2005: 69). Crucially, though, the emphasis on trauma and the attempt to manage trauma, which is shared by Oskar and his German grandparents, and embodied by the still photographs and visual trickery, reveals a thematic tension between the simple positing of an equality in traumatic rupture and the need to historicize 9/11 in an international context. In Kristiaan Versluys' reading, for example, the simple placing of 9/11 next to allusions to Hiroshima and Dresden positions 9/11 "in a line of historical catastrophes." Versluys argues that Foer's novel engages meaningfully with history in its account of 9/11: "This seemingly apolitical family novel has history palimpsestically inscribed in every sentence" (Versluys 2009: 81). However, the coming pages will demonstrate that, unlike the clear links to other historical traumas that Spiegelman is able to establish, Foer's allusion to history is largely superficial.

As stated, the primary concern of this chapter is to move beyond a concern simply for the stylistic aspects of the texts in order to illumi-

Two. A Crisis in Representation

nate what we might genuinely see as a crisis in representation in these novels. Despite the conspicuousness of the postmodernist or metafictional aesthetics or narrative devices of these novels, these decades-old stylistic conceits surely do not amount to what we could legitimately call a "crisis in representation" in these texts or, for that matter, in a wider sense, particularly given the dominance of realism in the rest of the 9/11 canon. There is a crisis in representation evident here, though, which is more illuminating than the difficulty or impossibility of finding a suitable form or style for representing what is deemed incomprehensible or traumatic.

The crisis here does stem from the problem of representing 9/11 and is to some extent signaled by the aesthetic qualities of the texts. The real difficulty revealed in these texts, however, is the difficulty in negotiating a broader tension that is generated by the compulsion to deploy two polarized narrative trajectories. The flagrant stylistics and structural gimmickry of both novels is clearly intended to mark a break and to cast the narratives as epochal trauma narratives or narratives of discontinuity, and these stylistic and formal gestures are supported by certain thematic strands and ideas within both texts. However, just as these stylistics are rooted in precedents and literary history, the transnational strand of the narratives also at least gesture toward contextualization and history. Furthermore, while the texts do to some degree bear out the promise of the experimental pretenses of difference or the difficulty in engaging with the "unrepresentable," the texts do not follow through on the suggestions they make to this effect, and they both gesture with equal strength towards historicizing and contextualizing narratives— narratives of continuity. What we can see as a "crisis in representation" is the fundamental conflictedness of the texts and the failure to reconcile these narratives or the powerful impulse they reveal towards both strands. The real crisis in representation here is the two narrative strands pulling against each other on many different and interrelated levels—notions of epoch, trauma and the personal against history, context, politics and continuity.

This chapter will map out the tension between continuity and discontinuity in each of the two novels, exploring the way this tension characterizes the wider "conflictedness" of the post–9/11 social and political realities of the time.

Windows on the World: Dualities and Hyperrealities

As illustrated above, *Windows on the World* is eager to present itself as a "hyper-realist" novel. This notion is expanded on sporadically in the early chapters of the book. For example, Carthew muses at one point:

> In America, life is like a movie, since all movies are shot on location. All Americans are actors, and their houses, their cars, and their desires all seem artificial. Truth is reinvented every morning in America [Beigbeder 2004: 21].

This is another clearly referential passage, in this case to the French cultural theorist Jean Baudrillard, whose theoretical writings have long been at the center of the theoretical discourse of "hyper-reality." This particular notion in the quoted passages evokes Baudrillard's famous assertion that Hollywood or theme-park America is more real than America itself: "Disneyland is presented as imaginary in order to make us believe that the rest is real, when in fact all of Los Angeles and the America surrounding it are no longer real but of the order of the hyper-real" (Baudrillard 2001: 175). As Holloway states, though, both narrators in *Windows on the World* are "too alarmed or pessimistic to take any decadent postmodern delight in the empty play of surfaces or endless deferrals of authentic meaning" (Holloway 2008: 120–21). However, irrespective of Beigbeder's insistence on referring to postmodernist discourse on several occasions (part of what constitutes these meta-fictional pretenses), what makes the narrative genuinely unconventional or unusual is the dual narration, and this is also at the heart of its conflictedness. The dual narration gives the text its transnational perspective, which articulates differences and commonalities in national perspective with almost equal weight. However, despite the clear similarities between Carthew and Beigbeder (particularly in their shared crises of masculinity), a clear and resonant dichotomy between the two narrations emerges. At the most basic level, it is set out from the beginning that Carthew dies, and in this respect his story lies in the realm of the discontinuous. "Beigbeder," on the other hand, lives on in the sense that he does not die in the towers, as the author is forever attached to the text. Also, though, his meditations, which become more and more meandering as the narrative progresses, begin to look back for origins and forward toward the reality of the aftermath, and provide continued conjecture regarding differences in international perspectives. This dichotomy emerges and builds throughout the text so that it climaxes with a real starkness, though there are also subtle dichotomies within both characters, internal polarizations which connect to this larger conceit.

Carthew's inevitable, ultimate demise is yet another tenet of the story that is presented in referential terms, as Beigbeder evokes the opening narrative conceit of Sam Mendes' film *American Beauty* (2000): "In two hours I'll be dead; in a way, I am dead already" (Beigbeder 2004: 5). The phrase "in a way, I am dead already" is, of course, a double entendre, and this complicates the simplistic division between the two characters of one who lives and one who dies. The suggestion of being "dead already" while alive is powerfully resonant in both Beigbeder and Carthew, and this becomes an important part of the back-story or context of both characters. They share an acknowledged moral bankruptcy and shallowness in their pursuit of wealth and status, and their relationships with women. Carthew's narrative is not just about the final two hours of his and his son's lives, but also about his privileged position in the hierarchy of American capitalism and subsequent clichéd disillusionment with the American Dream. However, as the narrative progresses, it is the Beigbeder character that attempts to bring the *American Beauty* conceit into a more universal, political discussion, and to extend discussion of his moral bankruptcy to a wider discourse. While the Beigbeder character continues to get more meditative, both in personal terms and also in a political sense, the Carthew narrative quickly gives way to a real-time realism that is similar to Paul Greengrass' real-time film *United 93* (2006) in the way it focuses strictly on the urgency and emergency of a short time period, and functions as a count-down narrative (chapters are not titled but rather bear the heading of each minute between 8:30 and 10:30 a.m.). Carthew is still occasionally omniscient, but the focus becomes progressively trained on the playing out of the tragedy for him and his sons on the top floor of the World Trade Center. As Holloway states, "The novel climaxed with real, visceral, human emotion, conveyed with an economy and punch" (Holloway 2008: 123–4). There is a well-known prescription for this mode of representation of 9/11 in Don DeLillo's initial essay response "In the Ruins of the Future." DeLillo asserted in this essay (long before any novelist had attempted a 9/11 novel): "The writer begins in the towers, trying to imagine the moment, desperately. Before politics, before history and religion, there is the primal terror" (DeLillo 2001: n.p.). Not only does the Carthew narrative move toward the representation of this "primal terror" in its gruesome images of "fountains of blood" and "falling limbs," "animal cries, like pigs with their throats cut," but it also mostly avoids the "politics" and "history and religion" aspects of the attacks (Beigbeder 2004: 265).

The move towards minimal realism in the Carthew narrative is evidently a conscious one, explicitly preempted not by reference to DeLillo but by the epigraphs or "Lightning Rods," as they are titled. *Windows on the World* has two. The first is a quote from Tom Wolfe: "A novelist who does not write realistic novels understands nothing of the world in which we live." This might be perceived as a sarcastic suggestion—given Beigbeder's explicit self-description as a "hyper-realist"—that Beigbeder actually knows nothing of the world in which we live; though the austere and sensitive realist prose used in describing the crucial moments of the event would suggest that, in this particular section at least, it is actually advice taken. This is certainly the case with the next "lighting rod" from Marilyn Manson: "The function of the artist is to plunge into the depths of hell." Indeed, it would seem that in *Windows on the World* these two ideas are deeply connected, as evidenced by passages such as the following:

> The lights go out, come on again. The bulbs start to flicker like strobe lights in a disco. Then, it's black as night. The kids scream inconsolably in the darkness. We are in the depths of hell. I have no choice anymore. Either we wait to die here or we go back down to the restaurant [Beigbeder 2004: 227].

There is no playfulness or self-reflexivity in passages such as this. As the terror and suffering inside the top of the North Tower of the World Trade Center increases, any playfulness or device gives way to unfettered realism, particularly marked in the short staccato sentences in the passage above. Carthew seems to be quoting directly from the epigraph here, describing the situation atop the skyscraper as being in the "depths of hell." This description is not inappropriate to the more and more disturbing nature of the situation. Furthermore, while Carthew's narrative does have a distinctly introspective facet, and is in many passages a depiction of a man's final racing thoughts, the crucial moments are always rendered in this realistic tone:

Two. A Crisis in Representation

> Since David died, Jerry won't let go of him, cries on his cold forehead, strokes his closed eyelids. I stand up, take him in my arms, a little prince with blond, lifeless hair. Jerry reads my thoughts, he shudders with grief [Beigbeder 2004: 295].

The continued turn toward realism is very marked in a text that is explicitly meta-fictional and full of stylistic flourishes. Like *Extremely Loud and Incredibly Close*, *Windows on the World* also features photographs and typographical playfulness. Carthew continues to occasionally muse about life in these closing chapters and make omniscient observations that resonate with some of Beigbeder's ideas or involve himself directly in the meta-fiction, but he generally works to reinforce the rhetoric of realism. For example, at one point Carthew states:

> You never saw us on TV. Nobody took photos of us. All you know of us are dishevelled figures scrambling down the walls, bodies hurled into the void.... You didn't smell the burning electrical cables.... You didn't hear the animal cries, like pigs with their throats cut, like calves torn limb from limb [Beigbeder 2004: 265].

Even in this passage it is clear that, ultimately, Carthew, addressing the reader, is attempting to evoke or advocate a kind of realism or fidelity in representing the attack and placing importance on faithfully rendering what happened inside the towers. Ultimately, *Windows on the World* pulls between wanting the reader to question the limits of fiction and representation in its meta-fictional guise and also wanting readers to immerse themselves into the reality of the brutality and finality of the last moments in the towers. This narrative tension is definitively delivered late in the novel where one page, headed "10:10," bears the two single sentences:

> In Windows on the World, the customers were gassed, burned and reduced to ash. To them, as to so many others, we owe a duty of memory. (Page cut.) [Beigbeder 2004: 278].

This is an explicit reference to the idea of the impossibility of representing atrocity and trauma. The visual unorthodoxy of the device betrays the sentiment that this is more than just a story or documentary account, and the "Page cut" itself suggests something omitted. It is ironic, though, and an embodiment of the narrative tension in the text, that visual devices like this, which usually denote a departure from realism, are embedded with the rhetoric of realism. Even more ironic is that ultimately, as previously suggested, it is not the playfulness or plethora of visual devices—the ostensible experimentalism—that evoke ideas of the absolute. As stated, it is the somber realism at the core of the Carthew narrative that posits this idea of discontinuity. It is not formally inventive but is loaded with apocalyptic imagery and the rhetoric of finality. Furthermore, the meta-fictional function of the text, which ostensibly is in place to indicate the difficulty of representing or understanding 9/11, is actually the aspect of the text that makes gestures toward locating the event on a continuum, toward context and history, both in its formal qualities and in terms of the subject the Beigbeder character discusses.

As stated, this dichotomy is emergent, and just as Carthew's narrative becomes more and more sparse and realist, pulling toward the bleak absolute, the Beigbeder narrative becomes more and more digressive and meditative, bringing out the real transnational tensions of the text in long passages devoted to musings on globalization, American identity and America's place in the world, and particularly to ideas of Western cultural identities. However, while the Beigbeder section interrupts the realism of the Carthew narrative, we can also see the rhetoric of the absolute interrupting Beigbeder's "hyperrealist" narrative. Not only does the apolitical realism of the end of Carthew's narrative pull against Beigbeder's meditations, but Beigbeder himself endlessly halts his contextualizing or musing by eliciting rhetoric of the absolute, framed continually in terms of the "uselessness" of "this book." Not long after the earlier quoted passage where he asserts that "nothing else touches us," he describes the text as a "useless book, like all books. The writer is like the cavalry, always arriving too late" (Beigbeder 2004: 27). In other words, no matter what kind of light his literary meditations throw on the attacks, the reality of death and trauma cannot be assuaged or undone. Nevertheless, Beigbeder continues to digress in this way, tempering his philosophical and historical musings with these notions of the irreducible; "it is simply an attempt—doomed, perhaps—to describe the indescribable" (Beigbeder 2004: 57).

Superficially, the most politically loaded factor in the dual narrative, particularly considering the geopolitical climate of the time when the novel was published, is simply that the Beigbeder character is French and Carthew is American. Ostensibly, the novel's perspective is widened through the dual narration's two nationalities. Certain points of view that might be unusual or jarring to American readers are indeed dispatched occasionally but are generally superficial. One example of this is when Beigbeder describes the reaction of a disparate group of colleagues as they watched French television coverage of the attacks unfolding:

> NARCISSISTIC: "Fuck—I was up there a month ago!"
> STATISTICAL: "My God, how many people are trapped in there? The death toll must be 20,000!"
> PARANOID: "Jesus, well, since I look like an Arab, I'm bound to get stopped by the cops every five minutes for the next couple of weeks."
> ANXIOUS: "We've got to call our friends over there, make sure they're all right."
> LACONIC: "Well, this is no joke."
> MARKETING: "This is going to be great for the ratings, we should buy space on LCI."
> BELLICOSE: "Fuck! This is it, it's the Third World War."
> SECURITY CONSCIOUS: "They need to put cops on all the planes and bulletproof doors on the cockpits."
> NOSTRADAMUS: "You see? I told you this would happen, I even wrote it."
> MEDIA SAVVY: "Shit, I have to get over to Europe 1 and give my reaction."
> KNEE-JERK ANTI–AMERICAN: "This is what happens when you try and control the world" [Beigbeder 2004: 88].

Some of these reactions are clearly "foreign" and almost adversarial. The tone here is satirical, though, and doesn't particularly widen perspective. Nevertheless, because of repeated episodes such as this, on the surface it remains tempting to see the dual narration as fundamental to the emergent dichotomy, as the French and American antagonism that emerged after 9/11 is certainly applicable in interesting ways to the paradigm of continuity and discontinuity. If we place the American post–9/11 political and military agenda, begun by President Bush's proclamation that on the evening of September 11 "night fell on a different world," or the repeated rhetoric of "you're either with us or you're against us," as firmly in the realms of discontinuity—an unprecedented response to an unprecedented event—then the French response to this response is most certainly firmly rooted in ideas of continuity (Bush 2001: n.p.). France was one of the most vocal opponents to the war in Iraq, with Foreign Minister Dominique de Villepin stating on January 20, 2003: "We think that military intervention would be the worst possible solution" (Villepin 2003: n.p.). France, with its large Muslim population and precarious relationship with post-colonial Algeria, wanted to look carefully at diplomatic possibilities and evoked powerful precedents in calling the war an "illegal occupation." Furthermore, the French were highly critical of the Bush administration's use of 9/11 as a catalyst. As Irwin Wall states, "Since 11 September, 2001, the pundits of the French have been telling them that the old United States is gone, replaced by a new unilateralist United States, willing to dispense with the United Nations and ignore NATO, trying to divide a Europe that it once did so much to unify, destroying the international order that it built after World War II" (Wall 2004: 2). However, when Beigbeder states early on that "war has been declared between France and the United States," it is with immense frustration (Beigbeder 2004: 17). Beigbeder characterizes himself as pro-American, at one point actually declaring: "I'm writing this book because I'm sick of bigoted anti-Americanism" (Beigbeder 2004: 17). Furthermore, he frequently seeks to recoup the French and American relationship as part of a larger European "us": "We are the same: even if we are not all Americans, our problems are theirs, and theirs ours" (Beigbeder 2004: 302). Indeed, the authenticity of the transnational perspective of the text has been frequently questioned, and rather than articulating or engaging with differing perspectives, the text has been accused of homogenizing. For example, Birgit Däwes accuses it of "confirming transatlantic hierarchies" in this emphasis on the French/American relationship (Däwes 2007: 528). Versluys echoes this, stating that "as an international novel, the book depicts September 11 as a historical episode that re-establishes the category of the transatlantic west" (Versluys 2009: 137).

Indeed, Beigbeder is pro-American, and Carthew has French ancestry, and any simple polarization in this facet of the dual narration is compromised. However, as previously suggested, the Beigbeder character's meditations or commentary does make powerful and more convincing suggestions of context and origin, and the most striking of these are the evocations of globalization which undoubtedly are among the novel's boldest uses of its transnational framework. Beigbeder begins discussion by emphasizing the media's importance in making the world aware of disproportions in wealth and evoking his own nation's history in his rhetoric:

> Television makes the world jealous. In the past, the poor, the colonized, didn't spend their nights in shantytowns staring at wealth on a screen. They didn't realize that some countries had everything while they slogged their guts out for nothing. In France, the revolution would have happened a lot earlier if the serfs had had a little screen where they could see the opulence of kings and queens [Beigbeder 2004: 115].

Beigbeder continues using the term globalization directly:

> Nowadays, all over the world, filthy countries hover between awe and contempt, fascination and disgust for the clean countries whose lifestyles they watch on satellite with hacked decoders, using sieves for satellite dishes. It is a recent phenomenon: we call it globalization, but its real name is television. Economics, broadcasting, cinema, marketing are all globalized, but the rest—the politics and the social policies—doesn't follow [Beigbeder 2004: 115].

Two elements of this passage make it as suggestive of origins and international context as any part of any of the existing literary representations of 9/11. First, it boldly makes a historical reference and comparison in evoking the French revolution. And second, in referring to "the poor, the colonized," it even more boldly alludes to American imperialism, explicitly evoking the popular Chalmers Johnson "blowback" theory.[6] Furthermore, this passage evokes Frantz Fanon's classic formulation of colonial violence in *The Wretched of the Earth* (1963). Fanon states, referring particularly to French-colonized Algiers:

> The settler's town is a strongly built town, all made of stone and steel. It is a brightly-lit town; the streets are covered with asphalt, and the garbagecans swallow all the leavings, unseen, unknown and hardly thought about.... The settler's town is a well-fed town, an easy-going town; its belly is always full of good things. The settler's town is a town of white people, of foreigners.... The town belonging to the colonized people, or at least the native town, the Negro village, the medina, the reservation, is a place of ill fame, peopled by men of evil repute. They are born there, it matters little where or how; they die there, it matters not where, not how. It is a world without spaciousness; men live there on top of each other, and their huts are built one on top of each other, the native town is a hungry town, starved of bread, of meat, of shoes, of coal, of light. The native town is a crouching village, a town on its knees, a town wallowing in the mire. It is a town of niggers and dirty Arabs [Fanon 1961: 30].

What makes Beigbeder's evocation of Fanon's logic of "compartmentalization" so powerful is that he frames it in the contemporary, within the discourse of globalization and the immediacy of television. However, while this is a clear gesture towards exploring contextualization and continuity in understanding 9/11, it is halted abruptly and never allowed to develop. A few pages later Beigbeder states the following, negating this contextualizing strand and reverting again to terms of the absolute: "Even if I go deep, deep into the horror, my book will always remain 1,350 feet below the truth" (Beigbeder 2004: 124). Toward the end of the narrative, after a digression on American materialism, Beigbeder makes another, similarly absolute conclusion: "Our future has vanished. Our future is the past tense" (Beigbeder 2004: 284). So while the duality in the narrators isn't necessarily strengthened by their international difference, it does play an important role in this ongoing conflictedness of the narrative; the tension between the stark realism, trauma and finality of the Carthew strand and the geopolitical and philosophical musings of the Beigbeder strand. As we can see, though, each of the narrators carry their own conflicts and divisions.

This tension which characterizes the text as a whole reaches its nadir in Beigbeder's continued discourse with what he at one point calls "raging liberalism," a condition that is also associated with Carthew and is again articulated through this transnational perspective (Beigbeder 2004: 282). Much of this discussion is couched in an ongoing discussion of the 1970s, itself a historical discourse and, for Beigbeder, the place where the shallowness that defines contemporary culture, and particularly masculinity, has its origins. The novel is actually preoccupied with this to the extent that at one point Beigbeder states, "I think I'm writing about September 11 but actually I'm writing about the seventies: the decade that spawned the WTC, the Tour Montparnasse and Concorde which connects them: of these three, two no longer exist" (Beigbeder 2004: 156). This again works to consolidate what Versluys calls "the transatlantic west," though it also subtly evokes the "clash of civilizations" conceit in the way that the licentiousness that Beigbeder describes is often identified—notably in John Updike's *Terrorist* (2006)—as the element of Western society that Islamists deplore. As stated, much of Beigbeder's discourse on the seventies revolves around issues of masculinity and sexuality, and he points to the seventies as the decade of origin for what he calls "THE INTERNATIONAL PLAYBOY": "the arrival of the contraceptive pill, relaxed divorce laws, the feminist revolution, the sexual revolution ... you get THE INTERNATIONAL PLAYBOY" (Beigbeder 2004: 142). Beigbeder goes on to describe some of what he sees as the lasting psychological impact of this kind of masculinity on the individual:

> What use is love in a civilization based on desire? Why burden yourself with a family if freedom is the ultimate principle? What is the purpose of morality in a hedonistic society? ... If the individual is king, then only selfishness makes sense [Beigbeder 2004: 143].

Indeed, there are suggestions of a more general societal moral decline originating in the seventies, and Beigbeder stretches to a precipitous condemnation of liberalism and contemporary ideas of freedom: "The West booms that we must be free! Free! Shout from the rooftops how free we are, brag about how free we are. Die to defend that freedom. All well and good. But I am not happy when I am free" (Beigbeder 2004: 281). This is an evocative statement, particularly at a time when the White House's declaration that "our very way of life, our freedom is under attack" was still resonating powerfully (Bush 2001: n.p.). This is not a universal notion of personal freedom, though, but his own sexual freedom that he refers to. Any universal rhetoric in this discourse is ultimately diluted by the two protagonists reining it in to clearly personal spheres. The final sections show Beigbeder and Carthew in contrition for their lack of commitment to marriage and relationships, and finally Carthew recalibrates this expression "I am not happy when I am free": "I liked it better having Candace hold me in her arms, so that I could forget the terror of being me. I wasn't happy when I was free" (Beigbeder 2004: 282).

While the possibility of a more general moral decline in "the West" seems to hang obliquely over several sections of the novel, the gestures toward the universal in these accusations of "raging liberalism" are never fully substantiated and related directly to 9/11. For example, the truism that Islamic extremism and Jihad amounts to a war against the perceived licentiousness of Western societies is never addressed in these sections, which are invariably reduced to discussions of the individuals. These two characters, in narrative corroboration and contrast, reveal powerfully the impulse to simultaneously declare epoch and probe for context, and these conflicting impulses cancel each other out, leaving a distinct sense of disorientation and frustration in the characters and with the reader. But while several ideas or gestures are never fully developed or invested in, the conflictedness does, as Versluys states, provide "arresting testimony to the mental crisis 9/11 provoked and to the moral confusion left in its wake" (Versluys 2009: 148).

Extremely Loud and Incredibly Close: *Trauma, Photography and Performativity*

As in *Windows on the World*, the transnational narrative of *Extremely Loud and Incredibly Close* is at the heart of the tension between the rhetoric of continuity and discontinuity. Integral to this is the chapter-by-chapter narrative alternation between Oskar and his German Grandparents, but it is useful to begin discussion with the most prominent aesthetic feature of the novel—its use of still photography, which correlates to each narrative strand. Still photography appears variously throughout the text and is the most prominent of the many visual and textual devices that Walter Kirn somewhat derisively describes as the novel's "avant-garde tool kit" (Kirn 2005: n.p.). There is, however, much discourse around the importance of still photography in representing, responding to and documenting 9/11, particularly in relation to trauma, and the use of the medium does have a prescience that goes deeper than the superficiality for which the text is often criticized. Firstly, the still photography can be seen as marking a deliberate opposition to mainstream media coverage. In the introduction to *Here Is New York: A Democracy of Photographs* (2002), the book collection anthologized from the celebrated proletarian exhibition of 9/11 photography that began just a week after the attacks, Michael Shulan states: "In order to come to grips with all of this imagery which was haunting us, it was essential, we thought, to reclaim it from the media and stare at it without flinching" (Shulan 2002: 1). The idea here is that while the constantly repeated images of the planes crashing into the towers, people jumping from the towers, and the towers falling perpetuated and contributed to the trauma of the attacks, the still photography allowed engagement. In this light,

Two. A Crisis in Representation

Extremely Loud and Incredibly Close is, ostensibly, oppositional in its use of photos; it is explicitly critical of this media coverage within the text as well. In one of the "My Feelings" chapters of the novel narrated by Oskar's grandmother, she describes the experience of watching the initial 9/11 news coverage using the phrase "Planes going into buildings. Bodies Falling. Buildings Falling" over and over through two pages (Foer 2005: 106).

Aside from being counterpoint to the most obvious and well-known images of 9/11, as stated, the still photos in the text can be related to discourse that frequently places still photography as particularly adept at representing or engaging with trauma, especially the much photographed events of 9/11. As noted previously, trauma is most often seen as a condition of temporality. In the introduction to her seminal work *Trauma: Explorations in Memory* (1995), Cathy Caruth writes, "The event is not experienced fully at the time, but only belatedly, in its repeated possession of the one who experiences it. To be traumatized is precisely to be possessed by an image or event" (Caruth 1995: 4). Marianne Hirsch incorporates this logic in describing the way still photography might respond to trauma:

> If still photography is the visual genre that best captures the trauma and loss associated with September 2001—the sense of monumental, irrevocable change that we feel we have experienced—it is due to the photograph's temporality. Photography interrupts, actually stops time, freezes a moment: it is inherently elegiac. The feeling that time stopped around 9:00 a.m. on September 11 has created an immeasurable gulf between the before and the after [Hirsche 2003: 71–72].

Hirsch here is following on from Susan Sontag's claim in *Regarding the Pain of Others* that "Memory freeze-frames; its basic unit is the single image ... the photograph provides a quick way of apprehending something" (Sontag 2003: 22). Hirsch, though, is clearly describing 9/11 as a moment of discontinuity and advocating still photography as a medium equipped to represent this kind of moment. In the only repeated photograph in *Extremely Loud and Incredibly Close,* the famous image of the "falling man," which is inserted three times and shows a man who Oskar believes may be his father, this logic is to some degree manifest.

However, still photos are not always registered as representing a discontinuous moment, and those used in *Extremely Loud and Incredibly*

Close, individually or compiled, carry a strong narrative function. Holloway, writing about the "here is new york" exhibition, locates a kind of "narrativity" in these images:

> *Here Is New York*'s intimate snapshots of people caught up in immense human drama often took forms reminiscent of "street photography," offering single frames, fleeting moments stolen from stories that were self-evidently much "bigger" than the snapshots on show—stories that were evoked by the image but that remained pregnant and untold within it ... [Holloway 2008: 134].

The photographs in *Extremely Loud and Incredibly Close* are not, of course, all centered on 9/11, but they also have a "street photography" quality to them in the way they infer a larger narrative, and the central image of the falling man is most certainly a definitive example of this. Furthermore, these photos, including that of the falling man, are explicitly narrativized by Oskar, as they comprise his diary, *Stuff That Happened to Me*. Therefore, while the photographs of the falling man, as well as many of the others, clearly signify or symbolize the traumatic break or moment of discontinuity in Oskar's life, they also remain loaded with this "narrativity"—particularly as Oskar believes the falling man may be his father, and that his quest to find the lock for his father's key (which ultimately proves to be a MacGuffin) is built around his need to understand how his father died.

In the text's frequently criticized inclusion of these still photos, there is a pronounced tension between Oskar's and his Grandparents' experience of trauma, and Oskar's need to inject narrative into his personal catastrophe in order to come to terms with it. This striking dichotomy is discussed by Laura Frost, who acknowledges Foer's awareness of the still photograph as a "tool for the resolution of trauma" but also suggests that the novel illustrates the "failure" of still photography: "Foer expresses longing for the 'still time' of the photograph as a form of memorialization; however, his novel also radically questions photography's efficacy to resolve the trauma of the falling people" (Frost 2008: 185). This open "question" is again indicative of the narrative tension; the prescient question here, though, is whether or not this marked tension can be extrapolated by the reader from simply the story of a traumatized nine-year-old boy and his quest to come to terms with "the worst day," as he repeatedly refers to it, and applied to wider or further

Two. A Crisis in Representation

reaching ideas about a societal or government response to 9/11. The answer to this may lie in Foer's use of the falling man photographs. As stated, not only does the falling man appear three times in stills throughout the course of the narrative, but this image is also the focal point of the device used in the finale, a fifteen-page flipbook of photographs of the falling man in reverse order—playing out Oskar's fantasy of going back in time or reversing time so that the falling man flies up and into the Windows on the World restaurant, back down the elevator and so on. While Frost believes that ultimately the falling man imagery "reflects a tendency to think of 9/11 as a moment frozen in time, as a city's and a nation's disaster, rather than as part of a political process that is still unfolding," the flipbook in *Extremely Loud and Incredibly Close*, to some extent at least, suggests the opposite in its narrativity.

Oskar's desperate wish to go back in time can't necessarily be related to a need to look back for origins or political context in regards to 9/11, but it can perhaps be related to the much discussed national fantasy of wanting to go back to the day before, to be prepared, a desire felt by many immediately, which subsequently gave way to a desire to understand why, nationally, America was not prepared—a desire that eventually led to the *9/11 Commission Report*. Furthermore, Oskar's compulsion to act, to embark on his quest, also allegorically reflects ideas of America's need to act in order to preempt further attacks (which, as many commentators have noted, was driven by the Bush administration and a complicit, conservative media). Mitchum Huehls argues that the flipbook is an embodiment of a "performativity" that is a major function of the text as a whole, and describes the novel as "performatively coextensive with Oskar's journal." Huehls states:

> Oskar thinks he will be healed if he can reverse time. While this reversal is clearly just so much wishful thinking, its temporal form—the flip-book's cinematic, real-time performance of motion—proves crucial to Oskar's healing process. He must relegate the event to the past by embracing time's forward progress into the future [Huehls 2008: 52].

Huehls' argument is that through these various devices the entire novel has a performative aspect, like the flipbook. However, his interpretation of Oskar as having an allegorical function, which constitutes a possibility for American national post–9/11 acting and understanding, is predicated on what he describes as a "quasi-performative" quality or "internally conflicted performativity" in the textual device and narrative (Huehls 2008: 52). The conflict comes, he suggests, in a kind of lack of consistency in the performative aspects of the texts—which are, again, largely the visual devices. On some occasions Huehls argues, "A thing is what it is, and at other times it represents something else" (Huehls 2008: 50). For example, when Oskar states, "I pulled *Stuff That Happened to Me* from the space between the bed and wall, and I flipped through it for a while, wishing I would finally fall asleep," the text then shows the fifteen photographs that he flips through, performing what has been described (Foer 2004: 52). In other instances the photographs have a more symbolic and less performative function, or, as suggested at the beginning of this chapter, actually interrupt the narrative flow. The image of the bridge is a perfect example, as the photograph is placed after the episode, causing an interruption, and the crossing of a bridge it depicts is metaphorically loaded and symbolic; thus, this image doesn't have the performative quality that many others do. Ultimately, Huehls posits the implications of this "conflicted peformativity" on the text as an allegory:

> If Foer's novel posits a performatively cinematic real-time as an ideal temporal mode for knowing and healing 9/11's timely traumas, it also reveals that adopting this mode comes with great risks: formal incoherence, an unknown and thus potentially dangerous future, and an equivocal relation to the world and its objects. These are precisely the risks that the Bush administration has refused to take, choosing instead to manage risk with a policy of preemption that is coherent, known, and unequivocal [Huehls 2008: 52–53].

This is an astute reading, and the possibility of a subversive quality in the text's performativity has been largely ignored by its many critics and commentators. However, the conception of "conflicted performativity" can be reduced more clearly to the level of the narrative dichotomy. As stated, this is a quest narrative, and perhaps the most important part of the meta-fictional qualities of the text's performativity is that, as Huehls does acknowledge, the reader is implicated; the text "channels readers into their own contingent search for knowledge." However, we and Oskar do not know what we're searching for, bar the most opaque reductions; Oskar is searching for some insight into his father's death, and the reader, perhaps, is searching for or expecting a more universal insight into the collective trauma of the attacks. This search for understanding and knowledge, on a core level, is rooted in continuity, though this is undoubtedly problematic or compromised, as is Huehls' notion of a "performatively cinematic real-time as an ideal temporal mode for knowing and healing 9/11's timely traumas," because the search is never stabilized and remains bound to the continued rhetoric of the absolute. If we accept the "value of gaining knowledge in real time and charging head first into those unknown unknowns," we must also accept that this charge never comes untethered from the traumatic, absolute break: the discontinuous moment. Even if there is some healing in the quest's "unexpected" resolution of Oskar's discovery of unknown depths in his relationship with his mother, on a macro level this is like the compensatory foregrounding of a positive sense of community or the heroics of rescue workers and firemen; it distracts and can be restorative but doesn't resolve the trauma or provide answers for questions of how and why.

History and Foer's Transnational Split

While the still photography and performativity of the novel clearly perpetuate its fundamental conflictedness, the aspect of the text that most clearly articulates its tensions and divisions is its transnational split. The alternation in chapters between the narratives of Oskar and his German grandparents facilitates the important references the text makes to previous historical moments of trauma and allows the possibility of comparison of 9/11 to the fire-bombings at Dresden and atomic bombing of Hiroshima. Before discussing this, though, it is necessary to turn to the highly synthetic characterization of both Oskar and the entire narrative framework (another aspect of the text which embodies its postmodernist pretenses). The way the characterization of Oskar and many of the novel's generic conceits connects literary tradition and convention to the story's historical reference points is integral to the ultimate impact of the transnational narrative.

The characterization of Oskar is widely cited as being a synthesis of several modern or contemporary literary creations; many reviewers associate him with Holden Caulfield or Oskar Matzerath, who Gessen cites as his "namesake." Michiko Kakutani states:

> He comes across as an entirely synthetic creation, assembled out of bits and pieces of famous literary heroes past. Like J.D. Salinger's Holden Caulfield, Oskar wanders around New York City, lonely, alienated and on the verge, possibly, of an emotional breakdown. Like Günter Grass's Oskar Matzerath in *The Tin Drum*, he plays a musical instrument (in this case a tambourine) while commenting on the fearful state of the world around him. And like Saul Bellow's Herzog, he writes letters to people he doesn't know [Kakutani 2005: n.p.].

Not only is Oskar a synthetic character, but the supporting cast and milieu are clearly derivative. As Kirn states, *Extremely Loud and Incredibly Close* is "a conscious homage to the Gotham wise-child genre, the book features several beloved stock characters, down to the nice doorman and other service folk who help their upper-middle-class young wards get around the urban jungle safely" (Kirn 2005: n.p.). Furthermore, despite the device of alternative narrators that force occasional leaps back in time pertaining to their respective subplots, *Extremely Loud and Incredibly Close* is a classic quest narrative, or, more specifically, it lies in the realm of a subgenre, the detective novel. As Däwes states, it is a "postmodernist pastiche of genres—combining bildungsroman and anti-detective novel, epistolary novel and memoir" (Däwes 2007: 529). However, despite the highly referential nature of the text, what Oskar does is personalize 9/11 as his own private tragedy. The novel is virtually apolitical, and the attacks are, for Oskar, simply "the worst day" (Foer 2004: 104). The significance of 9/11 is reduced to the fact that Oskar has lost his father. However, because of the stock characters, archetypal structure and synthetic nature of his character, the highly personalized and apolitical account of 9/11 affects a more generic air and is afforded some reach. Kirn actually suggests that this is where the novel makes its wider impact; discussing the fantasy or innocent New York of children's stories in which the novel is undoubtedly set, he states:

> Foer chose this quaint template for an ingenious reason: it evokes, at a primal cultural level, the benevolent, innocent New York that was vaporized, even as a fantasy, when the towers were toppled. Not all the victims, Foer knows, were real, live people. Eloise and Stuart Little died, too [Kirn 2005: n.p.].

A more severe interpretation of the effect of the synthetic and referential nature of the text on its wider messages is that its morality is

Two. A Crisis in Representation

reduced to the sentimental suggestion that all tragedy or trauma is horrible, and that there is equality in death, suffering and loss. This is a trope the text frequently falls back on, and the presence of these stock characters and familiar genre conceits reinforces it. Additionally, as we will see, this simplistic rhetoric ultimately characterizes the transnational aspect of the novel as well. For example, in a scene narrated by Oskar's grandmother, on the morning of 9/11 she describes sitting and watching a man on the news being interviewed about his missing daughter, the suspected victim of murder. As the breaking story of the attacks took over, she "kept thinking about the father of the missing girl. He kept believing" (Foer 2004: 225). Watching the attacks, her thoughts return to the aftermath of the Dresden fire-bombings, which her family had suffered; and as she meditates on this, Oskar's mother calls with the news that Thomas, her son and Oskar's father, is in the World Trade Center. This is one of many generic connections that are made between losses and suffering in the text, and while this is a story of one family's loss on 9/11, the generic and endlessly referential aspect of the characters and story opens them up. As Kirn points out, the synthetic nature of the text is also fundamental to its basic message:

> This hyperactive impersonation of Holden Caulfield, who dreamed of catching suicidal children as he trod the same sidewalks that Oskar does and tried to shake off a funk that also traced back to a family tragedy, connects with the photographs of the terrorist victim in a nifty, Rubik's cube sort of way that gives a chilly intellectual thrill but doesn't penetrate the bosom. This accords with what appears to be the novel's quite difficult grand ambition: to take on the most explosive subject available while showing no passion, giving no offense, adopting no point of view and venturing no sentiment more hazardous than that history is sad and brutal and wouldn't it be nicer if it weren't [Kirn 2005: n.p.].

This generic sentiment is, of course, related directly to the previously discussed generic search for understanding that the performativity of the text facilitates. It is also powerfully rooted in the narrative dichotomy in the way the stock characters and milieu, the archetypal narrative framework, and these repeated references to other fictional characters all seem to drive toward opening the story up and relating it to other narratives, showing commonalities and lines of continuity. Simultaneously, Oskar (as well as both of his grandparents) is so apolitical and existential that his concerns never approach a macro level, and this pulls the rhetoric in the opposite direction. On the rare occasions that Oskar alludes to wider post–9/11 society, it is always presented in the terms of his limited (as a sheltered nine-year-old) point of view:

> Even after a year, I still had an extremely difficult time doing certain things, like taking showers, for some reason, and getting into elevators, obviously. There was a lot of stuff that made me panicky, like suspension bridges, germs, airplanes, fireworks, Arab people on the subway (even though I'm not racist), Arab people in restaurants and coffee shops and other public places, scaffolding, sewers and subway grates, bags without owners, shoes, people with mustaches, smoke, knots, tall buildings, turbans [Foer 2004: 36].

As he qualifies these fears, it is all in terms of "I" or "me": "I'd get that feeling," "I started inventing things," "I couldn't stop," "which I know about," "that's how my brain was." These hints at real post–9/11 issues such as racism or paranoia, as provocative as they may be, are limited to one traumatized boy. The final dimension of the text that underpins this dichotomy is, as stated, its evocation of other historical moments of political violence or trauma.

There are references to two such moments, the continued subnarrative strand of the grandparents' traumatic experience of the Dresden fire-bombings of 1945 (by the RAF and USAAF) and their subsequently traumatized lives; and also, in two striking passages, to the atomic bombing of Hiroshima (by the USAAF). Both are potentially provocative points of references, considering they are perhaps the two most controversial bombing campaigns by American or Allied Forces during World War II, with civilian death tolls that vastly outnumber the 9/11 victims. Furthermore, the mere inclusion of events such as these seems to demand comparison of impact—particularly as these are World War II events which recall the widespread media headline in the days after 9/11—"A new day of infamy"—which evoked, of course, Pearl Harbor. The first reference to the atomic bomb comes in an episode that does make an indirect reference to 9/11. Oskar is describing his relationship to his grandmother and mentions that "a couple of days after the worst day, when I was on my way to my first appointment with Dr. Fein, I saw Grandma carrying a huge rock across Broadway" (Foer 2004: 104). This is never explained, though a few lines later the narrative moves to

Two. A Crisis in Representation

a scene where Oskar's grandmother gives him a collection of stamps of "Great American Inventors," one of whom is J. Robert Oppenheimer: "Who's he?" "He invented the bomb." "Which bomb?" "*The* bomb." "He wasn't a great Inventor." She said, "Great, not good" (Foer 2005: 105). The simple proximity in the text of "the worst day" to "*The* bomb" is striking. However, the contexts of either, the history, or even the way each of the individuals remember the events are not elaborated on, and the text quickly moves on. A more sustained account of "*The* bomb" comes in another episode, when Oskar presents an oral history of the bombing of Hiroshima for a school project. This episode employs a kind of delayed decoding, as the chapter in which it appears opens with the lines: "INTERVIEWER. Can you describe the events of that morning?" (Foer 2004: 187). In a novel revolving around 9/11, this is a clear evocation of the attacks. It is revealed to be a taped interview Oskar is playing out on a tape recorder of a graphic account of a mother and child's experience of the Hiroshima bombing. The interview ends with the following lines:

> That is what death is like. It doesn't matter what uniforms the soldiers are wearing. It doesn't matter how good the weapons are. I thought if everyone could see what I saw, we would never have war anymore [Foer 2004: 189].

This is as direct as the text gets in its approach to the politics of 9/11. It is a powerfully rendered message, and coming from a Japanese woman on a tape played on a boom box by the idealistic Oskar, it does seem to connect Hiroshima to 9/11 in this final meditation on parity in death. However, there is no explicit connection drawn, and the rhetoric remains of the opaque or generic variety discussed above.

There is more possibility for sustained comparison in the narrative of Oskar's grandparents, who lived through the Dresden fire-bombings. Oskar's Grandmother suffered the loss of her older sister, who was Oskar's Grandfather's first lover. They later met in New York where Oskar's father was conceived. His Grandfather's deeply damaging trauma soon causes him to leave Oskar's grandmother shortly before his father was born. The unraveling of this narrative (which also, to a much further extent, employs delayed decoding tactics, again involving the reader in the quest) lasts the length of the novel and does draw occasional parallels to Oskar's trauma. The narratives of Grandpa and Grandma are narratives of severe traumatic ruptures—both characters are clearly prisoners of the past. As Versluys states, "Dresden has become an absolute event, so totalizing in its impact that it no longer has a definable place in space or time" (Versluys 2009: 96). The fact that Oskar's father, the grandparent's son, dies in the World Trade Center suggests a cyclical narrative of history based on political violence or war. This is certainly the logic Versluys posits when he states that "this seemingly apolitical family novel has history palimpsestically inscribed in every sentence." However, any real connections between these historical events are limited to accounts of the psychological suffering of the individuals and their loss. There is nothing in the accounts of either the Dresden fire-bombings or 9/11 to distinguish them as major historical instances of political violence. Either of these traumas could be from a natural disaster or tragic accident. Keith Gessen sums this up concisely: "The effect of these other catastrophes in the novel is to suggest that all human suffering is equivalent, be it American, German, or Japanese" (Gessen 2005: 72). In accounts of the text that are more positive this is interpreted slightly differently. For example, Versluys emphasizes the way these two events, Hiroshima and Dresden, are acts of violence committed by Americans and how this shows opposition to "fetishistic narratives that simplistically reduce the issue involved to a pitched battle of 'us' versus 'them' or good versus evil" (Versluys 2009: 83). Similarly, Matthew Mullins articulates an equality in terms of trauma: "Since trauma is an experience common to all people regardless of social, political, or cultural difference, however, it seems logical to suggest the events of 9/11 as an opportunity to foster community." Gessen's argument, however, that the "effect of the book as a whole is in fact precisely to pull the September 11 attacks out of history," is perhaps hyperbolic, but, as Holloway states, there is no doubt that the emphasis on trauma in *Extremely Loud and Incredibly Close* looks inward and away from any "meaningful contextualizing of 9/11 in public or historical space" (Mullins 2009: 298). Ultimately this becomes the defining tension of the novel's general conflictedness. While the historical events referenced could indeed be apolitical incidents in the way they function in the text, the specificity of this parallel narrative, the setting up of the Dresden story as a novel-spanning sub-plot, forces the reader to think politically and to try and make connections. The text's refusal to concede any conclusions regarding competitive memories, collective memory or multidirectional memory heightens its conflictedness.

Foer, Beigbeder and the Paradigm of Conflictedness

While *Extremely Loud and Incredibly Close*'s reviewers and critical commentators have held disparate views, and readings of the text have been wide-ranging, one conviction brings them together—the identification of some kind of deeply rooted tension. The most critical of the reviews saw this in terms of the novel's lack of coherence. Kakutani wrote in the *New York Times* that "the novel as a whole feels simultaneously contrived and improvisatory, schematic and haphazard" (Kakutani 2005: n.p.). Laura Frost, in her article focusing on the use of the falling man imagery, finds it to be "by turns precious and poignant," and more specifically identifies a "struggle between visual evidence and narrative evidence, between discontinuous time and narrative time, between knowledge and uncertainty, and between traumatic repetition and narrative resolution" (Frost 2008: 185). Mitchum Huehls' account of the performativity of the text again identifies this tension as an "internally conflicted performativity." There are many more accounts which highlight oppositional pulls in the text, though, as we have seen, this tension is always identified in connection with its experimental pretenses, and the common denominator is clearly the basic oppositional pulls inherent in the attempt to locate 9/11 as both continuous and discontinuous. *Windows on the World* is a very different novel, and this tension is perhaps easier to identify in this text, as it can be aligned with the duality of the narrative—"a strange diptych," as Stephen Metcalf described it in *The New York Times* (though, as we have seen, it is much more sophisticated than this) (Metcalf 2005: n.p.). The way that the two narrative strands in *Windows on the World* begin to diverge and pull against each other, declaring the absolute at one turn and groping for context at the next, creates an effect that is similar to that in *Extremely Loud and Incredibly Close*. What really binds the two texts, though, and creates this effect in both, is their shared deployment of a deliberately playful and searching aesthetic, and the ways in which it relates to the transnational, which is where the central dichotomy is most prominently revealed. These two novels clearly reflect the widespread disorientation felt in U.S. and Western society in general in attempting to come to terms with 9/11—what Versluys describes as "the mental crisis 9/11 provoked" and the "moral confusion left in its wake." Both texts powerfully evoke the tension between the compulsion to declare epoch and trauma, and to simultaneously want to narrativize or contextualize. The disorientation is also illuminating in the way it suggests a possible logic in the initial approval and appeal to a large section of American society, of the unilateral and Manichean post–9/11 strategies of the Bush administration. It also is suggestive in considering the literary representations of 9/11 that would follow and the trends that define them. While this chapter has identified the conflictedness of these novels and failure to reconcile the oppositional narrative pulls they contain, it must be acknowledged that they are clearly ambitious in their allusions, attempting to evoke history through transnational narratives. The novels that follow not only contrast starkly in their aesthetic commitment to realism but also in the micro-focus of their themes and subjects.

THREE

Marriage, Relationships and 9/11: The Seismographic Narratives of *Falling Man*, *The Good Life* and *The Emperor's Children*

Aesthetically, *Windows on the World* and *Extremely Loud and Incredibly Close* stand out in the canon of 9/11 fiction, and the novels that have appeared subsequently are formally very different. However, in one shared thematic strand, at least, there is a marked continuity. This is the discourse of the American family, "the sacred cornerstone of the American social project," according to Kenneth Millard, and something that "is perceived as fundamental to the happiness of the individual, the nation, and corporate life" (Millard 2000: 9). However, while the American family forms the general milieu of *Extremely Loud and Incredibly Close*, which foregrounds the perspective of a child, and while *Windows on the World* relies on the importance of the protagonist's children for its emotional core, the later examples of the literary representation of 9/11 place much more emphasis on relationships between man and woman. Indeed, within this emerging canon there is no more widely explored theme than marriage and relationships. Three of the most significant of these novels, in terms of literary authorship and volume of readership, Don DeLillo's *Falling Man* (2007), Jay McInerney's *The Good Life* (2005), and Claire Messud's *The Emperor's Children* (2006), focus centrally on this subject. This discourse is so generally prevalent, though, that in a 2007 survey of 9/11 fiction, "The End of Innocence," Pankaj

Mishra asks disbelievingly, "Are we meant to think of domestic discord, also deployed by DeLillo and McInerney, as a metaphor for post–9/11 America?" (Mishra 2007: 5). Mishra's remark is to some degree representative of wider criticism of the generally narrow focus of these texts; many of them are frequently cited as lacking any wider historical context or political insight, and certainly in the case of the three texts studied here, any allegorical possibilities are conflicted or oblique. Discussing these three novels in particular, Richard Gray describes how "cataclysmic public events are measured purely and simply in terms of their impact on the emotional entanglements of their protagonists" (Gray 2009: 134). Additionally, apart from the protagonist of *The Reluctant Fundamentalist* (2007) or the cricketers of Joseph O'Neil's *Netherland* (2008), and certain small tokenistic sections of the other novels, the literary fiction of 9/11 focuses not just on New York and New Yorkers but on a very elite and unrepresentative bourgeois section of New York. The central protagonists comprise here of: *Falling Man* (a Manhattan lawyer and a freelance editor), *The Good Life* (literary editor, writer, stockbroker, society socialite) and *The Emperor's Children* (a large cast of privileged New York literati). Indeed, this trend extends to many of the other examples of 9/11 fiction, *A Disorder Peculiar to the Country* (two Manhattan lawyers) or *Netherland* (banker and a lawyer), for example. Nevertheless, this enterprise of dramatizing privileged American domesticity in the specter of the mourning city, exemplified by *Falling Man*, *The Good Life* and *The Emperor's Children,* is revealing and useful in a more meaningful and far-reaching way than perhaps the micro-focus of these relationship narratives might suggest. Analyzing Ulrich Baer's suggestions regarding the possibilities of literary representation of 9/11, Alex Houen develops three "clearly divergent" modes for fiction that could theoretically be employed in a novel representation of 9/11 (Houen 2004: 421). The first is a "transformative realism—it honors the 'shocking singularity' of the event while turning it into a story." This evokes Jenny Edkins' description of the first of two ways in which people respond to trauma: "The first involves an attempt to forget trauma and to incorporate what happened into the narrative forms we already have available. It means telling the story, fitting the event into a linear narrative framework" (Edkins 2002: 248). Despite the clear differences between the three texts, particularly the relative narrative complexity of *Falling Man*, these are logical ways of reading them all, as 9/11 is the backdrop for relationship narratives which ostensibly act as social barometers measuring the impact of the attacks and the pressures they exert on the domestic and banal. This chapter, however, will suggest that it is a variation of Houen's second category which is able to elucidate the lasting significance of these three texts. Houen states, "The second is a kind of seismographic registering of events, in which writing is subject to them as a form of unconscious, historical symptom" (Houen 2004: 421). In spite of the seemingly narrow domestic focus of these novels and their intent to primarily explore traumatic rupture, the narrative arcs of the relationship stories have an underlying compliance with the more contentious notion that the social realities of 9/11 and post–9/11 can be more accurately understood in terms of temporary disruption rather than an epoch or rupture, as so many felt or feel it was. What is manifest in these texts is not allegory but rather a subliminal or unconscious restoration of equilibrium, evoking ideas of continuity, history and a return to normality.

In *9/11 and the War on Terror* (2008), David Holloway illustrates his previously-quoted argument that "9/11 was long in the making, and the pre–9/11 and post–9/11 worlds were broadly continuous not discontinuous," by moving through separate fields of discourse—history, politics, mass media, literature, cinema and photography. These novels, however, do not afford themselves this kind of panorama and are not directly pointing to this kind of continuity. Nevertheless, even pertaining strictly to domestic drama, the restoration of equilibrium within narratives that are clearly entangling their emotional upheavals with the events of 9/11, there is a clear seismographic paralleling. As stated, these novels are actually narratives of marriage or relationships that build 9/11 in as a background or context. However, they are explicitly presented as "9/11 novels," the titles and book jackets alone establishing the two discourses as inseparable, and the narratives of 9/11 and the relationships are undoubtedly correspondent.[7] Even then, if they cannot carry explicit national allegories, the implications and suggestions in the narrative structure and plotting of these domestic dramas demand analysis.

The argument here—that despite their narrow focus and clear intent to examine the rupture caused by 9/11, these novels are rooted in ideas of continuity—is further complicated but ultimately given weight by the media-generated notion of post–9/11 shifts in gender roles, and the important critical accounts of these media interpretations, particularly Susan Faludi's *The Terror Dream: What 9/11 Revealed About America* (2008). Indeed, several notable theoretical works across a wide range of fields explore the myth-making capacity of the post–9/11 American media. Edkins generically emphasizes the enormity of media influence and its propensity for bombast in post–9/11 journalism: "In many parts of the world September 11 represented not so much a traumatic discontinuity but the beginning of a season of hyperbole and exaggeration in the western media" (Edkins 2002: 245). Faludi, though, meticulously details the way that the media relentlessly propagated a notion of a widespread return to particular American gender archetypes and crucially questions the urge to revisit classic World War II or Cold War gender stereotypes: "Why were independent female voices censured and a bugle call sounded to return to Betty Crocker domesticity? Why were our political and cultural stages suddenly packed with Lone Ranger leaders, Davy Crockett candidates, and John Wayne 'manly men?' Why, in short, when confronted with an actual danger, did America call rewrite?" (Faludi 2008: 199). Faludi uses National Consensus statistics to carefully reveal the line of demarcation between reality and media fantasy regarding notions of increased birth rates and women migrating from the workplace to establish themselves as homemakers. However, there clearly cannot simply be on the one hand the realities and on the other hand the media hyperbole, as lived lives are affected by media (as fictional or complicit as it may be with a neo-conservative government seeking military conflict). Therefore, while theoretical texts such as *The Terror Dream* or Derek Gregory's *The Colonial Present* (2005) offer empirical accounts of the way certain indisputable realities amount to powerful continuity narratives of 9/11 that lie beneath the media hyperbole, this chapter will show how these three novels reflect murkier social realities, probing the space between myth and empirical fact. And while the worlds they explore are, as stated, unrepresentative, it is precisely because of the social "set" that they dramatize (those with the closest proximity to 9/11 and who might be perceived as having the most to lose in the attacks) that the eventual restoring of equilibrium in the novels becomes an equally powerful statement about the impact of the attacks.

Three. Marriage, Relationships and 9/11

Terror Sex

While the main focus of these novels is long-term relationships, they all contain important passages discussing purely sexual relationships and respond to varying media tropes of post–9/11 sexuality. This includes a frequently alleged phenomenon of the immediate post–9/11 that the media quickly termed "terror sex"—the idea that New York, gripped by collective trauma, was experiencing heightened sexual activity through a desperate need for human contact and intimacy in the immediate aftermath of 9/11. Ostensibly, the terror sex myth and the media's role in it directly contradicts Faludi's account of a neoconservative media advocating very gendered moral obligations, though this is largely explained by the fact that it was a very early phenomenon occupying just the initial weeks after 9/11. Ultimately, this was quickly superseded by media-propagated archetypes of "protector" masculinity and "domicile" femininity that gained momentum as the mainstream media quickly aligned itself to the strategies of the Bush White House. The representation of sex or "terror sex" in these novels is usefully examined preliminarily, though, as it reveals a way in which these novels lay out the literary parameters and positions of distance from the media "hyperbole" that they attempt to hold throughout the narratives while also establishing an important tone of knowingness or self-reflexivity that underpins the relationship narratives.

A *Salon* article from September 21, 2001, is typical of these early accounts of "terror sex." The article describes an anonymous woman's experience: "She had been noticing a new phenomenon among her close friends since Tuesday. The world had changed; so had relationships. Now, just about everyone she knew was having what she and her friends call 'terror sex'" (Kazdin 2001: n.p.). In *The Good Life*, descriptions of this kind of activity come through similarly gossip-based situations. In one scene rescue workers evoke terror sex as a big media story: "'I hear everybody's fucking their brains out uptown,' Jerry said. 'There was an article about it today'" (McInerney 2005: 134). Nothing of this nature happens to any of the characters in these novels, however, and the "terror sex" discourse retains for the characters and for the reader the distance of speculative newspaper articles—gossip and myth. DeLillo addresses the notion of a heightened sexuality in the second chapter of *Falling*

Man, which begins with a long cerebral paragraph describing the ordinary or mundane as being exceptionally sexually charged in the days after 9/11:

> Sex was everywhere at first, in words, phrases, half gestures, the simplest intimation of altered space. She'd put down a book or magazine and a small pause settled around them. This was sex. They'd walk down a street together and see themselves in a dusty window. A flight of stairs was sex ... [DeLillo 2007: 2].

This is a very different kind of passage that ultimately maintains a similar distance from actual events in the narrative, as do the conversational episodes of *The Good Life,* by describing a kind of aura rather than actual experience. DeLillo's evocation of this "aura" is very suggestive in that it posits an alternative to the gossip and hyperbole. The kind of reckless, spontaneous episodes described in the *Salon* article and evoked frequently in all of these texts bears some relation to what Kai Erikson describes in "Trauma and Community": "Traumatized people calculate life's chances differently ... traumatized people often come to feel that they have lost an important measure of control over the circumstances of their own lives" (Erikson 1995: 194). However, accounts of terror sex remain gossipy and anecdotal, and the novels explicitly handle them as media exaggeration. Furthermore, there are other facets of collective trauma that we might apply to this discourse; Erikson also describes a sense of euphoria sweeping traumatized survivors:

> A "stage of euphoria" quickly follows.... The energy with which rescuers work and the warmth with which neighbours respond act to reassure victims that there is still life among the wreckage, and they react with an outpouring of communal feeling, an urgent need to make contact with and even touch others by way of renewing old pledges of fellowship [Erikson 1995: 189].

This bears more resemblance to the earlier quote from *Falling Man* where DeLillo describes a heightened aura of sexuality attached to everyday life. It is also suggestive of a more subtly underpinning reality behind both the initial "terror sex" and subsequent "baby-boom" strains of media mythologizing, as it suggests that in scenarios of collective trauma there may be a palpable need for intimacy and contact—not necessarily a reckless sexuality but enough of a general shift in mood for media interpretation to begin generating this kind of mythology.

Another important facet of the sex scenes, particularly in *The Good Life* and *Falling Man*, is a certain self-reflexivity. These relationship narratives, which shift or unsettle markedly with the advent of 9/11, carry a distinct knowingness or inevitability regarding the post-traumatic reevaluation of core values. This is foretold in allusions to this heightened need for contact and intimacy—there is the distinct feeling that this is a tried narrative. In *The Good Life,* Russell evokes this as he walks through a crowded street:

> The enforced intimacy of sweating bodies was strangely comforting. Russell found himself pressed against a beautiful, nameless girl he recognized—dark and delicate, of Indian extraction, he imagined—from shared trips on the elevator, enveloped in her musky scent. Was this to be the legacy: wartime couplings, sudden intimacies, frenzied couplings in stairwells and broom closets? [McInerney 2005: 199].

This passage clearly alludes to a historical precedent in this image of "wartime couplings."

In *Falling Man* the idea of a sudden need for intimacy is necessarily more closely tied to the larger relationship narrative. On 9/11 Keith and Lianne instinctively move back in together after Keith miraculously walks out of the burning towers, and their desire for contact isn't necessarily spontaneously passionate or unconsidered:

> And it's interesting, isn't it, the way you move about the bedroom, routinely near-naked, and the respect you show the past, the deference to its fervors of the wrong kind, its passions of cut and burn. She wanted contact and so did he [DeLillo 2007: 39].

When Keith and Lianne do have sex it isn't spontaneous or reckless but inevitable, and afterward, when Lianne pragmatically considers the man next to her, what comes through is again this sense of knowingness: "My husband. He wasn't a husband. The word spouse had seemed comical, applied to him, and husband simply didn't fit" (DeLillo 2007: 70). This is a different kind of knowingness to the one Russell conveys in *The Good Life*. Where Russell sees a historical precedent in "wartime couplings," Lianne, in a first sexual encounter with her estranged husband in years, admits that it was the "tenderest sex" she'd known but hints at an underlying reality in their relationship that even great tragedy and a subsequent need for companionship and meaning cannot negate.

Rupture and Re-evaluation

Re-evaluation of relationships and marriage in a post–9/11 condition of uncertainty become the primary themes of *The Good Life* and *Falling Man*. Characters explore meaning in their relationships through the course of the narratives, which ultimately reveal the degree to which 9/11 has effected genuine change in their lives. In a promotional interview in support of *The Good Life*, McInerney is explicit in his wish to explore this:

> *The Good Life* is first and foremost a love story. It's about the way in which the collective trauma of 9/11 prompted many of us, especially those of us here in New York, to re-evaluate our lives, to re-examine our values, our careers, our marriages [McInerney 2006: n.p.].

DeLillo has also explicitly stated his intention to create characters that are preoccupied with re-evaluation. Describing them individually, he states:

> The question Keith asks himself for the first time after the terrorist attacks: *Who am I? What's my identity?* Suddenly he realizes how much he loves his son, that he wants to be close to him. Lianne always wanted to be like other people, until through 9/11 she seems stronger to herself [DeLillo 2007: n.p.].

Both texts document the impact of the attacks on the banal or domestic, but what is revealed, ultimately, underneath the detailed reporting on the impact of trauma on domesticity is a complex narrative combination of evocations of continuity. On the one hand there is the illumination, under the pressures of post–9/11 disorientation, of long-standing relationship issues—the suggestion that the attacks have brought to the surface latent marital discord. On the other, there is an eventual restoration of equilibrium, a reversion back to previous patterns of pre–9/11 normality. Both of these strands are extremely evocative in their respective underlying suggestions and do contain allegorical possibilities. Kristiaan Versluys's chapter on *Falling Man*, "American Melancholia: Don DeLillo's *Falling Man*," disputes any restoration of equilibrium in this text. For Versluys, the "endless re-enactment of trauma presented in *Falling Man* allows for no accommodation or resolution" (Versluys 2009: 30). Versluys' use of the term "melancholia" is astute, and the analysis of the solemnity and lassitude of DeLillo's milieu in *Falling Man* is precise, particularly the way his assertion that "September 11 figured as the collapse of everything that is familiar and, in its familiarity, comforting" emphasizes DeLillo's focus on the "familiar" (Versluys 2009: 21). It must be acknowledged, as well, that in spite of this concern for the familiar, the social context of DeLillo's novel is more extensive than McInerney or Messud's; he includes a sub-narrative thread that follows a character called Hammad, one of the 9/11 terrorists, and also another couple in Lianne's mother and her partner, who provide important counterpoints. Crucially, though, Versluys' reading ignores the importance of the carefully plotted prehistory of the relationship between Keith and Lianne, which is an important aspect of the text. Furthermore, the assertion that "in *Falling Man*, trauma is not healed; it spreads like a contagious disease" misses the importance of the repeated patterns of working-through in which the characters participate, and, vitally, Lianne's eventual emergence from her traumatic haze which breaks the traumatic cycle (Versluys 2009: 30). This will be examined in the following pages, but it is worth noting here that, additionally, Gray illustrates the way that the knowingness of *Falling Man* detracts from its depiction of trauma: "The structure is too clearly foregrounded, the style excessively mannered, and the characters fall into postures of survival after 9/11 that are too familiar" (Gray 2009: 134). What Gray doesn't recognize, though, is that this knowingness—or what is "too clearly foregrounded"—is an important part of the architecture of the novel, setting up the restoration of equilibrium.

The process of working through is also integral, and much of this revolves around this idea of re-evaluation. Andrew O'Hagan draws attention to the importance of this in his lengthy review of the novel. Referencing passages of the text which describe the relationship between Keith and Lianne, and its history, he states:

> These descriptions are among the best things in the book: they have the force of felt life, and through them we begin purely to understand what estrangement really means with this Manhattan couple. They each have known a little hate. But how can they relate to each other now that hatred means something else, now that it means flying planes into public buildings? [O'Hagan 2007: n.p.].

Amidst the melancholic landscape of *Falling Man*, this theme of reevaluation is constant. Keith describes "what he'd lately taken to be the truth of his life, that it was meant to be lived seriously and responsibly, not snatched in clumsy fistfuls" (DeLillo 2007: 137). Similarly, Lianne "listened to what he said and let him know she was listening, mind and body, because listening is what would save them this time, keep them from falling into distortion and rancor" (DeLillo 2007: 104). Indeed, both of these novels feature protagonists that have a renewed sense of the importance of "meaningful" relationships after 9/11. In *Falling Man*, Keith literally walks out of the burning towers and back into his marital home from which he had been estranged for years. In *The Good Life*, Corrine and Luke begin an affair, searching for a more meaningful, authentic love than the stagnant home lives that they have suffered for years. While the characters in *Falling Man* reconstitute their marriage, re-evaluation in *The Good Life* means the beginning of an affair. As Louis Menand states, "McInerney's premise is that after September 11 anything seemed possible to the survivors.... They could start over, and have the life that they had always felt too scared or dependent or guilt-ridden to have" (Menand 2005: 43). Perhaps the aptness of Versluys' term "melancholia" is not in its Freudian sense of arrested mourning, but rather accrues its fullest meaning in the underpinning theme of reevaluation in both texts, the pervading inevitability that the process of renewal will be temporary and short lived.

Before and After 9/11

Narratively, *Falling Man* and *The Good Life* are structured very similarly; both contain three sections or acts, beginning with the events of 9/11 and going on to cover similar chronologies. In *The Good Life* these are literally titled "Indian Summer," "That Autumn" and "Holidays." The first two sections cover, respectively, the day before 9/11 where, over five chapters, much of the back-story is established, and the weeks after the attacks where Corrine and Luke meet while assisting in a soup kitchen for rescue workers and embark on their affair in this mood of reevaluation. In the final section, covering Christmas, the affair collapses. In *Falling Man* the three sections are more cryptically titled "Bill Lawton," "Ernst Herchinger" and "David Janiak," and while the time span of the action of the novel is wider, ending in 2004, the narrative arc is similar.

Three. Marriage, Relationships and 9/11

DeLillo's section titles refer to symbolic or mythical characters but also pertain directly to a similar chronology. Bill Lawton is the mythical name made by Keith and Lianne's son, Justin, for Bin Laden as he anxiously searches the skies in the initial weeks after; and, as in *The Good Life*, much of the back-story for the couple is established in this section. Ernst Herchinger is the real name of Martin Ridnour, the shadowy European art dealer who is Lianne's mother's partner, who is revealed to have once been involved in terrorist activities himself and whose presence forces Lianne into increasingly uncomfortable reflection which carries over into the domestic setting, where Keith and Lianne are re-starting their marriage. David Janiak is the symbolic performance artist known as the Falling Man who appears throughout the novel and divides public opinion: "Falling Man as Heartless Exhibitionist or Brave Chronicler of the Age of Terror," reads one fictional headline. In the final section, in 2004, which ends with Lianne's recovery, David Janiak, the Falling Man, dies. This death is symbolically important in its paralleling of Lianne's recovery; as the Falling Man epitomizes the spectacle and divisiveness of 9/11, his dying evokes a decline in 9/11 media hyperbole and a waning of post–9/11 disorientation.

The two texts cover slightly different time frames but follow a very similar arc and teleology, and both texts provide substantial insight into the protagonists' relationships before the attacks. In *Falling Man*, after Keith walks away from the towers, we quickly learn about the couple's history, "the eventual extended grimness called their marriage" (DeLillo 2007: 7). In fact, as if to demonstrate the novel's intent to use the couple's marriage as a kind of barometer, the narrative moves directly from the opening scene in the towers to a discussion between Lianne and her mother, Nina, just days after, about the history of their marriage.

The opening five chapters of *The Good Life* alternate between domestic scenes of Corrine and Russell Calloway, and Luke and Sasha McGavock, on September 10, dramatizing the unhappiness and delineating the discontents in both of these marriages that will underpin the affair between Corrine and Luke. The novel is, of course, revisiting the couple that was the subject of McInerney's *Brightness Falls* (1992), though *The Good Life* is not a conventional sequel and works without consideration of *Brightness Falls*. The emphasis on the prehistory in the novel is important, though, as it facilitates a very conventional arc; the image of the couples before the attacks, a period of reaction to the catastrophe, and then the restoration of equilibrium, or return to normal patterns and habits.

"Seismographically," these texts are at their most suggestive in the fact that they are not simply using tried narratives to, as Edkins states, "incorporate what happened into the narrative forms we already have available," but rather are making subliminal suggestions that this also may be the narrative of 9/11, a narrative with history and a kind of resolution. As Houen states, the writing is "subject to them [the events of 9/11] as a form of unconscious, historical symptom" (Houen 2004: 421).

The most striking aspect of these conventional narrative arcs and their restoration of equilibrium is the return to normality or convention in the characters themselves. Initially, both sets of couples make significant changes in their relationship or marital situations, and express new views regarding the importance of relationships. Corrine embarks on an affair with married man Luke because her experience with him feels more "meaningful." "Her conversations with Luke were more engaging than any she'd had with Russell for years" (McInerney 2005: 148). Lianne, in *Falling Man*, expresses a renewed need to have Keith at home with her: "She wanted to go home and talk to Keith.... Talk to Keith or not talk at all. But she wanted him to be there when she got home" (DeLillo 2007: 69). These are marked behavioral turns, both based on a renewed importance in relationships. The two narratives actually evolve in different ways and are even opposites in the crude sense that one relationship is dissolving and the other reforming; though the sense of re-evaluation and renewed desire for meaning in the protagonists is central to both. Furthermore, both texts underpin a surface emphasis on change and rupture, what *The Good Life* describes as "the trauma that had ruined their sleep and clouded their dreams," with sustained allusions to the characters' pre–9/11 problems (McInerney 2005: 147). As stated, some of the most affecting passages measure the effect of the attack on the banal in the aftermath, and these can overshadow the importance of the plotting of prehistory: Luke's thought in *The Good Life*, for example, that "it seemed nothing short of miraculous that you could still pick up the phone and conjure up moo-shu pork, shrimp toast, and fried dumplings" the Sunday after the attacks (McInerney 2005: 74). Or, similarly, in *Falling Man*, Keith, watching runners in Central Park, muses: "The ordinariness, so normally unnoticeable, fell upon him oddly, with almost dreamlike effect" (DeLillo 2007: 51). This is perhaps what we expect in the 9/11 novel—images of the banal in the traumatic aftermath. Underneath these descriptions, though, of the palpable effects of the attacks, the narratives build in the couples' histories, devoting significant space to pre–9/11. Corrine and Russell are deeply unhappy long before 9/11, as evidenced by their bickering in the early chapters, the revelation of Russell's infidelities, Corrine's near infidelity in one of the opening scenes, and her overt statement, "Long before the eleventh, he had been growing increasingly preoccupied and short-tempered" (McInerney 2005: 148). Keith and Lianne were, of course, separated before 9/11 brought them back together, and there is sustained allusion to their past problems. The strange gambling addiction and detached personality that consumes Keith after they reunite is crucially shown to have pre–9/11 roots:

> He used to come home late, looking shiny and a little crazy. This was the period, not long before the separation, when he took the simplest question as a form of hostile interrogation.... He carried that glassy look in his eyes and a moist smile across his mouth, a dare to himself, boyish and horrible [DeLillo 2007: 103].

This is particularly suggestive, as Keith's slide into numbness and gambling addiction, which could readily be identified as symptomatic of post-traumatic stress disorder (or simply as a coping mechanism or form of escapism), is clearly shown to have deeper origins. Versluys points to Keith's eventual residence in Las Vegas and gambling addiction as emblematic of his trauma and of the novel's "portrayal of enduring loneliness and unresolved melancholy" (Versluys 2009: 38). There is no doubt that much of Keith's post–9/11 decline is emblematic, but it is also clear that Keith's eventual maudlin post–9/11 existence, living "inside a bubble and outside of time," was predictable without the advent of 9/11, or at least that the condition he succumbs to in the desert originates from years before (Versluys 2009: 39). The idea that there are preexisting problems that are exacerbated by 9/11 is perhaps the single most provocative aspect of these texts. The impact of this suggestion of preexisting issues is somewhat blunted, though, by the other clear suggestion in the relationship narratives—the return to pre–9/11 conditions, or normality.

Both couples try and find new, lasting meaning in relationships after 9/11, but ultimately the shadow of the fallen towers doesn't amount to an impact big enough to effect lasting change and eradicate familiar behavioral patterns. There is an important scene in *Falling Man* where Keith is contemplating telling Lianne about his new, intimate relationship with a fellow survivor, Florence, and simultaneously trying to convince himself that he genuinely wants to reestablish the marital home:

> She would say, after we've just renewed our marriage. She would say, after the terrifying day of the planes has brought us together again. How could the same terror? She would say, how could the same terror threaten everything we've felt for each other, everything I've felt these past weeks? [DeLillo 2007: 162].

Ultimately, after attempting to rebuild his marriage, Keith drifts away, and Lianne expresses not only her readiness to be single again but also her readiness to end the period of rupture and let life resume as it had before Keith returned: "She was ready to be alone, in reliable calm, she and the kid, the way they were before the planes appeared that day, silver crossing blue" (DeLillo 2007: 236). This is not Lianne wishing she could be transported back to the security of pre–9/11 America but rather accepting that she doesn't need her husband and that she can resume life without him.

Luke and Corrine's romance also disintegrates at the end of *The Good Life*, also through characters falling into familiar patterns. On the afternoon of Christmas Eve they lie to each other, deploying the kind of routine deception that characterizes their married lives, both claiming to be doing "nothing really" later on. When they meet each other at a performance of the Nutcracker with their respective families, the affair is over. Benjamin Strong states that "*The Good Life* may be the most provocative novel yet about September 11, precisely because it dares to suggest that most of us weren't changed at all" (Strong 2006: n.p.). This is certainly supported by one explicit instance where Luke questions the lasting significance of the attacks:

> It seemed to him both hopeful that he could once again imagine the city as a backdrop to the dramas of daily life and sad that the satori flash of acute wakefulness and connectedness that had followed the initial confrontation with mortality in September was already fading behind them [McInerney 2005: 353].

This is the most overt suggestion of a wider return to normality in the text. As stated, the emphasis on the arc of the relationship throughout is overshadowed by the disruption 9/11 causes in the lives of the characters, and the suggestion of a return to ordinary life is clandestine. The attention to the details of the effects of the attacks on lived lives—the references to "terror sex," the fears of anthrax or the characters talking of leaving the city—almost distract from the creeping return of balance in the protagonists' lives.

In *Falling Man* the final chapter sequence works toward an even more clandestine suggestion that normality has resumed for Lianne and her son. The penultimate chapter, quoted earlier, finds Lianne emerging from her dazed, post-traumatic state. Again, she asserts that she was "ready to be alone, in reliable calm, she and the kid, the way they were before the planes." The final chapter, following this directly, is a four-page account of one of the planes speeding through the Hudson corridor toward the World Trade Center. It describes the plane hitting one of the towers from inside the plane and ends with Keith's frantic escape. This act of textual repetition has encouraged readings that rely on the discourse of trauma and trauma theory. It is important to bear in mind the power of Lianne's statement, though, and what it means for this vivid scene to come just after it. This juxtaposition does have the effect of bringing the trauma of the day back to the fore but with the underlying scene, fresh in our minds, of Lianne moving on—almost in spite of the vividly rendered image. Furthermore, it feels to some extent like a forced reminder of the horrors of the day, placed strategically to balance such an explicit statement. The reality, though, for the main protagonist is that despite the novel's lengthy focus on the rupture of 9/11, her life is not fundamentally changed and is no longer strictly characterized by uncertainty or trauma.

The Emperor's Children

There are many notable inversions of and departures from *The Good Life* and *Falling Man* in *The Emperor's Children*, though ultimately it reinforces and strengthens the idea of the texts operating as literary seismographs. The most notable departure is the novel's strong satirical element, which is pointed directly at the set of liberal New York literati that comprise the main characters. The "emperor" of the novel's title is Murray Thwaite, highly regarded author of numerous books and scholarly articles on world affairs and politics, tenured professor, adulterer, drinker, smoker. Thwaite is a clear caricature of the eminent American cultural critic: the archetypal *New Yorker* or *New York Review of Books* contributor. His status is described by his nephew as follows:

> From the civil rights movement and Vietnam right down through the Iran Contra and Operation Desert Storm, from education policy to workers' rights and welfare to abortion rights to capital punishment—Murray Thwaite has voiced significant opinions. We have believed him, and believed in him [Messud 2006: 343].

The clumsily condescending tone of this extract from Bootie's (Murray's nephew) article on his uncle, "Murray Thwaite: A Disappointed Portrait," bolsters and layers the general satire of Murray but also is part of the satirizing of Bootie as well. Bootie is one of four of the emperor's "children" who all have their own various literary or cultural pursuits. Murray's daughter Marina is beautiful and basks in her father's celebrity, and has been half-heartedly working on a cultural studies book of her own (about children's clothes) for nearly eight years. She exposes her naivety and superficiality early on by deliberating on whether or not to get a job: "Should I even have one when I'm trying to finish the book and then, you know, a real job would be so demanding, after all, that's what an interesting job is supposed to be; and an easy job, a dumb job, well, at that point, who am I kidding?" (Messud 2006: 90). The satire is less prevalent in the characterization of her friend Danielle, though it is evident in the clichéd way in which she embarks on an affair with Murray, seduced by his genteel preeminence. However, the satirical evocation of cliché borders on the politically incorrect in the depiction of Julius, characterized, for Amanda Claybaugh, as the "bitchy gay friend." Julius, a freelance *Village Voice* style critic, embarks on a drug-addled, sexually promiscuous period of his life throughout the course of the novel that relies heavily on a clichéd vision of male homosexuality. These various gradations of satire in *The Emperor's Children* have been widely recognized. Claybaugh astutely describes how the text relies on dialogue: "the spoiled princess and her bitchy gay friend; the philandering husband and his loyally oblivious wife.... Messud allows these shallow people to speak for themselves devoting a significant portion of the novel to dialogue" (Claybaugh 2006: 15).

Indeed, these are largely stock characters whose superficialities are self-evident, but the impact of the satire goes further than the individuals, extending to the characters as a group, a New York "literary set." There is every reason to believe that the social milieu in which they circulate would include people like McInerney, Messud herself, and, to a lesser extent, DeLillo—particularly during the twenty-first chapter, "Awards Night." This is a long chapter describing an unnamed literary awards evening where Messud pays careful attention to the "milling, crowing glitterati, assembling for their annual fete" (Messud 2006: 200). This satiric element is important because it clearly presents a chance for the author to discredit the views of this set and also to question the viability of them as representative or suitably microcosmic. Ultimately, though, as Joyce Carol Oates writes, "Even as she unmasks them, Messud can't resist evoking sympathy for her mostly foolish, self-deluded characters; and can't deny even the fatuous Bootie the possibility of regeneration in the chaotic aftermath of September 11" (Oates 2006: 30). The satire is not so much dulled by the good revealed in characters as overshadowed by the misfortune or suffering that they experience. Marina is manipulated into courtship and marriage by Ludovic Seeley, the Australian magazine editor who is using her name and prestige for his professional ambitions; Murray is sabotaged by Bootie; Julius is violently attacked by his new boyfriend, David; and Danielle is seduced by Murray.

What effect does this satire actually have then? David Simpson suggests that it may "be taken as a fitting acknowledgment of the limits of fiction in the face of an appalling and indescribable event ... or it might be read as a cry of quiet rage against the capacity of these people not to be radically moved or changed" (Simpson 2008: 218). To understand how it operates, though, it must be considered as coextensive with the equally deliberate structure of the novel. *The Emperor's Children* is a countdown narrative, and there are clear temporal indicators, such as the reference to the election of George W. Bush and the sections titled chronologically in months, which begin the countdown to 9/11. The morning of 9/11 happens in the final stages of the text, and while it does test the characters' temperaments and composure, and evoke sudden change, the drama of the novel is largely conducted before the attacks, which occur in Chapter 58 (out of 67). In the preceding chapters all of the major characters enter a new phase of their lives, establishing new relationships, which could represent, in every case, a major life change or personal epoch. The book culminates simultaneously with the advent of 9/11 and with the sudden climax or culmination in the character's changed personal lives, and ostensibly there are various degrees of direct connection between the two. Unlike *Falling Man* or *The Good Life*, then, in which 9/11 happens at the beginning, the novel takes some 500 pages to reach the attacks, and when it does happen there is already this sense of near culmination in all of the plotlines. Therefore, at the conclusion of the novel there is a blurred sense of what actual impact the attacks have had on the close of each narrative strand, and the powerful suggestion that individuals all bring their own personal concerns or psychic dispositions to an experience of collective trauma (though this suggestion is not fully developed). In one of these strands, charting the relationship of Julius and David, a startling episode of violence committed by David on Julius occurs just before 9/11. There is the possibility here for a study of what E. Ann Kaplan calls the "aggregation" of traumas or the entanglements of personal and public traumas—"the way that symptoms of prior traumatic events are triggered by new ones" (Kaplan 2005: 2). However, after 9/11 occurs in the text, this strand is largely over and, clearly, equilibrium is restored. Julius has a permanent scar, but he returns to the disposition in which he was introduced—not just before 9/11 but before his dangerous relationship with David. "Julius was the same, at least.... He seemed in all aspects more sober for his Conehead [David] interlude—more cynical, if that were possible. And he still didn't know what he was doing wasting his talents on trivia, like the piece on nightclubs he'd resold to *Interview*" (Messud 2006: 545). Rather than a comparison of the effects of his personal incident of violence and the impact of 9/11 on him, or a depiction of the blurring of two traumas, he is shown to have recovered from both. There is, though, a powerful suggestion in his description of his scar:

> You don't think of yourself as scarred. You forget. And you think you can just keep being your same self. But everyone sees you, and they see a changed person, and the ones who know the story see you as changed in a very particular way, which isn't so nice (Messud 2006: 545).

Three. Marriage, Relationships and 9/11

Like the novel as a whole, this passage hints at the psychic sophistication of this experience, but again, Julius is clearly depicted as largely unchanged.

The reality of the satiric countdown narrative of *The Emperor's Children* is that it replicates the setting up of ostensibly life-changing absolutes that appear in *The Good Life* and *Falling Man,* which, despite accordant rhetoric, reveal characters that return quickly to their pre–9/11 conditions. What binds the satire to the advent of 9/11 and the relationship narratives in *The Emperor's Children* is the idea of the satirized "children," Marina, Julius, Danielle and Booty, all ostensibly pursuing a new seriousness—the kind of seriousness embodied by Murray Thwaite. This combination, then, of satire and countdown narrative sets up an ultimate test in the novel, of this idea of 9/11 as an epochal moment: does 9/11 usher in a new era of seriousness in these characters who have seemingly been seeking it long before the attacks? In the first instance, it does seem to be the reality. Marina's by now husband, Ludovic, immediately scraps his magazine project *The Monitor*: "Nobody wanted such a thing in this new world, a frivolous, satirical thing" (Messud 2006: 542). This follows a clear logic in the text after repeated references before 9/11 to "criminally uninteresting times" and "people who aren't *for* anything, just against everything"—that 9/11 should usher in a new era of gravity (Messud 2006: 49). More powerfully, after watching the attacks from Danielle's apartment, Murray leaves Danielle, who has become his mistress, and returns to his wife:

> She had seen the second plane, like a gleaming arrow, and the burst of it, oddly beautiful against the blue, and the smoke, everywhere, and she had seen the people jumping, from afar ... and she had seen the buildings crumble to dust ... she had seen these things and had been left, forever, because in light of these things she did not matter, you had to make the right choice, you had to stay on the ground ... and now there was nothing but sorrow and this was how it was going to be, now, always [Messud 2006: 501–2].

Thus the relationship is over amid the shock of 9/11 and terms of "forever" and "always." But while Danielle is hurt the most by 9/11 and the demise of her relationship, after a few short chapters she and the others recover. They are revealed, in spite of each of their personal melodramas and the advent of 9/11, to be returned to their beginning dispositions. Marina discusses new plans with Julius in the November after 9/11: "'Our goal for next year will be to get you into a proper apartment.' 'And get me a proper job, too?' 'I'm unemployed myself, remember.' 'With a book coming out, thank you very much.' 'Well, but…' 'It will change everything. It's huge.' 'Or will slip into the bookstores and out of them just as fast'" (Messud 2006: 546). They are clearly returned to the concerns that preoccupy them in Chapter 3, when they were first introduced. Danielle takes time off work but decides ultimately to return: "She had a film about liposuction to make. It seemed, in some lights, trivial, but it wasn't really. By the time it was finished, people would be tired of greater tragedies and would be ready to watch it again. Mostly people's tragedies were small. She'd be doing the right thing" (Messud 2006: 572). Danielle here announces her recovery from her post–9/11 depression, which suggestively has hidden her post-relationship depression. When Marina, standing at Danielle's window, speculates that "maybe seeing it all so clearly was more traumatic," we know the real reason for her depression, which, like Julius's scar, hints at personal problems entangling themselves in public trauma (Messud 2006: 544). While Murray and Danielle split on 9/11 under the weight of this new seriousness, the novel has repeatedly suggested that they would inevitably have done so in spite of 9/11. Furthermore, the advent of 9/11 doesn't inspire any truth-telling among Marina and Danielle regarding the latter's affair with the former's father. The other relationships that have formed the "stories" for each character are not affected by the attacks. Just as a succession of precarious situations involving Danielle's friendship with Marina always seems to threaten Murray and Danielle's relationship, there are clear signs from the beginning of the novel that the manipulative Ludovic will ultimately disappoint Marina, and that the indulgent David will likewise let down Julius.

The Emperor's Children goes one step further than *Falling Man* or *The Good Life*. Not only do we see a restoration of equilibrium in the characters and in their relationships after the rupture of 9/11, as well as a clear suggestion of the importance of previous circumstance and conditions, but we can see this in spite of the attacks. In other words, things do not fundamentally change despite major disruptions in the character's personal lives, and furthermore, the ostensible new seriousness of life after 9/11 does not shed light on these disruptions either. There is one character in the novel for whom 9/11 is epochal—at least provisionally.

Bootie Tubb uses the chaos of the aftermath of 9/11 to flee to Florida, leaving his family to assume he's perished in the attacks. However, while Bootie begins life anew in Florida, the novel ends with the revelation that his regeneration is predicated on re-entering his previous life and redressing his long-held obsessions. The final sentences—"Take them by surprise. Yes. He would"—reveal not a new life and identity but an obsession with problems left unaddressed in his pre–9/11 life (Messud 2006: 581).

Seismographic Narratives

Bootie's paradoxical situation is emblematic of the narrative paradigm that all three texts carry. 9/11 has exacerbated what is clearly a pre-existing condition in Booty, causing quite dramatic action. Also, though, it becomes clear that despite his "new life" he is returned to the exact obsession he holds when first introduced—his need to prove himself to his family and particularly his uncle. In all three texts the suggestiveness or allegorical possibilities of pre-existing issues and concerns brought to the surface by or unrelated to 9/11 are tempered by the suggestion of a return to normality, which has its own suggestiveness. As we have seen, these strands do not sit comfortably together in these novels and render this underlying seismographic suggestion even more oblique then it already inherently is. One reason for this relates to what David Simpson has identified as another fundamental element of conflictedness in *The Emperor's Children*—the idea that "nothing has changed, and that life is not very interesting or stratifying" (Simpson 2008: 216). Simpson goes on to state:

> In this they show themselves suspicious of the rhetoric of 9/11 as a world changing event and not at all confident that the lives of these fictional Americans have been transformed by the tragedy or even by the spectacle. The question they raise is whether this response (or lack of it) is a tribute to the resilience of ordinary life or a more damning indictment of the sheer indifference and self-centeredness of the homeland mainstream [Simpson 2008: 216].

The seemingly apolitical aspect of the surface action or stories in all of these novels, the focus on marriage or relationships and ordinary life in general, is underpinned by this conflict, which is complicated by the larger "seismographic" tension. The combination allows the texts to ask whether it is a characteristic courage or a long-running lack of recognition or "indifference" that allows recovery.

The distinction of the "seismographic" aspect of the narratives is illustrated concisely by *Falling Man*. Keith, as stated, slides into numbness and gambling addiction, which, it has been suggested, is emblematic of a national condition. In this reading Keith could be said to carry a national allegory of trauma or to represent a nation suffering from collective trauma. Lianne, though, is seen to recover from the initial impact of the attacks on her life, working through her trauma, and her equal (if not greater) narrative importance weakens the possibility of national allegory. However, in a more underlying sense, at the end of the novel, narrative equilibrium is restored. Keith and Lianne were estranged before 9/11 and are now estranged once more—just as Corrine and Luke return to their marriages and families in *The Good Life*, and the "children" of *The Emperor's Children* resume their superficial pre-9/11 concerns. While these novels do not operate as unified national allegories, the "seismographic" evocations of continuity and context are certainly revealing in novels that, on the surface, clearly want to study rupture and change. Despite being for the most part narrow in their outlook and lacking in explicit historical or political insight, there is enough occurring beneath the surface of these narratives for them to, as Simpson suggests, be read as subversive of the "everything's changed" rhetoric that the Bush administration propagated. It must be emphasized, though, that these are unconscious evocations, and the texts seem to unknowingly follow an integral aspect of Ulrich Baer's manifesto for 9/11 literature: "Literature is called upon here as the unconscious history-writing of the world: as a form of expression that uncannily registers subtle shifts in experience and changes in reality before they can be consciously grasped or have fully taken place" (Baer 2004: 5). In this seismographic respect, the novels also counter or oppose the theoretical accounts which understand 9/11 and the literary response to 9/11 in terms of trauma and trauma theory. However, the seismographic registering of continuity in relation to 9/11 is not enough to make decisive statements about any specific causes or the origins of the attacks. The novels cannot explicitly be applied to political or historical theories of continuity, such as

Chalmers Johnson's thesis in *Blowback* (2002), which points to "the nature and conduct of U.S. foreign policy over the previous half century" (Johnson 2002: vii). There is no doubt, though, that they all evoke a more general notion of continuity which crucially elucidates aspects of conflict and tension within it, centered on the depiction of both prehistory and recovery and the question of whether it is characteristic steadfastness or strength that underpins the recovery, or a lack of recognition of the continuing relevance and connection to the past. Finally, the seismographic readings of these novels also provide another strand of insight in elucidating the conflicted subconscious desire to understand 9/11 in terms of continuity and context. This comes in the possibility or suggestion that the tension within these seismographic narratives betrays a difficulty the novelists may have had in making even an indirect political suggestion about 9/11 within what is clearly a deliberate and determined "continuity" framework. Additionally, this may also reflect both a wider need to begin imagining the prehistory of 9/11 and the recovery from 9/11, and the difficulty within American or Western consciousness of doing this. If *Windows on the World* and *Extremely Loud and Incredibly Close* are examples of a failure to reconcile narratives of continuity and discontinuity, then *Falling Man, The Good Life* and *The Emperor's Children* clearly depart from this, though only on a limited basis, in their "seismographic" suggestiveness. Because the evocations they make are encased in narratives that are so decidedly circumscribed and focused on rupture and change, they too betray a residual conflictedness. Like the novels by Beigbeder and Safran Foer, these texts reveal a struggle to engage with polarized narratives, though in this case it is in the way they obliquely deploy one under the cover of the other.

FOUR

The Road: Disaster, Allegory and the Exhaustion of the Early 9/11 Novel

Cormac McCarthy's *The Road* (2006), an unsettling vision of a bleak post-apocalyptic America, has frequently been read as a central post–9/11 novel. Of all the early post–9/11 novels that do not directly discuss 9/11, including such high-profile novels as Ian McEwan's *Saturday* (2005) or John Updike's *Terrorist* (2006), which also have very clear resonances with the social and political climate of the aftermath of the attacks, it is *The Road* which endures as the most powerful allegorical or symbolic narrative of the attacks. This chapter argues that McCarthy's novel is most usefully read as a conservative allegory of 9/11 that marks the exhaustion of the early paradigms of 9/11 fiction; and as such, it is an important turning point in the way the attacks have been represented in fiction. Nevertheless, McCarthy's apocalyptic novel carries its own fundamental conflictedness in the way that its conservatism simultaneously represents the culmination of the trend of "indirectly" representing 9/11 and exhausts the possibility of doing so, signaling change. *The Road* signals a new direction in the 9/11 novel while also encompassing and embodying the characteristics of the early 9/11 novel. Before any textual analysis of *The Road*, however, it is productive to first examine the ways in which we can position it as a 9/11 novel, and the ways it relates to earlier narratives of 9/11, particularly to two key cinematic narratives of the attacks. These films are essential texts of this era, 2005–2006, an era which marked the rapid decline in the popularity of the George W. Bush administration and included the playing out of an event that has had an enormous bearing on the cultural representation of 9/11: Hurricane Katrina and the post–Katrina flooding of New Orleans. As Jeffrey Melnick states in the closing pages of *9/11 Culture* (2009), "It seems possible that the pivotal moment for our study of 9/11 art will turn out to have been the moment of the next American tragedy, Hurricane Katrina's devastation of New Orleans and other sites on the Gulf Coast and the abandonment of the region and its people by the United States federal government" (Melnick 2009: 157). *The Road* was published almost exactly a year after Hurricane Katrina (though McCarthy began writing it years before), and it has a fraught connection with that catastrophe. As stated, this chapter will locate McCarthy's novel as the culmination of the first phase of the 9/11 novel, and Hurricane Katrina plays an important role in this reading. By looking first at the way *The Road* absorbs some of the central themes of the early literary and cultural representation of 9/11, we can position it as a pivotal text in the development of the 9/11 novel, which has changed fundamentally in the post–Katrina years. Read in the cultural context of Hurricane Katrina, the post–Katrina flooding of New Orleans, and the political fallout of that disaster, *The Road* simultaneously speaks to the apocalyptic images of flood-wracked New Orleans and also exhausts the possibility of examining disaster through indirect or symbolic means. After Katrina it would not be possible for national or foreign government policy to avoid scrutiny in narratives of disaster and crisis, including and particularly narratives of 9/11 and the War on Terror.

Richard Gray states that rather than "domesticating" the crisis, as, he argues Ken Kalfus' *A Disorder Peculiar to the Country* (2005), *Falling Man*, *The Good Life* and *The Emperor's Children* all do, McCarthy's novel sets out to negotiate the traumas of 9/11 through a process of defamiliarization:

> It is surely right to see *The Road* as a post–9/11 novel, not just in the obvious, literal sense, but to the extent that it takes the measure of that sense of crisis that has seemed to haunt the West, and the United States in particular, ever since the destruction of the World Trade Center. And whereas writers like DeLillo, Kalfus, McInerney, Messud and Schwartz try to domesticate, to shepherd that sense of crisis into the realms of the familiar, McCarthy's alternative strategy in *The Road* is not to domesticate but to defamiliarize. His way of telling a story that cannot but has to be told is to approach it by circuitous means, by indirection [Gray 2011: 25].

While Gray is careful to distinguish *The Road* from the "domestic" novels he is so critical of, he is clear in his position that like those texts, the novel does not engage politically with the attacks, and he includes it in his discussion of texts that try variously to mitigate and contain the traumas of the attacks, effectively depoliticizing the events of 9/11. Furthermore, Gray is ultimately critical of the novel's hopeful ending for reasons that are similar to those that he gives in his criticism of DeLillo, Kalfus, McInerney and Messud: "It is as if, at this moment, McCarthy has withdrawn into the sheltering confines of American myth: a myth that is, in this case, a curious but not uncommon mix of the heroic and the domestic" (Gray 2011: 47). This is an astute observation that will be revisited later in this chapter, but for our purposes here, the crucial point is that Gray locates *The Road* broadly within the same frame as the "domestic novels," and certainly it shares their "indirect" approach to 9/11. David Holloway also locates *The Road* as a 9/11 novel that sits comfortably next to the "domestic" novels of 9/11 in its focus on the relationship between parent and child; though in his reading there is an obliquely political subtext. Holloway sees a clear pattern evident in the entire body of early 9/11 fiction that is manifest both symbolically and literally, where parents struggle to care for children. In a wider allegorical sense this is identified as the story of a government struggling to care for its citizens. *The Road* is seen by Holloway as the nadir of this trend:

> The novel pushed the generic conventions of early 9/11 fiction about as far as some of them could go, partly because McCarthy extended the 9/11 novel's generic stress on the flimsiness of Western modernity into full-blown apocalypse and partly also because *The Road* fetishized, and in the process heightened to an almost unbearable degree, the genre's central concern with children/citizens divested of parental/state protection [Holloway 2008: 110].

This reading of *The Road* links it to the very early texts by Safran Foer, Beigbeder and Spiegelman, where parent and child relationships are integral to the plots of the novels, and also to the "domestic" novels, simply in the allegorical importance it places on familial relationships. Crucially, though, it shares their general avoidance of the politics of 9/11 (at least any kind of direct political engagement), preferring to focus on the trauma of disaster.

Cinematic Narratives of Disaster and Trauma and the "Bush Doctrine"

As suggested, given that McCarthy's novel is frequently anchored to the context of 9/11 and the War on Terror, yet doesn't directly discuss these events, and as a long-awaited response to this turbulent part of American history by one of the most revered practitioners of contemporary literature, it is particularly tempting to want to read *The Road* in conjunction with John Updike's *Terrorist* and Ian McEwan's *Saturday*. Indeed, one could argue that *Saturday* and *Terrorist* feature more explicit discussions of the "age of terror" in their more direct approaches to important post–9/11 social and political issues. As we will see, however, while these novels are very much post–9/11 novels, *The Road* is very much a 9/11 novel—even if it is so allegorically. It is useful, however, to contextualize and to compare the novel with other 9/11 narratives of its era, and as a disaster narrative, *The Road* can perhaps more fruitfully be linked to two early Hollywood representations of 9/11, Oliver Stone's *World Trade Center* (2005) and Paul Greengrass' *United 93* (2006). These films do engage directly with the attacks, and, like *The Road*, they are starkly minimalist, share some of the generic tropes of the Hollywood disaster narrative, and, crucially, have prominent allegorical components that relate in different ways to the novel. Despite dramatizing the actual events of September 11, *World Trade Center* and *United 93* focus directly on the emergency, chaos, and disaster of the attacks; and in doing this, like the domestic novels, they eschew any kind of wider interrogation of how or why the attacks occurred. What makes them particularly relevant here, though, is that despite the progressive, leftist political leanings of other works by Stone and Greengrass, these films both reinforce specific strands of the Bush administration's post–9/11-rhetoric, or the "Bush Doctrine" (Holloway 2008: 4). *United 93* is a real-time "docudrama" that focuses simultaneously on the passengers and hijackers of United Airlines Flight 93 (which was forced by a passenger uprising to crash-land near Shanksville, Pennsylvania), and responses from the military and various air-traffic control and aviation authorities during the first hours of the attacks. The film dramatizes the two critical hours on the morning of 9/11, and what is prioritized is the documenting of the minutiae of this single flight and the chaos surrounding its hijacking, in real-time realism. As Douglas Kellner states, "It is highly specific and does not engage with broader contextual issues" (Kellner 2009: 117). Oliver Stone's vision is equally singular in *World Trade Center,* which dramatizes the true story of two Port Authority police officers, Will Jimeno and John McLoughlin, who were among the first responders to the emergency on the morning of 9/11, and who were trapped beneath the rubble of the towers. B. Ruby Rich states in a *Sight and Sound* review: "*World Trade Center* is a movie so determinedly circumscribed, so micro-focused, as to constitute not a historical epic but rather a classic disaster movie. Men are trapped. Families await word. Help is on the way" (Rich 2006: 14).

The allegorical functions of both these minimalist films are very different but ultimately reinforce the rhetoric of American heroism, American exceptionalism and, in the case of *United 93,* the theory of a "clash of civilizations" that had such alarming currency after 9/11. *United 93* actually goes to great lengths to avoid the then-popular conceptions of individual heroism and patriotism, which is remarkable given that one of the passengers, Todd Beamer, was widely hailed as one of the American heroes of 9/11. Beamer famously coined the phrase "Let's roll," as the passengers stormed the cockpit, a phrase which was subsequently appropriated by President Bush in his presidential address on November 8, 2001; *United 93* downplays this moment to the point that it is barely audible. The film also carries a sharply critical agenda in its damning portrayal of the inability of the authorities to successfully intervene. There is, however, one aspect of the film which powerfully reinforces the "Bush Doctrine": the allusion to the "clash of civilizations" narrative. It will be useful here to establish some context, as this theory is also an important context for *The Road.* David Holloway describes the post-9/11 appeal of this clash of civilizations "abstraction" as an easy way of understanding an impossibly complex geo-political dynamic: "With so many overlapping and unstable factors in play, an abstraction like "clash of civilizations" was attractive because, like all sound bites, it reduced complex and opaque historical forces to a more manageable form" (Holloway 2008: 11). The rise of this abstraction can be attributed to a variety of sources, mostly beginning with the post–9/11 appropriation of the writings of Samuel P. Huntington, who published an article entitled "The Clash of Civilizations?" in *Foreign Affairs* (1993) and then an expanded book-length version called *The Clash of Civilizations and the Remaking of World Order* (1997), which was quickly updated and reprinted after 9/11. Huntington defines civilization by drawing on opaque ideas of culture rather than ideology or government, ultimately reducing his definition to "culture writ large" (Huntington 2002: 41). Huntington is careful to differentiate between government and ideology, and posits that religion is the primary cultural element of a civilization: "Of all the objective elements which define civilizations, however, the most important usually is religion" (Huntington 2002: 42). The crux of Huntington's thesis is that the contemporary global political landscape is characterized by the volatile relationships between seven different civilizations, and that the West needs to be aggressive and strategic, creating alliances between some of them in order to maintain its stability and global preeminence against particularly the "Islamic" and "Confucian" civilizations—essentially the Middle East and China. Furthermore, Huntington's rhetoric is frequently homogenizing, designed, it would seem, to characterize certain "civilizations," such as "Islam," as monolithic and all-encompassing. Huntington's section on "Islam and the West" is particularly inflammatory in his analysis that there is no possibility of reconciliation between these two "civilizations": "The underlying problem for the West is not Islamic fundamentalism. It is Islam itself, a different civilization whose people are convinced of the superiority of their culture and are obsessed with the inferiority of their power" (Huntington 2002: 209). This thesis is prone to abstractions, but was and is validated by the credence it has been given and influence it has exerted. Edward Said was quick to identify the increasing cachet the "clash of civilizations" would gain after 9/11, publishing "Islam and the West are Inadequate Banners" in *The Observer* on September 16, 2001, continuing his long-standing debate with and criticism of this theory. Nevertheless, the "clash of civilizations" abstraction garnered unprecedented popular currency, appearing everywhere from newspaper articles to President Bush's repeated citation of an attack on "our way of life" and "good" and "evil" (Bush 21.09.2001: n.p.).

The opening sequence is crucial to the narrative of *United 93*. The film opens on a dimly-lit close-up of the Qur'an, fades to black, and then features an establishing shot of an Arab man praying on a bed in a hotel, the Qur'an open in his hands. He is shown to be praying in Arabic, but it is not subtitled for the understanding of non–Arabic speakers; the camera studies him intently. Another Arab man enters the room and says, "It's time," which is subtitled. The un-subtitled praying continues as voiceover while the camera moves to an overhead shot of the New York skyline. It then alternates between aerial shots that glide in between skyscrapers in the pre-dawn light, and shots of the men, clearly establishing them as terrorists, preparing: shaving their chests and genitalia, and praying on prayer mats inside the hotel room. The dominant images and sounds in this opening sequence are a conflation of Islam and terrorism. As the prayer chants are not subtitled, they are, to the non–Arabic speaker, religious abstractions. After this ominous sequence the scene changes to Newark airport, and the narrative of 9/11 begins, emerging out of these abstractions.

The subtitling (or lack of subtitling) remains largely the same throughout the entire film, only appearing during tactical statements: "We have to do it now" or "Wait for the sign," for example. During the action sequences on the flight, it could be argued that it reinforces the realism of the film. The passengers (who we presume cannot speak Arabic) do not understand what the terrorists are shouting, and this adds to the chaos of the clash. Consequently, as these scenes are not subtitled, the audience (who we also assume, for the most part, cannot speak Arabic) is immersed in the drama. But the arbitrary nature in which subtitling is employed is particularly important in the opening sequence, which contributes to the abstraction of Islam. It is also important to consider that the prominence of religious imagery highlights the conspicuous absence of any mention of political motives. While the terrorists are only given minimal characterization, it is entirely split between tactical dialogue and religious abstraction.

United 93 focuses on group dynamics, and it is precisely this, combined with the heavy emphasis on Islam which opens the film, that speaks to the clash of civilizations theory. As the film hurtles towards its finale, the passengers huddle together in the rear of the plane while the terrorists hold down the front; two locked in the cockpit and two guarding it outside, one strapped with explosives. As the antagonism between the passengers and terrorists palpably escalates, in an extraordinary sequence of rapid-cut editing, there is a polarizing montage alternating between shots of the terrorists praying feverishly in un-subtitled

Four. Disaster, Allegory and Exhaustion

Arabic and the passengers saying the Lord's Prayer. The images are powerfully antithetical. Shortly after these scenes play out, the film culminates with a violent clash, as the passengers charge the cockpit and a literal clash between oblique Huntingtonian conceptions of Islam and the West ensues. Because of the lack of distinction between Islam and Islamism, the lack of characterization and the Manichaeism of the finale, *United 93* clearly evokes the "clash of civilization" theory. Martin Amis' commentary on the film, "What Will Become of Us?" brings this out via some alarming speculation. Amis imagines what the film may have looked like if there had been a child on board, and his reductive interpretation of the terrorists (as he imagines explaining the situation to a child) is revealing: "What's happening? Well, you see, my child, the men with the bloodstained knives think that if they kill themselves, and all of us, we will stop trying to destroy Islam and they will go at once to a paradise of women and wine" (Amis 2009: 135). Amis' interpretation clearly chimes with the "clash of civilizations" narrative and is an example of how it is perpetuated by cultural representation.

World Trade Center also has a distinctly revanchist rhetoric in the portrayal of Dave Karnes, who famously, as a civilian ex-marine, found the two trapped officers. Karnes closes the film by declaring his intent to re-enlist in the marines, stating, "They're going to need some good men out there to avenge this." Allegorically, though, it is the story of the two trapped policemen that clearly becomes the story of the nation. From the very beginning of the film, Stone establishes the two protagonists as connected to the towers and to New York. The opening sequence depicts them waking up as the city wakes. They are identified as family men, and as shots alternate between the men driving to work and the sun rising over the city, their ethnic difference is reflected in the depiction of a culturally diverse city. As Rich suggests, they are cannily representative:

> They couldn't have been scripted any better than they lived it: a veteran and a rookie, one with four kids and the other with a pregnant wife, one Irish and one Colombian.... They're not only suitable stand-ins for all the New Yorkers who survived or perished on 9/11, but they're perfect movie characters—ordinary guys raised to greatness by extraordinary trials [Rich 2006: 16].

As the opening sequence develops, the shots continue to alternate between the two men and the iconography of New York, particularly the World Trade Center, which has the effect of unifying them. When the final cityscape shot appears featuring a title stating "September 11, 2001" over the newly sunlit city, the two men and the city are firmly established as connected. Ceylan Özcan identifies this as a strategy the film employs to help its audience work through the collective trauma of the attacks:

> By dealing with the collective trauma microcosmically, through the individual stories, Stone is able to capture a sincere and effective account, as opposed to concentrating on it on a massive scale ... the strength and survival of these two individuals becomes synonymous with the strength and survival of America as a nation [Özcan 2008: 209].

Masculinity and Crisis

This brief reading of the way *World Trade Center* and *United 93* allegorically reinforce the rhetoric and values of the George W. Bush administration is valuable as context, as my argument in this chapter is that through a messianic allegory and portrayal of a retrograde, frontier masculinity, *The Road* endorses the Bush administration's rhetoric of heroism, it's focus on "American values," and its Manichean vision of "good vs. evil." A useful starting point for this reading of *The Road* as a conservative allegory of 9/11 is its vision of frontier masculinity. There is a clear connection in the novel's vision of masculinity and messianic allegory in that its masculinity is that of the mythological American West and Manifest Destiny. McCarthy is well known for his preoccupations with the American West, the frontier and masculinity; and as well as borrowing from these mythologies, it is also possible to read *The Road* as a "reversed story of the conquest of the American West" (Ibarrola-Armendiariz 2011: 2). Ibarrola-Armendiariz points out that, "Like the earlier pioneers, these two characters face an inhospitable land and all kinds of cruel enemies" (Ibarrola-Armendiariz 2011: 2). The main protagonist, the unnamed man, is characterized by the classical frontier masculinity of cowboys, trail-blazing pilgrims, and even adventurers. He navigates the open road with a pistol and a map, he is a protector and a provider, and actually resembles a kind of post-apocalyptic cowboy, the decrepit shopping cart replacing the horse. Michael Chabon articulates this can-

Four. Disaster, Allegory and Exhaustion

nily in his review-essay for the *New York Review of Books*, identifying a general likeness in *The Road* to an archetypal adventure narrative—particularly in the characterization of the man:

> There are strong echoes of the Jack London–style adventure, down to the novel's thematic emphasis on the imperative to build a fire, in the father's inherent resourcefulness, in his handiness with tools and guns, his foresight and punctilio, his resolve—you can only call it pluck—in the face of overwhelming natural odds, savage tribesman, and the despair of solitude [Chabon 2007: 26].

It may be somewhat tenuous to classify *The Road* as an "adventure" story, but there is no doubt that the man has certain characteristics of the archetypal Western protagonist, and that this seems oddly congruous in the novel's post-apocalyptic landscape. This is partly because the Western hero is conventionally "at odds with regulated society," and the man's natural capabilities in the hostile, uncivilized environment of the novel certainly strengthen this characterization (Coy 1997: 4). This is emphasized through a combination of skills and traits—his abilities with tools and weapons, his general resourcefulness and his uncompromising, minimally emotional and persevering character—that place him in the realms of the Western protagonist. As Gray notes, in "his weathered face, his assured carriage … his bluntness of manner, and breadth of personal experience he … recalls any number of American heroes from Natty Bumpo to Randle McMurphy or the characters played by John Wayne" (Gray 2011: 46). The novel's dialogue continually reinforces this, as the man repeatedly emphasizes his singular drive and purpose, and unwillingness to compromise his objectives: "My job is to take care of you.... I will kill anyone who touches you" (McCarthy 2006: 80). John Hillcoat's 2009 film version of *The Road* includes an explicit image of the man in traditional Western apparel in a part of the narrative that it embellishes and develops from McCarthy's novel. In a brief pre-apocalypse scene that shows a glimpse of life before the disaster, the man is seen in jeans and a flannel shirt, stroking a horse, a colorful and almost idyllic image of the American cowboy. In the novel, however, it is the man's actions that most clearly characterize him as a Western hero. One memorable scene describes the man demonstrating his self-reliance and skills to the onlooking boy who is observing and learning:

They collected some old boxes and built a fire in the floor and he found some old tools and emptied out the cart and sat working on the wheel. He pulled the bolt and bored out the collet with a hand drill and resleeved it with a section of pipe he'd cut to length with a hacksaw. Then he bolted it all back together and stood the cart upright and wheeled it around the floor. It ran fairly true. The boy sat watching everything [McCarthy 2006: 15–16].

The man's work under the observing eyes of the boy serves as a demonstration of his masculinity and extends his role from protector and provider to also emphasize his resourcefulness and classically American self-reliance.

The enduring appeal of the Western frontier myth is often related to various socio-political needs to articulate a clear vision of American identity. Classic Hollywood Westerns, from *Stagecoach* (1939) to *The Wild Bunch* (1969), are often thought to have anchored American identity in its frontier past in order to mitigate the disorienting speed of American modernity and to reinforce quintessentially American "frontier" identity and values during the uncertain war years (Coy 1997: 9). In a similar way, *The Road*'s characterization of the man as a Western hero resonates with the resurgence of the Western myth after 9/11. As Susan Faludi comprehensively assesses in her account of post–9/11 gender formulations, *The Terror Dream: What 9/11 Revealed About America* (2007), the image of frontier, "protector" masculinity was being actively advocated by the Bush administration after the attacks, and this image seemed to permeate society at the time: "The attack on home soil triggered a search for a guardian of the homestead, a manly man, to be sure, but one particularly suited to protecting and providing for the isolated American family in perilous situations ... a frontiersman whose proofs of eligibility were the hatchet and the gun" (Faludi 2007: 148). One of the fundamental tenets of Faludi's thesis is that America's recourse to mythologies such as this "frontier masculinity" deflected harsh social and political realities in favor of popular images of heroism and power. However bleak *The Road* may be, its heroic ending gives nobility to the man's frontier masculinity and is a resonant endorsement of this mythology. This is part of the reason that Gray finds the novel's ending so objectionable: its recourse to the "the sheltering confines of American myth" (Gray 2011: 47). *The Road*'s vision of American masculinity goes to great lengths to reinforce this dominant image of early post–9/11 masculinity—the same retrograde vision of frontier masculinity that was appropriated by the 2004 presidential candidates President Bush and democratic nominee John Kerry, who both delivered a variety of well-document PR performances dressed as cowboys and hunters on the 2004 campaign trail.[8]

The Messianic Allegory of The Road

In a range of different manifestations, religion—and particularly Christianity—is an integral theme in *The Road*. The most frequent and frequently alluded to Christian imagery in the novel comes in the form of two often-repeated phrases from the man and boy: "carrying the fire" and "good guys and bad guys." These phrases are not direct Biblical quotations and are in keeping with the text's "circuitous" or "symbolic" nature. It is possible that "carry the fire" could be a direct reference to the Puritan pastor Ezekiel Culverwell, who preached that "God's children go limping in their knowledge, and carry the fire of zeal in a flinty heart" (Evans 2001: 71). However, alone the phrases remain nebulous in their theology and simply evoke a generally spiritual or religious tone. Indeed, their key function may simply be their repetition. As Ashley Kunsa notes, the phrases become "incantatory in the manner of a litany or prayer" (Kunsa 2009: 59). So while these incantatory phrases cannot alone be cited as explicitly Christian, they become integral to the text when read as a Christian allegory, serving as a constant refrain to which the protagonists frequently return.

While numerous explicit references to "God" and to Christianity can and have been identified in *The Road*, the Christianity of the novel is most completely expressed as a messianic allegory. The symbolism of the novel undoubtedly finds its locus in the boy, who is characterized as explicitly Christ-like throughout the novel. This is established early on by the man when we learn that "he knew only that the child was his warrant. He said: if he is not the word of God, God never spoke" (McCarthy 2006: 3). The allegory is developed and sustained through the use of the phrases mentioned above, "carrying the fire" and "good guys and bad guys." The objective to "carry the fire" and to find more "good guys" ostensibly gives the journey its purpose, though it is really only the boy that truly believes in these objectives; the man perseveres by focusing on the immediate objectives of survival, avoiding starvation and keeping the boy alive at all costs. The boy constantly seeks to reinforce what he sees as the purpose of their existence, and when his father makes decisions that are morally questionable within this framework in order to preserve their lives, the boy reproaches him, questioning whether they are still "good guys." One example of this is when they encounter the traveller Ely and the boy begs his father to give the starving stranger some of their scant supply of food. When the man reluctantly concedes to his son's wishes, he tells Ely:

> You should thank him you know, the man said. I wouldn't have given you anything.
> Maybe I should and maybe I shouldn't.
> Why wouldn't you?
> I wouldn't have given him mine.
> You don't care if it hurts his feelings?
> Will it hurt his feelings?
> No. That's not why he did it.
> Why did he do it?
> He looked over at the boy and he looked at the old man. You wouldn't understand, he said. I'm not sure I do.
> Maybe he believes in God.
> I don't know what he believes in.
> He'll get over it.
> No he won't [McCarthy 2006: 184–5].

The boy's essential selflessness, purity, innocence and sheer incorruptibility are distinctly Christ-like. Steven Frye sees the messianic aspect of the boy as explicit: "The messianic quality rather unambiguously presented in the boy's character … implies … the moral purity and self-sacrifice of Christ" (Frye 2009: 168). The allegorical or symbolic aspect of *The Road*, and in particular the boy, is reasonably widely accepted, though some critics have suggested that it might relate to a different kind of Christian narrative—that of the grail legend. The most obvious evidence of this is an oft-quoted passage where the man refers to the boy as a "Golden chalice, good to house a god" (McCarthy 2006: 78). Lydia Cooper has made this argument convincingly and suggests that *The Road* should be interpreted as such: "a dying father embarks on a quest to preserve his son, whom he imagines as a chalice, the symbolic vessel of divine healing in a realm blighted by some catastrophic disease" (Cooper 2011: 221). This is a provocative reading and certainly highlights the importance of the father in establishing the symbolism in the boy. However, surely the father's repeated assertions of the boy's purity and goodness indicate that he is also, at least, projecting a messianic role onto him. It is certainly the case that the man continually emphasizes the boy's preternatural goodness, and that he dies attempting to ensure the survival of the boy. As Richard Crownshaw states, "The novel's end suggests the messianic meaning of the boy's survival, with which the father figure had invested his son" (Crownshaw 2011: 773). In the aftermath of the man's death the messianic quality of the boy is soon reinforced when, after finally meeting (what we assume are) more "good guys," the mother in the family clearly identifies this in him: "She said that the breath of God was his breath yet though it pass from man to man through all of time" (McCarthy 2006: 306).

The Road is undoubtedly anchored in Christian imagery throughout, some of which relates to this allegorical function and some of which doesn't. At times this imagery brushes with fundamentalist, right-wing Christianity. This is particularly apparent in the descriptions of the depraved "blood cults" (or bad guys) as savage "cannibals" leading chained "catamites" (or male sex-slaves): it is an odd and particularly conspicuous association of evil with homosexuality (McCarthy 2006: 96). While this could be a small link to the prominence of the Christian Right after 9/11, the novel's portrayal of the blood cults as savage "others" is also closely linked with its echoes of the classic Western or frontier narrative, where the role of the hostile other was usually played by Native Americans. In one scene the man and boy encounter a group of slain men, and the description carries echoes of a frontier massacre marked by a strange tribal otherness: "The wall beyond held a frieze of human heads, all faced alike, dried and caved with their taut grins and shrunken eyes. They wore gold rings in their leather ears and in the wind their sparse and ratty hair twisted about on their skulls ... the crude tattoos etched in some homebrewed woad died in the beggared sunlight. Spiders, swords, targets. A dragon" (McCarthy 2006: 80). The description of the blood cult approaching is an even more explicit evocation of a savage, amoral tribe: "all wearing red scarves at their necks. Red or orange, as close to red as they could find.... An army in tennis shoes, tramping, carrying three-foot lengths of pipe with leather wrappings. Lanyards at the wrist" (McCarthy 2006: 95).

However, it is undoubtedly the allegorical aspect of the novel that links *The Road* so clearly to a post–9/11 context. It is not the intention of this chapter to criticize, specifically, the Christian elements of *The Road* or Christianity in general, but rather to note the singularity of this allegory. It is this singularity that links the narrative to the George W. Bush project of reestablishing grand narratives after 9/11, grand narratives that post-modernism had allegedly disrupted. Indeed, the novel has been frequently read as a challenge to the post-modern notion of plurality and difference. John Cant highlights "the author's willingness to address fundamental philosophical questions in a manner generally out of fashion in a culture that has lost faith in the very notion of the grand narrative," as indicative of *The Road*'s boldness as a minimalistic, philosophical and religious narrative (Cant 2009: 183). The problem here is that the novel's central grand narrative falls into alignment with the grand narratives that the Bush administration was trying to reestablish in the early post–9/11 era: Islam v. the West and the Huntingtonian logic of a clash of civilizations, which characterizes one civilization—a Christian civilization—as "the good guys." In *Framing Muslims: Stereotyping and Representation After 9/11*, Peter Morey and Amina Yaquin remind us that "at no time since the 1930s have questions about the position of 'the outsider' in Western society been raised so persistently, troubling fashionable postmodern notions of the decline of the nation-state" (Morey and Yaquin 2011: 18). When President Bush rallied Americans to defend "our way of life," characterizing America as the world's "good guys," his vision of America was, as many commentators have noted, homogenous and unashamedly Christian (despite its many cursory gestures toward the "diversity" and "multiculturalism" of America) (Holloway 2008: 4). Indeed, as Bradley and Tate have noted, President Bush was "the first Born Again Christian President," whose foreign policies were frequently seen to be guided by an "unholy alliance between Neo-Conservatism and Christian Zionism" (Bradley and Tate 2010: 4). The messianic allegory of *The Road*, with its insistence on "good guys" and "bad guys," and "carrying the fire," clearly speaks to the unilateral policies of the Bush Doctrine.

Four. Disaster, Allegory and Exhaustion

The Road is underscored by the rhetoric of a return to the grand narratives of Christianity, Manifest Destiny and American exceptionalism, and in this way is surprisingly compatible with the Bush administration's desire to grossly simplify a multifaceted socio-political landscape to a series of easily understandable imperatives and objectives. However, *The Road* also operates as a culmination of the depoliticized or domestic narratives of 9/11—the end of a mini-cycle of narratives that conclude after the political backlash to Hurricane Katrina. Hurricane Katrina created a cultural tipping point that has seen more recent representations of 9/11 become much more politically engaged and dissenting. As Wai Chee Dimock points out, "The nation-state seems 'unbundled' by the hurricane in ways both large and small—not only as a system of defense but also as psychological insurance, political membership, and academic field" (Dimock 2008: 36). For the 9/11 novel, and the politically engaged narrative of Katrina, this unbundling meant a movement away from the "unity scripts" inherent in previous narratives (Melnick 2009: 45). In fact, many narratives of Katrina emphasized the fact that despite the tragedy ultimately beginning with a natural disaster, it was the government that created catastrophe. This is memorably articulated by the character Creighton Bernette in the first episode of David Simon's series *Tremé* (2010–present): "What hit the Mississippi Gulf Coast was a natural disaster, a hurricane pure and simple. The flooding of New Orleans was a man-made catastrophe, a federal fuck-up of epic proportions." In order to demonstrate this adequately, and to reinforce this chapter's reading of *The Road*, we will conclude by examining Dave Eggers' work of narrative non-fiction, *Zeitoun* (2009), a narrative of Hurricane Katrina that responds to the conservative rhetoric of *The Road* and the depoliticized nature of the early 9/11 novel.

Dave Eggers' narrative is clearly both responding to and informed by *The Road*—he even includes a quotation from McCarthy's novel as one of his two epigraphs. In some ways the vision of apocalypse in *The Road* speaks to the deeply biblical descriptions of the flooding of New Orleans in *Zeitoun*. In general, though, *Zeitoun*'s emphatic rhetoric advocating a multicultural, pluralistic America is particularly stark in contrast to *The Road*, especially considering the narrative importance of the protagonist's Muslim faith. Just as *The Road* establishes its religious subtext early on, so does *Zeitoun*. In an early scene, the narrator describes how

Abdulrahman and Kathy Zeitoun first set up their painting and decorating firm using a rainbow motif in their corporate identity and branding: "Immediately they began getting calls from gay couples, and this was good news, good business. But at the same time, some potential clients, once they saw the van arrive, were no longer interested in Zeitoun A. Painting Contractor LLC" (Eggers 2009: 11). The Zeitouns considered changing the logo but quickly dismissed the thought: "We're a Muslim couple running a painting company in Louisiana. Not such a good idea to turn away clients.... Anyone who had a problem with rainbows, he said, would surely have a problem with Islam" (Eggers 2009: 12). So while Christianity in *The Road* comes in the form of the ultimate metanarrative, Islam (while integral to the identity of the Zeitoun family) is always discussed in personal terms and situated as part of a greater plurality. There is no doubt that the Zeitoun family's faith is an integral part of the text's narrative, as Abdulrahman was arrested as a suspected Islamist terrorist during the chaos of the post–Katrina flooding of New Orleans. However, the text explores this essential part of the protagonist's identity while very conspicuously depicting post-9/11 Islamaphobia and paranoia as a threat to a pluralistic, secular "melting pot" America and to the great American immigration story—a genre which *Zeitoun* both conforms to and subverts. The story of Abdulrahman's incarceration in Camp Greyhound, the temporary New Orleans prison camp modeled after Guantanamo Bay, is damning, and there are certainly passages that outrightly condemn practices that have characterized the War on Terror. *Zeitoun* recounts how the wars in Afghanistan and Iraq had created a sense of anxiety in Kathy long before Abdulrahman's incarceration. Kathy had always been anxious around groups of returning soldiers, for example: "She had not wanted their family to become collateral damage in a war that had no discernible fronts, no real shape, and no rules" (Eggers 2009: 252). This is the kind of depiction of the everyday realities of the post-9/11 "homeland" that the first wave of 9/11 fiction was unable to represent. Even *Falling Man,* which includes short inter-chapters describing the preparations of the terrorists, does not speak to this issue in any great depth. Reflecting on Abdulrhaman's incarceration at Camp Greyhound, though, *Zeitoun* goes much further:

> But it seemed every month another story appeared about a native of Iran, Saudi Arabia, Libya, Syria, or any one of a number of other Muslim coun-

Four. Disaster, Allegory and Exhaustion

tries who was released after months or years from one of these detention centers. Usually the story was similar: A Muslim man came to be suspected by the U.S. government, and, under the president's current powers, U.S. agents were allowed to seize the man from anywhere in the world and bring him anywhere in the world, without ever having to charge him with a crime [Eggers 2009: 254].

However, while the text does highlight Abdulrahman's faith as one of the reasons he was wrongly targeted, abused, beaten, incarcerated and deprived for weeks of basic human rights, it is equally at pains to emphasize his continued love of and belief in a multicultural community, of America, and of a city which Helen Taylor describes as "one of America's most extraordinary melting pots" (Taylor 2010: 483). Not only does the text ultimately keep faith in an idea of American multiculturalism, it conspicuously depicts the Zeitoun family's faith as belonging to their private domain: *Zeitoun* deliberately advocates for a split between the private world of religion and the public world of pluralism and multiculturalism. The early stages of the text, which recount Abdulrahman dutifully paddling around his submerged neighborhood rescuing its diverse citizens, revel in the beauty of this image of the immigrant American working tirelessly to save his adopted home, which is an archetypal image of American diversity. As Grandin states, "If Zeitoun was virtuous to a fault—tolerant, open, pluralistic, inquisitive, all the values the ideologues of the war on terror believed could be imposed on the Middle East with tanks and guns—then it was a fault encouraged by the Caribbean worldliness of New Orleans" (Grandin 2011: 27). Abdulrahman never loses sight of this, and in one of the final, memorable passages, which again evokes the rainbow branding, Abdulrahman's continued love, in spite of terror and torture, is clearly stated:

> More than anything else, Zeitoun is simply happy to be free and in his city. It's the place of his dreams, the place where he was married, where his children were born, where he was given the trust of his neighbors. So every day he gets in his white van, still with its rainbow logo, and makes his way through the city, watching it rise again [Eggers 2009: 324].

Hurricane Katrina has forced a panoramic scrutiny of American society, which is neatly articulated by the strap-line to Tia Lessin and Carl Deal's Katrina documentary *Trouble the Water* (2006): "It's not about a hurricane. It's about America." The way *Zeitoun* contributes to this scrutiny is by insisting on plurality in place of the unilateral.

Another aspect of *The Road* that *Zeitoun* responds to in particular is its representation of masculinity. As stated, one of its two epigraphs is from McCarthy's novel, but the other is from Mark Twain: "To a man with a hammer, everything looks like a nail." Abdulrahman's masculinity is very similar to the man's, and another passage, which also highlights Abdulrahman's love of his adopted city and neighborhood, evokes the kind of assuredness and capability that also characterizes the man in *The Road*. It describes how in the first days of the flood Abdulrahman was unaware of the atrocities occurring in parts of the city, and he was actually enjoying being useful and helping people in his immediate neighborhood:

> Zeitoun dropped Frank at his house and made for home. His paddle kissed the clean water, his shoulders worked in perfect rhythm. Zeitoun had traveled five, six miles already that day, and he wasn't tired. Night was falling, and he knew he had to be home, safe on his roof. But he was sorry to see the day end [Eggers 2009: 110].

This is one of many passages that characterize Abdulrahman as hardworking and capable, and in this image of the classically self-reliant man, *Zeitoun* shares some commonality with *The Road*. Both Abdulrahman and the man are self-reliant and skilled men, but the two fall into divergent archetypes, and there is a stark division here in the narratives to which these images of masculinity belong. While the man represents a kind of mythological frontier masculinity, Abdulrahman is the quintessential immigrant man who achieves the American Dream through perseverance and hard work—as well as the Emersonian self-reliance we see in the man. So while *The Road* plays its part in reinforcing a retrograde vision of frontier masculinity at a time of crisis (appealing to a sensibility that saw a host of politicians and public figures evoking this image), *Zeitoun* problematizes the stereotypical image of the self-reliant immigrant man. This, again, links *The Road* uncomfortably to its unilateral post–9/11 context and shows *Zeitoun* to be reflexive and political. Abdulrahman's industrious work ethic, his resourcefulness and sheer capability against the odds, are the kind of attributes that enabled him to successfully achieve the American Dream in New Orleans, and, tragically, were precisely the traits that led him to his incarceration in Camp Greyhound. Moreover, Abdulrahman's series of dramatic rescues, which are corroborated facts, have obvious resonance with the often-celebrated story of the New York firemen who heroically entered the World Trade Center. But while the surviving firemen were instantly transformed into icons of American heroism, Abdulrahman was arrested as a terror suspect and, with horrific irony, subjected to Guantanamo Bay-like conditions.

The Ending of The Road

To return to Gray's critique of the ending of *The Road*, it is worth also returning to the notion that it reverts to "a myth that is ... a curious but not uncommon mix of the heroic and the domestic." The odd deliverance of the messianic boy into the safety of a family is an obvious link to what have been described as the "domestic" novels of 9/11—the previously mentioned novels that depoliticize the attacks, deferring to narratives of trauma, mourning and domestic stories of marriage and the family. There is also an emphasis on trauma in *The Road* that reinforces this link to the domestic texts and disaster cinema of 9/11. As we have seen, trauma theory, popularized in literary studies by Cathy Caruth, posits that certain events are outside the realms of normal comprehension, short-circuiting normal response systems. Furthermore, we have noted that Kristiaan Versluys, one of many commentators who employ trauma theory as a way of interpreting 9/11 fiction, starts with the assertion that "in the instantaneity of its horror and in its far-flung repercussions, 9/11 is unpossessable. It is a limit event that shatters the symbolic resources of the culture and defeats the normal processes of meaning-making and semiosis" (Versluys 2009: 1). Much has been said about how the domestic fictions of 9/11 negotiate the traumas of the attacks by fitting them into tried and safe narrative formulas, such as relationship narratives, essentially by deferring the trauma or building it in to the narrative as a backdrop to a more familiar genre narrative. But as Gray notes, in deferring traumatic events, these texts can only be attached to "the preliminary stages of trauma" because traumatic memories cannot be contained and eventually will haunt or intrude upon the present. *The*

Road seems to acknowledge this in one of the early discussions between the man and the boy, which establishes their situation. The man says to the boy: "'Just remember that the things you put into your head are there forever,' he said. 'You might want to think about that.... You forget what you want to remember and you remember what you want to forget'" (McCarthy 2006: 11). In this respect *The Road* flirts with a meta-fictional aspect which begins to comment on the domestic novels, offering a coded suggestion that it is aware of the discourse. However, this early suggestion is never developed outside the literal story, where the man and boy repeatedly witness horrific events, inevitably returning to the story of "good guys" and "bad guys," and "carrying the fire," to absorb these traumas and sustain their journey. Moreover, the novel's messianic allegory, and ultimately redemptive conclusion, also avoids the interruption of the original traumatic event by using a tried and safe story. In contrast, *Zeitoun* dares to place its protagonists in a bigger picture and, in measured prose, directly discusses the damage that the events of Hurricane Katrina and its aftermath have caused the Zeitoun family. Moreover, *Zeitoun* provides the political and social context of a story that, like *The Road*, has a distinctly religious quality. Indeed, in its poetic images of the flooding of New Orleans, *Zeitoun* has great potential for allegory but resists this in favor of a documentary-style presentation.

Dave Eggers's work of narrative non-fiction responds to the early corpus of 9/11 fiction and, specifically, to *The Road*. In its very form it presents a way to narrate an American disaster reflexively without compromising an experiential, literary or poetic quality. Eggers deploys a style that is both literary and documentary, and, crucially, this narrative non-fiction demonstrates a way of recounting an individual's experience of catastrophe while also confronting the politics of the event and telling a larger story: what Grandin calls a "survey at once intimate and comprehensive" (Grandin 2011: 27). Most notable, perhaps, is the way that the very conspicuous presence in this story of the politics of 9/11 and the War on Terror is suggestive of how these events were circumvented or plainly avoided by the first wave of 9/11 literature and cultural representation. *Zeitoun*, and, indeed, many other politicized accounts of Katrina—from Spike Lee's documentaries *When the Levees Broke: A Requiem in Four Acts* (2006) and *If God Is Willing and da Creek Don't Rise* (2009), Carl

Four. Disaster, Allegory and Exhaustion

Deal and Tia Lessin's film *Trouble the Water* (2008), David Simon's ongoing series *Tremé* (2010–)—all incorporate the politics of 9/11 and the War on Terror into their stories. Jesmyn Ward's award-winning novel *Salvage the Bones* (2011) inverts the formula of the domestic novels of 9/11 in its representation of Hurricane Katrina; rather than a privileged, white, Manhattan family, the novel dramatizes the experiences of a poor, rural, African American family in Louisiana. As stated, one of *Zeitoun*'s epigraphs comes from *The Road*: "...in the history of the world it might even be that there was more punishment than crime..." (Eggers 2009: xiii). There is an obvious reference to Abdulrahman's crimeless punishment here, but this also ironically addresses the way that certain kinds of punishment, such as torture and rendition, racial profiling, invasion of privacy, and extreme military aggression, which were particularly prominent in post–9/11 America, are largely absent in early 9/11 representation.

Texts such as *Zeitoun* demonstrate that the U.S. government's handling of Katrina was so bad that it forced cultural examination and inquiry beyond the shortcomings of FEMA. Furthermore, Katrina exacerbated existing fears over whether or not the U.S. government was equipped to adequately deal with disasters of all kinds. As William Waugh states, "Clearly, Hurricanes Katrina and Rita raise serious questions concerning the capacities of local, state, and federal governments to deal with major hazards and disasters. Obviously, we are not prepared to deal with catastrophic events, including a terrorist attack or an avian influenza pandemic" (Waugh 2006: 10). Helen Taylor echoed this sentiment, writing retrospectively in a fifth anniversary special issue of the *Journal of American Studies*, "Katrina was seen as heralding the death of a unique city, exposing American racism and neglect of its poorest citizens; as the nation's loudest wake-up call to the realities of global warming; and the beginning of the end of Bush's popularity and credibly presidency (Taylor 2010: 483). *Zeitoun*, and many of the other Katrina narratives, engage with the politics of American society after 9/11 in a way that the first wave of 9/11 novels were unable to do. This is evidenced most clearly by the fact that after Hurricane Katrina there began to emerge a body of 9/11 fiction and cultural representation that has been reflexive and political. In the coming chapters we will examine the way Joseph O'Neil gives space to a previously marginalized group of New Yorkers in *Nether-*

land (2008); how Mohsin Hamid deploys a first-world national allegory in *The Reluctant Fundamentalist* (2008), which demands a more reflexive understanding of 9/11; and how Amy Waldman, in a stylistic register not dissimilar to *Zeitoun*, challenges the post–9/11 racism that many Muslim Americans were subjected to.

FIVE

First World National Allegory and Otherness in *The Reluctant Fundamentalist*

As suggested in the previous chapter, Mohsin Hamid's novel *The Reluctant Fundamentalist* (2007) marks a departure in 9/11 fiction; it carries a sharp critical edge and offers one of the first meaningful representations of "otherness" in the canon of 9/11 fiction. There are, however, two clear lines of continuity between the early instances of 9/11 fiction and Hamid's novel. Firstly, like the "domestic novels" of 9/11, *The Reluctant Fundamentalist* is very much a relationship narrative, and one of the two main protagonists, Erica, who suffers from great emotional upheaval in the aftermath of the attacks, would not be out of place in the respective milieus of *The Good Life*, *Falling Man* or *The Emperor's Children*. Secondly, like *The Road*, the novel has a very clear and resonant allegorical function that relates directly to 9/11. The way in which *The Reluctant Fundamentalist* diverges is that the relationship at the center of the novel is between a privileged Manhattan woman and a Pakistani emigrant (the novel's narrator, Changez). This allows the novel to dramatize an affecting experience of otherness in America after 9/11 and begin to shape what we could call, borrowing from Michael Rothberg, a "multi-directional" understanding of 9/11. This chapter will argue that *The Reluctant Fundamentalist* constructs a complex "first-world" national allegory of 9/11, which is given nuance and dialectical tension through a unique duality in its narrative point of view—that of the assimilated immigrant American and the mysterious Muslim "other." This allegory itself suggests that the U.S. must look to its past to understand its complex reaction to 9/11, and, provocatively, to engage with the questions of how and why the attacks happened. However, while the novel is overtly political in this respect, it also emphasizes the importance of honoring and examining a deeply felt sense of loss and the trauma of the attacks. To this effect, *The Reluctant Fundamentalist* is underpinned by David Holloway's suggestion that "9/11 was long in the making and the pre–9/11 worlds and post–9/11 words are broadly continuous not discontinuous, however much it suited politicians to claim that the attacks came out of the blue" (Holloway 2008: 4). Equally, though, the novel is anchored to the idea of 9/11 as traumatic rupture and the notion that 9/11 was a moment when "everything changed"; and through this unique narrative duality and first-world national allegory, the continuity and discontinuity narratives begin to converge.

The tension between the discourses of trauma and politics is apparent throughout the allegorical structure of the text, and the novel is able to explore some of the nuanced binaries contained within the larger paradigm of continuity and discontinuity. For example, it engages with the dialectical aspect of trauma—the understanding of trauma as both a "limit event" and something that works in aggregate, incorporating previous traumatic events. It is also acutely aware of the dichotomy within the "everything's changed" rhetoric of the Bush Doctrine, which seemed apocalyptic or epochal and yet simultaneously couched in a nostalgic appeal to return to a retrograde vision of American identity, as discussed in the previous chapter. While *The Reluctant Fundamentalist* explicitly engages with the conflictedness of the aftermath of 9/11, the clear tensions in the novel have also been identified as problematic; Anna Hartnell argues that "Hamid's Pakistani protagonist is not simply alienated but also simultaneously drawn to the isolationist and exceptionalist currents of the American national narrative" (Hartnell 2010: 36). Hartnell ultimately argues that *The Reluctant Fundamentalist* suggests that America is failing to live up to its "self-understanding as a post-colonial nation," while still acknowledging its potential to be an "exceptional" melting-pot (Hartnell 2010: 346). The conflictedness that Hartnell identifies not only adds further nuance to the series of tensions and divisions in the novel, but is also prescient to the argument here, and the duality of the narrative voice is vital to the development of a nuanced and multifaceted first world national allegory.

First World National Allegory

Firstly, I must delineate what exactly constitutes a "first world" national allegory and what makes this instance of first world national allegory unique. In order to establish this, it is useful to begin with Frederic Jameson's 1986 *Social Text* essay entitled "Third World Literature in the Era of Multinational Capitalism," which has been the subject of much scrutiny and criticism for its formulation of the "third world" and reductive reading of "third world literature," but which, as we will see here, also presents an equally problematic idea of first world national allegory. Jameson states:

> Third World texts, even those which are seemingly private and invested with a properly libidinal dynamic—necessarily project a political dimension in the form of national allegory: *the story of the private individual destiny is always an allegory of the embattled situation of the public third world culture and society* [Jameson 1986: 69].

This formulation has been fiercely criticized over the subsequent decades of postcolonial studies, particularly in Aijaz Ahmad's response, "Jameson's Rhetoric of Otherness and the 'National Allegory,'" which takes issue with the "binary opposition of what Jameson calls the first and third worlds" (Ahmad 1987: 3). The notion that all "third world" texts (a grouping which, according to Jameson's essay, evidently contains a vastly diverse selection of international literatures) are necessarily national allegories has been repeatedly cited as homogenizing and Orientalist. However, Imre Szemen's 2001 recuperation of Jameson's essay, "Who's Afraid of National Allegory," points out that Jameson's equally provocative statements regarding first world national allegory are often overlooked. Szemen highlights Jameson's statement that "in the west, conventionally, political commitment is re-contained and psychologised or subjectivised by way of the public-private split," and elaborates on this:

> Jameson believes that in the West, the consequence of the radical separation between the public and the private, "between the poetic and the political," is "the deep cultural conviction that the lived experience of our private existences is somehow incommensurable with the abstractions of economic science and political dynamics." In terms of literary production, this "cultural conviction" has the effect of limiting or even negating

entirely the political work of literature: in the first world, literature is a matter of the private rather than the public sphere, a matter of individual tastes and solitary meditations rather than public debate and deliberation [Szemen 2001: 807].

This is still a reductive and even Manichean formulation in that "third world" literature is inevitably allegorical and first world literature is incapable of national allegory. However, this idea that Western literature is "a matter of individual tastes and solitary meditations" could certainly be usefully applied to some of the texts from previous chapters that are so prominently focused on individual traumas or domestic scenarios, though this isn't relevant here. The following textual analysis will sit in opposition to this formulation, arguing that through the unique dual perspective of *The Reluctant Fundamentalist*, Jameson's "private-public split" is broken, and through the filters of "otherness," and a focus on American national identity, a politically engaged, first world national allegory is constructed.

The Dual Perspective of The Reluctant Fundamentalist

The Reluctant Fundamentalist was first published in English, has had a largely Western audience and may not constitute what Jameson would categorize as "third world literature." There is no question, though, that it is invested in exploring "otherness" and that it can lay claim to an authentic perspective of "otherness." Nevertheless, it is important here to establish a definition for the term "dual perspective," and to give specific meaning to such nebulous terms as "other" and "otherness." *The Reluctant Fundamentalist* is the first novel in the 9/11 canon to feature a non–American central protagonist, and it is the first of these novels to explore 9/11 and post–9/11 from a genuinely international perspective. Hamid's novel is essentially a first-person monologue told from a café in Lahore, from where its protagonist Changez originates. The majority of the story he narrates, however, takes place in New York, so in its structure alone there is a fundamental split. The ways in which the chapters alternate between the New York of the retrospective narrative and the Lahore of the present is emblematic of the narrative's dual perspective, as this is also the alternation between the assimilated young emigrant Changez pursuing and achieving his American Dream, and the disillusioned mature Changez describing his dream's post–9/11 disintegration. In some ways the narrative split here echoes the transnational narrative splits in *Extremely Loud and Incredibly Close* and *Windows on the World*. However, it differs in the sense that it is a temporal split where a single narrator alternates between the present and the past. Changez tells the story of his immigration to the U.S., his success at Princeton and then as a Wall Street consultant, his falling in love with an American woman, and his subsequent disenchantment with his adopted country in the tense aftermath of 9/11. In interview, Hamid has described the story as a "failed love story about somebody who desperately wanted to succeed in loving the United States but failed to do so," a revealing statement in terms of both the duality of the narrative point of view and the allegorical functions of the characters (Hamid 2008: 47). Certainly Changez is established in the opening chapter as a character who has been immersed in (or in love with) America and American culture to the extent that he is able to understand it in a sophisticated way. In the opening chapter (one of the "present day" chapters) he identifies his "interlocutor," the man he is telling the story to, as an American on account of his "bearing" (Hamid 2007: 2). It could be said that Hamid shares his protagonist's dual angle of perspective, and to some degree the novel is biographical; like Changez he is from Pakistan and attended Princeton (Hamid also studied at Harvard Law School), and worked for several years as a management consultant on Wall Street.

Allegories of Private and Public Traumas

The allegorical aspect of *The Reluctant Fundamentalist* functions through the relationships between Changez and his friend (and longtime romantic interest) Erica, whom he met at Princeton, and her deceased partner Chris. The novel also has another tangential allegorical strand which is important in key moments of the narrative; the Wall Street firm that Changez works for and at which he learns his fundamentalist approach to his consultancy work is called Underwood Sampson (U.S.). This aggressive New York firm, whose mantra is to "focus on the fundamentals," is clearly symbolic of the United States, and Changez's growing frustration with his employers after 9/11 parallels his increasingly fractious relationship with his adopted country. The most integral strand in the allegory, however, belongs to Erica—or, as James Lasdun has suggested, "(Am)Erica" (Lasdun 2007: n.p.). As well as assigning the national allegory function to Erica, Lasdun also factors her deceased ex-partner into the occasion: "It dawns on you that Erica is America and that Chris's name has been chosen to represent that nation's fraught relationship with its moment of European discovery and conquest, while the narrator himself stands for the country's consequent inability to accept, uh, changez" (Lasdun 2007: n.p.). In this reading, the immigrant, or what Jameson's essay might term "third world" narrator, tells the story of his relationship with an allegorical American woman—a first world national allegory, which challenges the established ideas of national allegory in several ways. Lasdun's *Guardian* review formulates this allegory in simplistic terms, and it is evidently more complicated than this. Hartnell positions Erica as a personification of "American nationalism," arguing that she provides a "compelling exploration of the narrative of American innocence" (Hartnell 2010: 346). There are certainly some very clear elements of allegorical traction that support this: Erica's profound turn inward after 9/11 (nationalism or American isolationism) and her nostalgia (the much discussed "return to core values"), as well as the essential goodness or innocence that Changez sees in her. However, Erica's obsession with deceased boyfriend Chris is more complex than Lasdun's notion of America's "fraught relationship with its moment of European discovery and conquest," and it makes her character more than just a personification of American nationalism or national innocence. Erica's post-9/11 depression or trauma is a combination of the collective trauma she experiences as a New Yorker, mourning the city's collective loss and her heightened feelings of her personal loss of Chris, which resurfaces powerfully after the attacks. This is another example of what has been identified as an "aggregation of traumas," where one trauma is in dialogue with or is filtered through another. As we have seen in Chapter One, this phenomenon is illustrated in Irene Kacandes' essay "9/11/01 = 1/27/01: The Changed Post-Traumatic Self," which describes the post-9/11 resurgence of the trauma of losing loved ones in a violent homicide some months before 9/11. Kacandes evokes Erica's trauma, stating, "For me, much of how I experienced September 11 was determined by events that had taken place months earlier" (Kacandes 2003: 68).

The allegorical function of Erica becomes highly evocative, as this

Five. First World National Allegory and Otherness

aggregation of traumas evokes the complexity of the social and political climate in America after 9/11. Furthermore, allegorically, the aggregation of traumas in *The Reluctant Fundamentalist* makes a pointed statement about the U.S. response to 9/11. Firstly, it clearly suggests that pre-existing, unresolved issues are affecting America's response to 9/11. It is clear that Erica's personal trauma of losing Chris years before stands for American domestic or national issues that had been dormant or subterranean, and the trauma she experiences so acutely after the attacks relates to both the impact of the attacks on the nation and these suppressed, hidden or unresolved issues. This allegory is given further complexity by two factors: Erica is disoriented by the merging of multiple traumas, one singular or private and one plural or public, and this becomes a canny articulation of the generally disorienting merging of individual crises and public events. Crucially, though, as she is unsure as to whether her post–9/11 decline is related to the powerful resurgence of emotion connected to the personal tragedy of her past, or to the attacks, her story becomes another articulation of a "continuity" narrative of 9/11 in dialogue with a "discontinuity" narrative. This question of whether this is an instance of rupture or an event that is part of a clear continuum hangs over, and resonates throughout, the narrative.

As Erica retreats within herself, her entangled traumas are reflected in and related to other key strands of the story. Internationally, the launch of the War on Terror and bombing of Afghanistan are watched on television by Changez, and a latent xenophobia and rampant nationalism in New York rises to the surface, affecting him everywhere he goes. The New York that Changez describes is covered in patriotic symbolism: "Small flags stuck on toothpicks featured in the shrines; stickers of flags adorned windshields and windows; large flags fluttered from buildings" (Hamid 2007: 79). Changez is unable to distinguish or pinpoint what precisely causes Erica's decline and, extending from this, has difficulty understanding the changes to his beloved, adopted country, as either a sudden shift or a rising to the surface of latent issues:

> I never came to know what triggered her decline—was it the trauma of the attack on her city? The act of sending out her book in search of publication? The echoes raised in her by our lovemaking?—but I think I knew even then that she was disappearing into a powerful nostalgia [Hamid 2007: 86].

Changez's attempt to come to terms with Erica's decline is integral to the novel, as the change in Erica is closely related to his own eventual disillusionment with his adopted country. Again, Changez is, as Hamid describes, "somebody who desperately wanted to succeed in loving the United States but failed to do so," and Erica's decline sheds some light on the national changes that incite his disillusionment (Hamid 2008: 47). Two of the possibilities that Changez lists above are crucial to the allegory of Erica: her experience of the "trauma of the attack" and the "echoes raised in her by our lovemaking." The trauma of the attacks is clearly the catalyst for Erica's decline, as it begins in earnest directly after they take place. The couple's "lovemaking," though, reflects the complexity of Erica's trauma and her decline.

Changez and Erica's sexual encounter is evocative and brings out the full allegorical weight of their relationship. After a long, steadily increasing friendship that is unable to blossom into romance largely due to Erica's prolonged grieving over her first love, Changez and Erica attempt to have sex for the first time, just after 9/11. The experience is awkward, and they are unable to engage in this physical intimacy:

> At times I would feel her hold onto me, or I would hear from her the faintest of gasps. Mainly she was silent and unmoving, but such was my desire that I overlooked the growing wound this inflicted on my pride and continued. I found it difficult to enter her; it was though she was not aroused. She said nothing while I was inside her, but I could see her discomfort, and so I forced myself to stop [Hamid 2007: 105].

Upon aborting this attempt at intercourse, Changez and Erica speak, and indeed it is thoughts of her ex-partner Chris that has inhibited Erica. A few weeks later, though, as they sit speaking of Chris, Erica enters a heightened state of emotion, and Changez makes the strange suggestion that she pretend that he is Chris, which leads to a much more physically successful intercourse:

> It was as though we were under a spell, transported to a world where I was Chris and she was with Chris, and we made love with a physical intimacy that Erica and I had never enjoyed. Her body denied mine no longer; I watched her shut eyes, and her shut eyes watched him [Hamid 2007: 104].

This episode is possibly the most richly symbolic in the novel. After the sexual act, Changez experiences conflicting emotions. He is both exhilarated and ashamed, and has difficulty understanding this: "Perhaps by taking on the persona of another, I had diminished myself in my own eyes; perhaps I was humiliated by the continuing dominance, in the strange romantic triangle of which I found myself a part" (Hamid 2007: 105). The metaphorical aspect of Erica and Changez's sexual encounters is clear; their inability to engage in physical intimacy represents a more general difficulty in intercultural relations, and much of it has to do with Erica's (or America's) inability to completely embrace the outsider or the "other." The sexualized language above could easily be transposed to a more general but pointed description of the experience of immigration in America—phrases like "I found it difficult to enter her," or "She said nothing while I was inside her, but I could see her discomfort." These are suggestive phrases, particularly considering the backdrop of escalating racial, national, ethnic and inter-cultural tensions after 9/11. Additionally, the suggestion that the only way the couple can enjoy genuine intimacy is by escaping from the realities of their racial difference and imagining that they are a white American couple evokes the fallacy of America's melting pot claims.

Changez and Erica's relationship suffers in general after 9/11, deteriorating with Erica's inward turn, and this is powerfully described by Changez just after the attacks: "She was struggling against a current that pulled her within herself, and her smile contained the fear that she might slip into her own depths, where she would be trapped, unable to breathe" (Hamid 2007: 86). As stated, this description of Erica comes in what Changez describes as a very particular backdrop: "Your country's flag was everywhere.... They all seemed to proclaim: We are America" (Hamid 2007: 79). At this point in the novel Erica is at her most allegorical, and Changez makes the explicit connection to what he had previously identified as Erica's "dangerous nostalgia" to what he here identifies as a symptom of the post–9/11 American national condition:

> It seemed to me that America, too, was increasingly giving itself over to a dangerous nostalgia at that time. There was something undeniably retro about the flags and uniforms, about generals addressing cameras in war rooms and newspaper headlines featuring such words as duty and honor ... [Hamid 2007: 115].

Erica's turn inward, while at odds with this hyperbolic, flag-waving patriotism, clearly reflects the dark or dangerous side of this national "nostalgia." The scenes Changez describes evoke James Der Derian's description of the "sepia tones" of World War II nostalgia. This nostalgia, as noted elsewhere, carries its own internal conflicts as a response to rupture, which is fundamentally historical.

Crucially, while Erica's depression begins after 9/11, it is presented as a problem that has deeper roots, and nostalgia, of course, is an emotion or expression of continuity, as it is rooted in an idealization of the past. There is no doubt of Erica's troubled psyche before 9/11, and weeks before the attacks Changez notices her "detachment": "I had come to suspect that hers were not merely the lapses of the absent-minded; no, she was struggling against a current that pulled her within herself, and her smile contained the fear that she might slip into her own depths" (Hamid 2007: 86). This statement that even before the attacks "she was struggling against a current that pulled her within herself" is loaded with the suggestion that even before 9/11, America was becoming isolationist on the international stage, and the allegorical rhetoric of Changez's experience supports this sentiment completely. Even considering that Erica's loss is a personal rather than social issue, if we do take her ex-partner, Chris, as symbolic of his "nation's fraught relationship with its moment of European discovery and conquest," as Lasdun suggests, then we can see a long-term issue of national identity aggravated by the events of 9/11 and the problematic relationship she embarks on with Changez. This may seem like a simplistic allegorical mapping of country to character, but these allegorical aspects, combined with the nature of the literal story, make complex suggestions that go beyond the singular notion of a new era post–9/11. It is the emotional experience of one person processing personal and "collective" trauma that is then projected onto a national identity, evoking the idea of a nation embroiled in a moment of crisis, that is defined by a tension between latent, pre-existing issues (a continuity narrative) and immediate, fundamental change (a discontinuity issue).

The "first world" national allegory in *The Reluctant Fundamentalist* concludes with an absolute, a moment of genuine rupture—Erica's death—and the individual narrative currents of "epoch" and "history" collide and meld. In the closing chapters, the retrospective story of Changez and Erica's relationship, and the impact of 9/11, gives way to the present narrative of Changez and the American man to whom he is telling

Five. First World National Allegory and Otherness

the story. Erica's death is clearly a powerful statement about the impact of 9/11, and as she has been such a vivid allegorical character, it casts a significant pall over the remaining chapters. Her death brings the notion of complete traumatic rupture back to the fore, and, in her allegorical aspect, represents "discontinuity" on a national level. However, the aspect of her allegory that has clearly illustrated the rising up of pre-existing racial antipathy and intercultural discord becomes a prominent part of the remaining narrative as it quickly moves toward its tense conclusion. Indeed, by the time Changez becomes aware of Erica's apparent suicide, the streets are hostile and Changez is brimming with anger at aggressive American militarization in the Middle East, the nationalism he encounters in the streets of New York, and the biases of the media:

> Sometimes I would find myself walking the streets, flaunting my beard as provocation, craving conflict with anyone foolhardy enough to antagonize me. Affronts were everywhere; the rhetoric emerging from your country at that moment in history—not just from the government, but from the media and supposedly critical journalists as well—provided a ready and constant fuel for my anger [Hamid 2007: 167].

Ostensibly, one of the most provocative strands of *The Reluctant Fundamentalist*'s rhetoric is the image of a wholly pro–American immigrant becoming disillusioned by his adopted country. Changez actively accentuates aspects of his physical appearance and character that mark him out as "other"—such as his beard. This part of the narrative demonstrates how media stereotyping becomes dialogical. As Amina Yaqin and Peter Morey point out:

> Negative images of Muslims do not cause alienation or radicalization. Nonetheless, substituting simplistic and politically manageable views of a sizeable portion of contemporary global citizenry in place of unwieldy and complex realities must have a detrimental effect on the quality of political decision-making, community relations and public debate" (Yaqin and Morey 2011: 19).

So while the rise of American nationalism does not radicalize Changez, it makes his existence untenable, stokes his defiance and, of course, is integral to his increasingly adversarial relationship with America.

The key moment of Changez's disillusionment comes from an epiphany he has on a business trip in Valparaiso just before Erica dies.

Continuing the kind of historical thinking and referencing that characterizes his thoughts throughout the novel, he realizes that he is a "modern-day janissary, a servant of the American empire at a time when it was invading a country with a kinship to mine and was perhaps even colluding to ensure that my own country faced the threat of war" (Hamid 2007:152). The significance of Underwood Sampson as symbolic of the United States as a whole is vital here: "I had thrown in my lot with the men of Underwood Samson, with the officers of the empire, when all along I was predisposed to feel compassion for those ... whose lives the empire thought nothing of overturning for its own gain" (Hamid 2007: 152). When Changez states that he has sided with the "officers of the empire," one cannot avoid the explicit association of Underwood Sampson, which Hartnell describes as the "pragmatic face of American state power," with the United States (Hartnell 2010: 340). Despite the narrative importance of this association, however, it is Erica's demise that consolidates Changez's decision to leave the country and return to his increasingly imperiled family in Pakistan, and it is through Erica that the nature of his relationship with America is defined. Firstly, Changez casts this in terms of diverging narratives, which has its own allegorical logic: "I had begun to understand that she had chosen not to be part of my story; her own had proven too compelling, and she was—at that moment and in her own way—following it to its conclusion" (Hamid 2007: 167). However, he eventually concedes to the lasting impact Erica, or America, has made on his life: "I had returned to Pakistan, but my inhabitation of your country had not entirely ceased. I remained emotionally entwined with Erica, and I brought something of her with me to Lahore" (Hamid 2007: 172).

The ambiguous conclusion of the novel contains layers of meaning and complexity, and the author has suggested on numerous occasions that the meaning of the ending is contingent on the biases of the reader. On the surface, Changez describes his increasing politicization in Lahore to the increasing suspicion of his "interlocutor," who is likely some kind of American agent. Changez had expressed his conviction that "America had to be stopped" and, until the final pages when he explicitly condemns violence, allows the possibility that he has become a different kind of "fundamentalist" (Hamid 2007: 168). The exact nature of the American man's intention is left unresolved, though the final paragraph leaves the reader with the possibility of him reaching for either a weapon or a business card. This open ending and unresolved relationship among the two men representing different nations is the logical, ambiguous conclusion to the allegory of Erica, which, as narrated by Changez, is laden with the issues of intercultural relations in the U.S. and international discord. The ambiguity reflects the conflictedness that pervades almost every aspect of the novel. Richard Gray points out a series of oppositions—"past and present, Muslim and American, East and West," for example. This conflictedness goes further, though, into the characters and was clearly an integral part of the author's design as he conceived of the allegory:

> I think countries are like people. Not that countries are monolithic—even people have fractured identities and conflicting impulses—but notions of pride, passion, nostalgia, and envy shape the behavior of countries more than is sometimes acknowledged. In the Muslim world, one sees love for things American co-exist with anger towards America. Which is stronger, politics or love, is like asking which is stronger, exhaling or inhaling. They are two sides of the same thing [Hamid 2007: n.p.].

The Reluctant Fundamentalist's first-world national allegory, which suggests that these issues have pre-9/11 origins (an evocation of continuity) is balanced by the absolute of death and permanent change (a discontinuity). The novel's dual perspective of American and "other" asks its readers to consider both perspectives from one narrator and at the very least problematizes the dominant perspectives and understandings of 9/11 in the West. There is also, clearly, an inherent advocacy for a multidirectional memory of 9/11 that acknowledges the impacts and experiences of a wider range of Americans and, indeed, citizens of other countries. In the introduction to *Multidirectional Memory*, Michael Rothberg discusses the need to "think about the relationship between different social groups' histories of victimization," and this need is at the heart of Hamid's novel (Rothberg 2009: 2).

National Allegory and the Dual Perspective in Spike Lee's 25th Hour

To reinforce this idea that Changez's unique "dual perspective" facilitates the first world national allegory, it is useful to make an unlikely comparison to one of the very first narrative representations of 9/11, Spike Lee's film *25th Hour* (2002), which was actually the first production granted access to Ground Zero. Lee's film is also a national allegory, and, like *The Reluctant Fundamentalist*, its complexities are brought to their full potential through a multifaceted narrative point of view characterized by an emphasis on otherness. The movie *25th Hour* is the story of drug dealer Monty Brogan, who is "touched" or convicted and faces his last twenty-four hours of freedom before beginning his seven-year sentence. His life is changed forever, and the film explores Monty's response to this change. The narrative follows Monty through these final 24 hours as he walks the streets of New York, spends time with the important people in his life, reflects on what has happened (much of which is dramatized in flashbacks), and meditates on his suspicion that it was his partner Naturalle who gave him up to the police. The unlikely reality of a convicted felon having this 24-hour period to ponder his sudden fate is one part of Monty's story that doesn't have any corresponding allegorical logic, though ironically it is precisely this plot device that allows the character the space to develop its allegorical meaning; it is almost a period of reflection that, one could argue, nationally, America didn't allow itself, and the narrative carries its own suggestion in this aspect. However, this depiction of a man, whose life has changed irrevocably, looking for answers gains allegorical traction immediately. The literal story takes place sometime in the months after 9/11 in New York, which is indicated by the opening title sequence that features powerful imagery of the New York skyline, with the prominent presence of the "Tribute in Light" memorial; and the imagery of 9/11 supports the allegorization of Monty throughout the film. After the long title sequence, this association of Monty and the imagery of post–9/11 New York continues as the narrative follows him around a New York covered in American flags and other images of 9/11 iconography—the same images that affront Changez in *The Reluctant Fundamentalist*. Soon after this, in a provocative scene, before meeting him for farewell drinks, Monty's two oldest friends discuss his future while looking down on Ground Zero, the camera's focus pointedly reflecting the subject of the dialogue. With the camera trained on the ongoing excavation of the site, Francis tells Jacob that Monty has three options—to run and never be seen again, to kill himself, or to go to prison where he will be killed. In any case, he argues, it is effectively

Five. First World National Allegory and Otherness

the end of Monty. This is one of many examples of instances in the film that position Monty as directly mirroring the story of New York or America, and this scene in particular emphasizes the allegory. The culmination of this discussion of Monty between his two best friends is powerfully set by the camera's focus and zoom in on Ground Zero. What is provocative and powerful in this film, though, is that allegorically the narrative of Monty or America is not only down to the absolutes that Francis and Jacob discuss but rather becomes the narrative of a man coming to terms with the fact that he has only himself to blame. Consequently for Monty (and America)—as in *The Reluctant Fundamentalist*—this is an exercise of looking within and looking back, evoking ideas of continuity and context.

This is established in one early scene which features Monty standing before a mirror in the bathroom of his father's bar and launching into an extravagant (and fairly comprehensive) rant against every minority culture in New York. Allegorically, this represents a rising to the surface of latent paranoia and racism in New York and America. This scene is the first depiction of the violent and aggressive part of Monty's character, and it breaks the stride of the film stylistically as well, rendered in a highly stylized montage using a more colorful and grainier film stock; it is clearly intended to be a set piece that disrupts the normal alignment of point of view with Monty. Ultimately it reinforces the allegorical aspect of Monty by using the device of the mirror to show what is inside of him (which appears to be all of the diverse citizenry of New York). The monologue he delivers is worth quoting in its entirety:

> Fuck the panhandlers grubbing for money and smiling at me behind my back. Fuck the Squeegee men dirtying up the clean windshield of my car. Fuck the Sikhs and the Pakistanis bombing down the avenues in decrepit cabs, curry steaming out their pores and stinking up my day. Terrorists in fucking training! Slow the fuck down! Fuck the Chelsea boys with their waxed chests and pumped up biceps, going down on each other in my parks and on my piers, jingling their dicks on my Channel 35. Fuck the Korean grocers with their pyramids of overpriced fruit and their tulips and roses wrapped in plastic. Ten years in the country, still no speaky English? Fuck the Russians in Brighton Beach, mobster thugs sitting in cafes, sipping tea in little glasses, sugar cubes between their teeth. Wheelin' and dealin' and schemin': Go back where you fucking came from! Fuck the black hatted Chassidim, strolling up and down 47 street in their dirty

Gabardine with their dandruff. Selling South African apartheid diamonds! Fuck the Wall Street brokers. Self-styled masters of the universe. Michael Douglas, Gordon Gecko wannabe motherfuckers, figuring out new ways to rob hard-working people blind. Send those Enron assholes to jail for fucking life! You think Bush and Cheney didn't know about that shit! Give me a fucking break! Tyco! Imclone! Adelphia! Worldcom! Fuck the Puerto Ricans. 20 to a car, swelling up the welfare rolls, worst fuckin' parade in the city. And don't even get me started on the Dominicans, because they make the Puerto Ricans look good. Fuck the Bensonhurst Italians with their pomaded hair, their nylon warm-up suits, and their St. Anthony medallions, swinging their Jason Giambi, Louisville slugger baseball bats, trying to audition for the Sopranos. Fuck the Upper East Side wives with their Hermes scarves and their fifty-dollar Balducci artichokes. Overfed faces getting pulled and lifted and stretched, all taut and shiny. You're not fooling anybody sweetheart! Fuck the uptown brothers. They never pass the ball, they don't want to play defence, they take five steps on every lay up to the hole and then they turn around and blame everything on the white man. Slavery ended one-hundred-and-thirty-seven years ago: move the fuck on! Fuck the corrupt cops with their anus violating plungers and their 41 shots, standing behind a blue wall of silence. You betray our trust! Fuck the priests who put their hands down some innocent child's pants. Fuck the church that protects them, delivering us into evil. And while you're at it, fuck JC! He got off easy! A day on the cross, a weekend in hell, and all the hallelujahs of the legioned angels for eternity! Try seven years in fuckin' Otisville, J! Fuck Osama Bin Laden, Al-Qaeda, and backward-ass, cave-dwelling fundamentalists everywhere. On the names of innocent thousands murdered, I pray you spend the rest of eternity with your seventy-two whores roasting in jet fuelled fire hell. You towel-headed camel jockeys can kiss my royal Irish ass! Fuck Jacob Elinski, whining malcontent. Fuck Francis Xavier Slaughtery, my best friend, judging me while he stares at my girlfriend's ass. Fuck Naturelle Rivera. I gave her my trust and she stabbed me in the back. Sold me up the river, fucking bitch! Fuck my father with his endless grief, standing behind that bar sipping on club soda, selling whisky to firemen and cheering the Bronx Bombers. Fuck this whole city and everyone in it. From the row houses of Astoria to the penthouses of Park Avenue; from the projects of the Bronx to the lofts in Soho; from the tenements in Alphabet City to the brownstones in Park Slope to the split levels in Staten Island. Let an earthquake crumble it, let the fires rage, let it burn to fuckin' ash, then let the waters rise and submerge this whole rat-infested place. No. No, fuck you, Monty Brogan. You had it all and then you threw it away, you dumb Fuck!

Five. First World National Allegory and Otherness

This scene is reminiscent of a similarly stylized set-piece in one of Spike Lee's other New York–set films, *Do the Right Thing* (1987). However, the presence of 9/11 hangs heavily over it, and it is crucial to the allegory for three reasons. As stated, the device of the mirror, which literally shows Monty to "mirror" and contain all of these cultures and minority groups he rants against and which we see on screen, consolidates his allegorical quality. Secondly, the monologue is Monty's first real gesture of self-examination; after ranting against "everyone" and assigning some blame to his best friends and father, and explicitly to his partner Naturelle, he blames himself. It is his placing of blame on himself that sets the course for a process of painful realization that plays out over the course of the narrative. This is a strong indictment allegorically, particularly when Monty eventually concludes that he "had it all" and "threw it away" because he was too "greedy." Lastly, because of the revealing of Monty's racism, homophobia, xenophobia and general aggression, the audience's alignment of POV with him is jarred, thus problematizing the narrative point of view and destabilizing the allegory. The audience is invited to subjectify Monty here after he had previously been the clear focalizer.

This is the first surfacing of Monty's unpleasant inner turmoil, which is well-masked by repeated emphasis on his friendliness and sensitivity in certain scenes. The film actually opens with a prologue that precedes the title sequence and features Monty rescuing an injured dog (not only does this immediately establish him as empathetic but it foregrounds the emphasis on recovery that is the focus of the film's conclusion). It is an explicit instance of the well-known screen drama device often referred to as the "pet the dog moment"—where an antihero, antagonist or rogue character establishes his ultimate inner goodness by "petting the dog" (or through some other demonstration or act of empathy). Monty keeps the dog, who he names Doyle, and he is with him at key moments throughout the film. Underneath his pleasant surface, though, this set piece reveals violent racial hatred and a multitude of bigotries which are all clearly identified as having pre–9/11 origins. As Monty is explicitly allegorical, this is another powerful and damning suggestion that underneath an appealing surface, and despite its "melting pot" pretenses, the U.S. houses violent racial and intercultural hostility. The narrative focus of the film is refigured at this point, and just as Changez has two registers as a narrator, the audience's identification with Monty oscillates in response to his own conflictedness. Narrative point of view is filtered through a continual foregrounding of post–9/11 identity issues (not least of which is the fact that Monty is deeply in love with his Puerto Rican partner yet reveals himself as being a racist), highlighting the post–9/11 position of the minority "other."

An important tangential element of the allegory of Monty is the fact that it is a Russian organized crime group that he has been involved with throughout his criminal career. The reflecting he does, then, about how what has happened has happened inevitably leads him to scrutinize his relationship with this Russian mafia. This gives even more weight to this suggestion that America needs to look within itself for answers and an understanding of 9/11 as it allegorically correlates to what David Holloway identifies as one of the popular historical strands of 9/11: "the truism that the CIA had created Osama bin Laden and Al-Qaeda by arming and training the guerrilla army of Afghan Muslims and international Islamic volunteers which waged jihad against the Soviet occupation of Afghanistan" (Holloway 2007: 21). This is not exactly allegorically symmetrical, but it is clear that Monty's downfall, which is brought on in part because of his relationship to the Russian criminals, alludes to the frequent connections made between 9/11 and U.S. Cold War involvement with Russia. The thrust of this aspect of the allegory in *25th Hour*, then, is again to emphasize history and context, and the only aspect of the film which tempers this (before the denouement) is the somber stylistic tone of the film.

The stark aesthetic palette of *25th Hour*, including the heavily stylized cinematography and epic quality of Terence Blanchard's score, conjures a sense of irreparable damage and trauma that balances the allegorical suggestions of continuity; and if the allegory of Monty represents continuity, then the world he inhabits represents discontinuity. Indeed, much of the limited amount of critical attention paid to the film revolves around its general tone and style. Mick LeSalle remarks on the tone of *25th Hour* in a recent re-evaluation of the film: "He weaves it [9/11] into the fabric of the story, not in a cosmetic way, and not as a cheap metaphor, but in ways that informed the mood of the film and its characters. That lassitude, that feeling of defeat and despair that pervades *25th Hour*" (LaSalle 2009: n.p.). This echoes a *Sight and Sound* review by Ryan

Gilbey which connects its access to Ground Zero and the imagery of 9/11 to the film's focus on collective trauma: "*25th Hour*, the first film production to be granted access to Ground Zero, is about the damage wreaked on New York's psyche" (Gilbey 2003: 58). It certainly is the case that the imagery of the film is deliberately engaging with or confronting traumatic subject matter. Ivan Cañadas points out that "in contrast to other filmmakers and studios, which deleted footage of the World Trade Center from films released in the wake of the attack—out of supposed deference to public sensibilities—Lee did the opposite" (Cañadas 2009: n.p.). Of course, the film doesn't include any footage of the towers but rather the fact of their absence. As Judith Greenberg states, "the towers now overwhelm in their absence," and this focus on Ground Zero in *25th Hour* directly confronts the viewer with potentially traumatic imagery (Greenberg 2003: 25). The emphasis on these images of the traumatic site and 9/11 iconography tempers the context-seeking allegory, though, as in *The Reluctant Fundamentalist*, the binaries converge in the film's final sequence.

Indeed, Monty's allegorical function gets more sophisticated toward the end of the film when he must face up to his new reality: prison. Monty's father picks him up in the morning to take him to prison, and as they drive he begins suggesting the possibility of "running" and starting a new life "out west." This begins a second highly stylized fantasy sequence that aesthetically recalls Monty's racist monologue and is clearly devised as another set piece, where again the narrative point of view shifts out of sync with Monty and he is subjectified. This is partly facilitated by a voiceover narration from Monty's father, played by the iconic Joseph Cox. The fantasy sequence revolves around ideas of regeneration and rebuilding one's life "out west" as the embodiment of the American dream or American "way." Monty's father's monologue explicitly evokes the origins of the nation: "So we drive west, keep driving till we find a nice little town. These towns out in the desert—you know why they got there? People wanted to get away from something else." The cinematography throughout this monologue sequence foregrounds the American flag, which flies from James' Jeep Grand Wagoneer, and images of "the West" and images of "going West," which further strengthen this clear allusion to the frontier myth and to America's national origins. Monty's father continues to monologue, and as he tells his son that he can "find God" and spirituality out west, the scars on Monty's face begin to heal in each frame.

The allegorical substance of this sequence is given further weight by the way Monty's father's monologue, in suggesting this return to historical narratives, again evokes characteristics of what Faludi has identified in *The Terror Dream: What 9/11 Revealed About America* (2008) as a mythical, archetypal American masculinity, which the Bush administration went to great lengths to promote in the immediate aftermath of 9/11 in the repeatedly foregrounded images and characterizations of "Lone Ranger leaders, Davy Crockett candidates, and John Wayne 'manly men'" (Faludi 2008: 199). This was a key aspect of the post–9/11 rhetoric of a return to core values, which, as Faludi demonstrates, relied on national myths. The movie *25th Hour* places particularly strong emphasis on this notion of starting anew with a traditional masculinity and patriarchal drive that is precisely in tune with the gendered rhetoric extolled by the U.S. mass media and government in the years following 9/11. One example of this came in the image of the president himself. Faludi states:

> In the post–9/11 effort to restore American's confidence in the country's impregnability, national politics would become increasingly deranged. The demonstrations, as often as not, were comically absurd, as witness the deskbound officeholders of the 2004 presidential campaign out in the woods, felling flora and blasting fauna to prove their virile bona fides. But the needs these staged exertions in the wild addressed ran deep in the American past, far deeper than the superhero fantasies we constructed around our leaders. The attack on home soil triggered a search for a guardian of the homestead, a manly man, to be sure, but one particularly suited to protecting and providing for the isolated American family in perilous situations. He was less Batman than Daniel Boone, a frontiersman whose proofs of eligibility were the hatchet and the gun—and a bloody willingness to use them [Faludi 2007: 148].

As Monty's father continues, the emphasis on a mythological masculinity increases: "You get yourself a new family and you raise them right, you hear me, give them a good life Monty, give them what they need. You have a son, maybe you name him James; it's a good strong name." Another feature of Monty's father's patriarchal rhetoric is that it seems designed to counter references to failed masculinity that appear throughout the film: his own admission to Monty in his bar to being a

Five. First World National Allegory and Otherness

"drunk father"; Monty's suspicion that Naturalle has betrayed him and his eventual tearful admission to Naturalle of "fucking everything up" as a provider and partner; Francis' admission of failing as a "best friend"; and Jacob's frequent references to what he perceives as his failure with women. Undoubtedly, *25th Hour* is deeply preoccupied with post–9/11 gender configurations throughout the film, particularly the representation of masculinity and heterosexual masculine fears. However, crucially, Lee's movie shows an awareness of the mythical element of these gender constructions in its finale, and the film as a whole highlights the absurdity of the characters' obsessions with macho masculinity. After Gilbey describes the movie's main concern as "the damage wreaked on New York's psyche," he goes on to state that it is "also about a heterosexual man living in fear of being sodomized. The biggest surprise is not that one movie should combine these wildly disparate subjects, but that it should contrive a point of convergence between them" (Gilbey 2003: 58). Gilbey is alluding to the frequent references to the likelihood of prison rape, and to the many misogynistic asides in the film. In the light of Faludi's research, though, the presence of these masculine fears converging with the trauma of 9/11 is not necessarily a surprise, and Monty's fears actually further strengthen his allegorical significance, representing a country that, in the face of crisis, is fixated on compensating for what Faludi describes as a "depleted masculinity" and also the fear of a failed traditional, heterosexual masculinity. Here *25th Hour*, provocatively, highlights both the absurdity of the aggressive, misogynistic and homophobic masculinity and the fantasy of this return to traditional archetypes. It is worth noting here, as well, that this fantasy is not entirely unrelated to the fantasy sequence in *The Reluctant Fundamentalist*: in allegorical terms, when Changez and Erica fantasize that Changez is actually her former lover Chris, they too are using a nostalgic fantasy to compensate for an unpalatable post–9/11 present.

As the fantasy sequence and Monty's father's regeneration monologue continues, the sequence becomes more and more unrealistic. Not only, it is suggested, could Monty find work and live, but maybe his partner could rejoin him and they could raise a large family in a large house and completely reinstate the "American Dream." At this point the images become much more surreal and symbolic. Monty and Naturalle stand with their large extended family, all dressed in immaculate white in front of a large, classically American, white house. A few frames later they sit together in the living room, again all dressed in white and surrounded by white. The clearly multiracial aspect of the family is aesthetically united or controlled by the images, a clear reference to the homogenizing nature of the politics of the post-9/11 Bush White House and American mass media. As if to play out the critical findings of *The Terror Dream*, the sequence becomes flagrant fantasy, and the dream breaks into reality when Monty and his father have passed the George Washington Bridge—where they would have to turn to go west—and they continue toward Otisville. The fantasy sequence, though, particularly the ultra-masculine portrayal of Monty's regenerative flight westward, is a concise foregrounding of Faludi's account of the "return to core values" rhetoric of the post-9/11 media and government, particularly as the film ends by showing the sequence to be fantasy. The foregrounding here of this aspect of Faludi's argument also embodies the film's engagement with the paradigm of "continuity" and "discontinuity," as this mythology carries the fundamental tension within Bush Doctrine's "changed world" rhetoric, which simultaneously evokes a new world order while also continually alluding to the 1950s and to centuries-old national myths. These same national myths that characterize masculinity in *The Terror Dream* are evident in the fantasy sequence in *25th Hour*.

Nevertheless, as in *The Reluctant Fundamentalist*, this problematic "continuity" and "discontinuity" paradigm is, to some extent, dialectically reconciled in the film's ending. The breakdown of the fantasy sequence acquiesces to the reality of prison at Otisville, which, again, had been emphasized as "the end of Monty." As we have seen, this absolute has been foregrounded by the movie's stark stylistic register throughout the film, which, through the course of the narrative, has been in dialogue with the divergent allegorical rhetoric of continuity. Simultaneously, just as the end sequence evokes the reality of America's nostalgic, nationalistic response to 9/11 as being a fantasy or contrivance, the vision of self-responsibility and genuine accountability that the allegorical narrative has built, which is clearly a continuity narrative, is consolidated. The reality of Monty (America) being irreparably damaged or "ended" in the film's conclusion is undeniable, though the historicizing allegory powerfully characterizes the epoch—Monty's "new" world as linked to a knowable past. The emphatic statement alone, though, that America must look to its own past is extraordinary (even if it is delivered in allegory), particularly for a film released as early as 2002.

Both of these first-world national allegories create dialectics between continuity narratives of 9/11 that very provocatively suggest that the U.S. needs to look internally at its own actions and assess its complex race relations issues for answers to the questions of how and why, and for context and understanding, while also upholding interpretations of 9/11 as an epochal or traumatic moment. The allegorical characters, in the case of Erica in the *Reluctant Fundamentalist*, who is narrated by "the other," and in the case of Monty in *25th Hour*, who is filtered through a narrative fixation on "otherness" and subjectified by an oscillating narrative point of view, allow these texts a unique plurality of perspective. When Changez states, in the novel's most quoted passage, that his "initial reaction" to the falling of the twin towers "was to be remarkably pleased," it does not necessarily provoke a response of disgust, as Changez has been firmly established as a "lover of America" and an adopted American. The complex identity of the narrator demands that the reader accept a complex and conflicted response to the attacks, and consider the implications of his feeling of being "caught up in the symbolism of it all, the fact that someone had so visibly brought America to her knees" (Hamid 2007: 73). Ultimately, through the combination of dual perspective and first-world national allegory, *The Reluctant Fundamentalist* approaches points of reconciliation in the paradigm of continuity and discontinuity. A particularly provocative statement by Changez highlights this:

> The destruction of the World Trade Center had, as she had said, churned up old thoughts that had settled in the manner of sediment to the bottom of a pond; now the waters of her mind were murky with what previously had been ignored. I did not know if the same was true of me [*Reluctant Fundamentalist*, p. 83].

Changez highlights two things here: the possibility of preexisting factors determining the impact of 9/11 in these "old thoughts that had settled in the manner of sediment," and the possibility of a plural response ("I did not know if the same was true of me"). *The Reluctant Fundamentalist*, and to some extent *25th Hour*, problematize the polarized paradigm of discontinuity and continuity, and locate points of reconciliation. Nevertheless, while Hamid's narrator certainly problematizes existing formulations of "otherness" in 9/11 fiction, the novel does not attempt to represent the wider or marginalized citizens of America after 9/11. It remains, for the most part, rooted in the elite spheres of New York, and the racial antipathy faced by an immigrant student at Princeton or high-earning consultant would likely be less severe than what was/is faced by immigrants working in the service industries. This is not to suggest that the novel should be obliged to offer some kind of panorama of post–9/11 otherness, and again it marks a sharp turning point in the 9/11 novel in its politics and challenge to the continuity and discontinuity paradigms. In the penultimate chapter we will examine Joseph O'Neil's *Netherland*, a novel which takes the next logical step as it opens up narrative space to examine 9/11 and its aftermath with a field of characters that represent new stratospheres of society for the 9/11 novel. Finally, we will turn to Amy Waldman's *The Submission*, which directly confronts the post–9/11 racism that many American Muslims and Asian-Americans were subjected to.

Six
Netherland and 9/11 Fiction

Like *The Reluctant Fundamentalist*, Joseph O'Neil's *Netherland* (2008) seeks points of reconciliation within the paradigm of continuity and discontinuity, and works toward a kind of dialectical balance in this framework. What makes *Netherland* unique in the 9/11 canon, though, is its clear awareness of tropes and trends that have been identified and criticized as problem areas in the growing body of 9/11 fiction—in particular, the way that, as Richard Gray states, "The crisis is in every sense of the word, domesticated" (Gray 2009: 134). In this aspect, *Netherland* is the first genuinely self-conscious 9/11 narrative, as it demonstrates an awareness, in several ways, of some of the perceived limitations of 9/11 fiction. Where novels such as *Windows on the World* and *Extremely Loud and Incredibly Close* have utilized the formal conventions of literary meta-fiction (what one review called the latter's "avant-garde tool kit"), *Netherland* operates as a straightforwardly realist novel that draws attention specifically to this emerging body of 9/11 fiction by subverting its dominant tropes and conceits (Kirn 2005: n.p.). O'Neil's novel does this in four ways. Firstly, like many of the first wave of novels that take 9/11 as their subject, it utilizes a marriage or relationship narrative, placing 9/11 and post–9/11 as the historical backdrop for a domestic drama. However, unlike the relationship narratives of *The Good Life*, *Falling Man* or *The Emperor's Children*, for example, which ostensibly use their decidedly micro, domestic settings to measure the impact of 9/11 on the everyday or banal, ultimately avoiding any direct political discussion, *Netherland* uses its relationship narrative to directly articulate two sides of a political polemic, making direct reference to this domestication of 9/11. Secondly, and extending from this, *Netherland* is clearly, keenly aware of the lack of representation, or minimal, cursory representation, of "otherness" in

9/11 fiction (excepting, again, *The Reluctant Fundamentalist*). The action of *Netherland* begins in a setting common to most of the 9/11 novels—the privileged world of the Manhattan or Wall Street elite. However, when protagonist Hans finds his marriage disintegrated in the aftermath of 9/11, he begins exploring a more marginalized or subterranean New York, and indeed his own status as a Dutch émigré, primarily through his emerging friendship and association with the Trinidadian Chuck Ramkissoon and the immigrant cricketers that he begins spending his time with. The novel scrupulously maps out what Michael Rothberg identifies as a "deterritorialized America," an alternative New York that is both new to Hans and new to 9/11 fiction. Thirdly, *Netherland* is very aware of the difficulty, in cultural representation of 9/11, in rendering trauma, particularly in making the distinction between private or personal and collective trauma, and the characters engage directly in making this distinction. Lastly, the characters in *Netherland* explicitly ask and explore questions that are implicit in all cultural representations of 9/11 but are infrequently engaged with directly—what is the lasting impact of the attacks? Are we meant to think of 9/11 as an epochal moment or an event with a past, present and future?

As stated, in addressing these concerns, O'Neil's novel sustains a dialectical aspect, working towards points of intersection in seemingly oppositional narrative drives. The principle thematic concern of the novel is uncertainty or anxiety, what Versluys describes as "the mental crisis" and "moral confusion" that was caused by 9/11 (Versluys 2009: 148). In *Netherland*, this anxiety evidently rests on the need to distinguish the experience of 9/11 in the frameworks of the continuity or discontinuity narrative, and there is a working dialogue between the anxieties characters feel because of either longstanding political, social or personal issues, and because of the immediate threats and fears brought on by the attacks. Certain episodes in the novel emphasize different sides of this paradigm, though rather than first world national allegory, as in *The Reluctant Fundamentalist* (where the actions of individuals are politically evocative in their correspondent national suggestion), or the "seismographic" allusion of *The Good Life*, *Falling Man* and *The Emperor's Children* (where political context is buried subliminally in the substratum of the texts), the realism of *Netherland* features the protagonists acknowledging the difficulty in distinguishing their anxieties and attempting to work them out themselves in the action of the narrative. As in many of the "domestic" fictions of 9/11, the story individualizes an experience that has repeatedly been described in terms of "collective trauma," a somewhat nebulous term for which Kai Erikson's "Notes on Trauma and Community" provides an adequate starting point. The characters in *Netherland*, however, particularly Hans, repeatedly attempt to locate their individual selves within a community, and overtly attempt to probe the points of intersection between personal and public issues. This entanglement of personal and public runs parallel to the novel's overt attempt to gauge the impact of 9/11 or to place it historically.

Netherland's pursuit of balance is explicit to the point that it is one of the novel's clearest manifestations of this self-consciousness. For example, protagonist Hans' generally apolitical disposition is juxtaposed with his fiercely politicized wife. Additionally, the passivity, disorientation and inwardness that characterizes his post–9/11 condition is tempered by his friend and counterpart, the extroverted Chuck Ramkissoon, whose defining characteristic is action. Furthermore, while Hans' professional circle is that of the wealthy, Wall Street elite, and his personal life (up until the main narrative action begins) has been that of the liberal bourgeois of London and New York, the novel spends most of the narrative exploring his relationship with the more marginalized characters and areas of the city: the Caribbean and West Indian immigrants that comprise his cricket club, and the strange and ultimately seedy underworld he enters into via Chuck. Ultimately these aspects of the narrative give the novel an alternative perspective that distinguishes it from the dominant narrative points of view in 9/11 fiction. This perspective is a key aspect of Hans' post–9/11 condition, well described by Alan Hollinghurst: rather than seeing Hans' condition as strictly trauma, depression or melancholia (which it seems to oscillate between), it embodies "the book's larger picture of our ability to drift sideways in the face of our great crises," again evoking the individual in context of public "crisis" (Hollinghurst 2008: 54). This chapter will argue that this drift sideways opens up a self-reflexive, balanced, dialectical exploration of post–9/11 uncertainty and anxiety, achieving the most convincing narrative reconciliation of 9/11 in the emerging corpus of 9/11 novels. It will move beyond Michael Rothberg's advocating of its "deterritorialized America" and argue that it is able to achieve this balance and dialectical aspect through a four-pronged, self-conscious exploration and interrogation of key aspects of this emergent canon, all within an essentially realist aesthetic.

The Domestic Narrative Refigured

Like so many of the 9/11 literary texts, *Netherland* is a relationship narrative, though unlike any of these narratives, the marital crisis in *Netherland* begins with an application of the "narrative" of the central couple's marriage to the larger encapsulating "continuity" and "discontinuity" paradigm, and thus to ideas of history, politics and context. Additionally, the marriage ultimately becomes an overtly politicized aspect of the text. At the very beginning of the novel, just after 9/11, Hans' wife decides to leave New York with their son Jake and move back to her native London. Ostensibly her reasons are 9/11 and the anxiety she feels after the attacks. Indeed, the uncertainty that Hans and Rachel both feel as to the larger significance of the attacks is something they consciously try to comprehend. Hans recalls this period retrospectively: "Very little about anything seemed intelligible or certain" (O'Neil 2008: 21). They engage in dialogue about the impact of 9/11 and attempt to locate the historical significance of the attacks comparatively:

> We were trying to avoid what might be termed a historic mistake. We were trying to understand, that is, whether we were in a pre-apocalyptic situation, like the European Jews in the thirties or the last citizens of Pompeii, or whether our situation was merely near-apocalyptic, like that of the Cold War inhabitants of New York, London, Washington and, for that matter, Moscow [O'Neil 2008: 21].

Hans and Rachel's sense of uncertainty, then, from the very beginning is rooted in historical thinking, though they ponder the possibility of being in an epochal or "pre-apocalyptic situation." (Hans's addendum in this sentence, "and, for that matter, Moscow," is also another example of the text's pervading emphasis on balance.) Hans even phones Rachel's father for information on how his generation had dealt with the Cold War nuclear threat. Hans "wanted to believe that this episode of history, like those old cataclysms that deposit a geologically telling layer of dust on the floors of seas, had sooted its survivors with special information"

(O'Neil 2008: 22). Soon after 9/11, though, Rachel's decision to move back to her native London, and the uncertainty they have both felt regarding the nature of the threat of the post–9/11 world, is extended to uncertainty about whether or not 9/11 or post–9/11 anxiety is the real issue at all. Despite the fact that she has palpable fears of terror and experiences trauma or PTSD clearly related to the 9/11 attacks ("a goods truck smashing into a pothole sounded like an explosion, and the fantastic howl of a passing motorbike once caused Rachel to vomit with terror"), Rachel's anxiety quickly extends to their relationship (O'Neil 2008: 16). Again, the re-evaluation of relationships or marriages in the wake of 9/11 is a common conceit in 9/11 fiction and occurs in *The Good Life*, *The Emperor's Children*, *Falling Man*, *Windows on the World* and many other texts. As we have seen, Jay McInerney, describing his ambition in *The Good Life*, illuminates the appeal of this phenomenon: "It's about the way in which the collective trauma of 9/11 prompted many of us, especially those of us here in New York, to re-evaluate our lives, to re-examine our values, our careers, our marriages" (McInerney 2006: n.p.). These novels generally focus on re-evaluation based on new circumstance and follow the logic of a memorable line from *Falling Man*: "Everything now is measured by after" (DeLillo 2007: 138). Intriguingly, though, Rachel views their domestic crisis not as the advent of a new condition or product of a post–9/11 re-evaluation, but instead questions the whole "narrative" of their marriage:

> She stated that she now questioned everything, including, as she put it, the narrative of our marriage.... "The whole story" she said. The story of her and me, for better and for worse, till death did us part, the story of our union to the exclusion of all others—the story. It had somehow been falsified [O'Neil 2008: 26].

This is a highly suggestive passage. Firstly, the conspicuous terms "narrative" and "story" are clearly setting up the marriage story as in dialogue with the larger story of the attacks, presenting a parallel need to think not just in terms of the absolute but also historically or about "narrative." Where many of the 9/11 novels in their narratives of post–9/11 domestic rupture and re-evaluation have only "seismographically" addressed the overall impact of 9/11, the story of Hans and Rachel is directly mirroring the political discussion here about the "narrative" of 9/11; is it "apocalyptic" or "near apocalyptic?" This evocation of the "narrative" of their marriage and its position in relation to the historical and political discussion of the attacks can be read as addressing or at least acknowledging an awareness of the dominance of marriage or relationship narratives in the 9/11 canon, and seems to address the pointed question Pankaj Mishra asks in his 2007 critique of 9/11 fiction, "The End of Innocence": "Are we meant to think of domestic discord, also deployed by DeLillo and McInerney, as a metaphor for post–9/11 America?" (Mishra 2007: 5).

Indeed, the relationship is deployed in a way that self-reflexively responds to narrative trends in 9/11 fiction. For example, as Rachel moves away to London in the opening stages of the novel, the majority of the narrative plays out in New York, and while some important episodes return to London and the relationship story, it is the marital crisis that opens up space for the world of Chuck and these marginalized areas that 9/11 fiction has avoided or excluded in its predominant privileging of the domestic sphere. Additionally, unlike the texts by DeLillo, McInerney, Messud, or Kalfus, the novel is told in retrospect, and from the beginning the reader knows that the relationship which disintegrates in the opening chapters is actually reconciled by the end. *Falling Man* and *The Good Life*, for example, both employ a three-act structure where the relationship stories are allowed to be disrupted, to undergo change, and, surprisingly (considering the emphasis on trauma, crisis and change), to restore a kind of equilibrium. As we have seen, Lianne in *Falling Man* announcing her readiness to leave her husband, who she had welcomed back in the traumatic aftermath of the attacks, "is ready to be alone, in reliable calm, she and the kid, the way they were before the planes appeared that day, silver crossing blue" (DeLillo 2007: 236). In *Netherland*, in terms of the relationship, the periods of rupture, crisis and change have a predetermined ending, which recalibrates the focus of the story. This narrative is therefore not only drawing attention to a dominant conceit but redirecting emphasis to how Hans responds to the break-up and the characters he meets in the intervening time.

As stated, despite their predetermined status, and the transatlantic separation placing emphasis on Hans' post–9/11 New York period, Hans and Rachel's relationship does remain an important strand of the novel, and to some degree we are invited to read this as a defense of the relevance or importance of exploring the pressure placed on the domestic and banal in the wake of 9/11. In fact, the way Hans experiences existential crisis, and Rachel becomes more and more politicized, contributes to the dialectical aspect of the novel in providing significant space for both a politicized and traumatized narrative perspective. This cuts through what Rothberg has identified as a danger of depoliticization in overemphasizing trauma: "the possibility that a focus solely on trauma as a structure of reception might ... actually end up unwittingly reinforcing the repressive liberal-conservative consensus in the United States, that attempting to explain the events amounts to ... excusing them" (Rothberg 2004: 150). Indeed, the relationship becomes a politicized aspect of the novel in more than one way. As well as the parallel discussion of the political reality of 9/11 in the opening scenes, which attempts to locate the attacks historically, in the heated discussions between Rachel and Hans that ensue, *Netherland* is also addressing the absence of overt political engagement in 9/11 fiction; the discussions that Hans and Rachel have just don't appear in other 9/11 novels. After Rachel and Hans split up, he has difficulty understanding his wife's increasingly politicized perspective. Rachel's continued rhetoric comprises of a scathing condemnation of U.S. foreign policy after 9/11 and the G.W. Bush administration in general, which firmly and in explicit detail places her perspective within the context of the continuity narrative of 9/11. During one of their many transatlantic phone calls, Rachel rants at Hans:

> The fact that Saddam is horrible and should be shot dead today is not the issue. The bad character of the enemy does not make the war good. Think politically, for once. Stalin was a monster. He killed millions of people. Millions. Does that mean we should have supported Hitler in his invasion of Russia? [O'Neil 2008: 94].

Rachel is thinking historically, interpreting 9/11 in contextual terms and thinking about the aftermath. Hans, on the other hand, feels disaffected by Rachel's position and can't bring himself to think politically:

> In this ever shifting, all enveloping discussion, my orientation was poor. I could not tell where I stood. If pressed to state my position, I would confess the truth: that I had not succeeded in arriving at a position. I lacked necessary powers of perception and certainty and, above all, foresight [O'Neil 2008: 96].

Hans' position here, his lack of orientation, his lack of "perception and certainty," are perhaps related to his clearly identified symptoms of depression and even trauma; he was, as he states, "lost in invertebrate time" (O'Neil 2008: 28). Furthermore, this description of Hans' inability to orient himself politically after 9/11 again emphasizes the novel's self-conscious aspect in its similarity to descriptions by critics, such as Richard Gray, of the lack of political engagement in the fiction of 9/11, "the sense of those events as a kind of historical and experiential abyss, a yawning and possibly unbridgeable gap between before and after" (Gray 2009: 130). But Hans' inability to think politically is also a reference to the inability of 9/11 fiction to engage politically and the criticism it has received because of this. It is important to reiterate, though, that as Hans is a sympathetic character. This isn't manifest necessarily as criticism—especially as this period of Hans' life is characterized from the beginning of the novel as temporary, an era of his life from which he has now moved on. It is, rather, dialectical—Hans' pronounced inwardness and depression is contrapuntal to politicization.

As the reader knows from the beginning of the novel that this polarization has, to some degree, been reconciled, as Hans and Rachel have settled their differences and reestablished their marriage, attention is drawn to the fact that while Hans is disillusioned by political discourse, he is drawn to the alternative world of Chuck, clearly framed as oppositional to Rachel.

> The sushi, the mistress, the marriage, the real estate dealings and almost inconceivably, Bald Eagle Field: it was all happening in front of my eyes. While the country floundered in Iraq, Chuck was running. That was political enough for me, a man having trouble putting one foot in front of the other [O'Neil 2008: 158].

While the antagonism between Hans and Rachel provides a dialectic aspect that negotiates political commitment and trauma, Chuck and Rachel provide a sense of balance within the politics of 9/11, which is important, given that the novel is oriented largely by Hans' perspective. Additionally, while there is a predetermined reconciliation of Hans and Rachel, which ostensibly could marginalize Chuck's lasting impact, the importance and regard Hans retains for Chuck as an integral part of the working through of his post–9/11 condition is clear in the way he speaks of him to Rachel. He repeats to her in one of the retrospective scenes: "He was a good friend. We had a lot in common. I took him very seriously" (O'Neil 2008: 161). In any case, the positioning of Rachel and

Chuck isn't the simplistic formulation of liberal and conservative—though if Chuck is to counter Rachel's liberalism, his Cadillac covered in American flag stickers is a start—but in more the sense of Rachel being preoccupied with post-9/11 public and political concerns, and the war in Iraq, and Chuck being an embodiment of individuality and quintessentially American enterprising spirit. Indeed, for much of the narrative Chuck seems to embody an appealing, if slightly caricatured, Americanness that to Hans has a certain authenticity. Furthermore, it is oppositional to what he perceives as almost anti–American sentiment from Rachel in comments such as "You want Jake to grow up with an American perspective? Is that it?" (O'Neil 2008: 93). The dialectical opposition of trauma and politics in Hans and Rachel's arguments, and the binary perceptions of America and Americans presented in Hans' understanding of Chuck and Rachel's angry perceptions of American consciousness, become enmeshed in the book's larger dialectic between continuity and discontinuity. This is prominent during one of Hans and Rachel's phone conversations when she seems to mistake his inability to engage politically with being "conservative": "You're constantly flailing around and changing the subject and making emotive statements. It's the classic conservative tactic" (O'Neil 2008: 93). When Hans denies this accusation of conservatism, she states, "You are a conservative.... What's so sad is you don't even know it" (O'Neil 2008: 93). This probing of the connections and lines of distinction between the sense of loss and uncertainty embodied by Hans, and the kind of unilateralism evoked by Rachel, is an important part of the dialectic, as it illustrates the difficulty in distinguishing them. It is also subtly didactic in the underlying suggestion that while national collective trauma may have compromised America's ability to think multi-laterally, the European Left may have not fully understood the national trauma of 9/11 during its aggressive criticism of American foreign policy. While certain aspects of *Netherland*, which will be discussed in the coming pages, depict the "deterritorialized" America that Michael Rothberg calls for in post–9/11 fiction, this sense of balance and dialectical opposition also creates another aspect of what Gray demands in his manifesto for a more politically engaging post–9/11 novel: "...the space between conflicting interests and practices" to "dramatize the contradictions that conflict engenders" (Gray 2009: 147).

Cricket, Otherness and American Identity

There is another aspect of Hans' domestic world which the novel pays much attention to and which also seems to conspicuously address a trend in 9/11 fiction: the divide in wealth and class that lies between Hans' social and professional spheres and the new world he enters through the Staten Island Cricket Club and Chuck. Like the central protagonists in *Falling Man* (a Manhattan lawyer and a freelance editor), *The Good Life* (literary editor, writer, stockbroker, society socialite), *A Disorder Peculiar to the Country* (two Manhattan lawyers), *The Emperor's Children* (a large cast of privileged New York literati), *Windows on the World* (wealthy realtor and famous author), and, indeed, most of the 9/11 novels, Hans' Wall Street position makes him part of the extreme elite or bourgeois and limits the scope for universality in his perspective. However, the entrance of Chuck and the Staten Island Cricketers, who represent the marginalized of New York, allows Hans an avenue into a previously unavailable culture or underground. The novels of the 9/11 canon are packed with elite Wall Street characters, but *Netherland* is the first to include the voices of cab drivers and doormen, let alone a whole group of immigrant cricketers. This is imperative to the larger dialectic of the novel and to Hans as a character, who admittedly lacks perspective. Reflecting on his pre–9/11 New York years, years of abundance, Hans states:

> We had plenty to feel smug about, if so inclined. Smugness, however, requires a certain reflectiveness, which requires perspective, which requires distance; and we, or certainly I, didn't look upon our circumstances from the observatory offered by a disposition to the more spatial emotions— those feelings of regret or gratitude or relief, say, that make reference to situations removed from one's own [O'Neil 2008: 89].

This could be a line describing characters in most of the 9/11 novels and gives the novel another self-conscious dimension. Hans, however, literally finds this position of remove in Chuck's weathered old Cadillac, shifting candy wrappers, coffee cups and other miscellaneous junk out of the way to take his seat as they navigate previously uncharted or unnoticed areas of the city.

Indeed, their first meeting outside the cricket club comes when Hans takes an "unfamiliar" route home, passing Chuck's office in the old "Tin

Pan Alley Quarter" (O'Neil 2008: 66). The sights he describes seem unfamiliar: "Arabs, West Africans, African Americans hung out on the sidewalks amongst goods trucks, dollies, pushcarts, food carts heaped with trash, boxes and boxes of merchandise. I might have been in a cold Senegal" (O'Neil 2008: 66). Almost immediately, though, Hans begins to familiarize himself with this hitherto "invisible" part of New York:

> I became familiar with the topical sights: the chiming, ceaselessly peregrinating ice-cream truck, driven by a Turk, the Muslim funeral home on Albemarle Road out of which watchful African American men spilled in sunglasses and black suits; the Hispanic gardeners working on the malls; the firehouse on Cortelyou that slowly gorged on reversing fire trucks; the devout Jewish boulevardiers on Ocean Parkway ... [O'Neil 2008: 147].

This is clearly different scenery from the Wall Street milieu that Hans is accustomed to, and, crucially, while he repeatedly refers to the "wretchedness" that he felt throughout the period of separation from his wife (during which he navigated this defamiliarized New York, and associated with Chuck and the cricketers), he chooses these associations over other more characteristically bourgeois company or pastimes (O'Neil 2008: 29). When Hans looks for ways to occupy his time after Rachel leaves, his Wall Street colleague, Rivera, "decided" that he "should play golf" (O'Neil 2008: 39). Hans, though, is drawn to the sight of a cricket bat in a West Indian cab driver's car and, after minimal enquiry and introduction, is invited for a game.

Another crucial balance that Chuck provides to the narrative is that of a voice from the underground, which not only counters Rachel's liberal perspective and Hans' elite Wall Street perspective but also provides a point of view from a new and previously marginalized position. Chuck's perspective is given weight by Hans' endorsement of it, which gathers strength from meditation on his own immigrant status. Chuck's early monologue at the end of a cricket match interrupted by a near violent encounter is worth quoting at length for the insight it gives Hans and the resonance it has throughout the novel—not only for what it states but because of who states it and because of its audience. It occurs in the opening pages of the novel when Chuck, after umpiring the cricket match, addresses both teams in the locker room:

> "But cricket, more than any other sport is, I want to say"—Chuck paused for effect—"a lesson in civility. We all know this; I do not need to say

more about it." A few heads were nodding. "Something else. We are playing this game in the United States. This is a difficult environment for us. We play where we can, wherever they let us.... In this country we're nowhere. We're a joke. Cricket? ... Every summer the parks of this city are taken over by hundreds of cricketers but somehow nobody notices. It's like we're invisible. Now that's nothing new, for those of us who are black or brown. As for those who are not"—Chuck acknowledged my presence with a smile—"you'll forgive me, I hope, if I say that I sometimes tell people, You want a taste of how it feels to be a black man in this country? Put on the white clothes of the cricketer. Put on white to feel black" [O'Neil 2008: 13].

This is a very significant extract for several reasons. Firstly, this is precisely what Hans does—he puts on "the white clothes of the cricketer" for the first time since he moved to New York, and indeed he is the only white man on this team full of immigrant cricketers. Hans' approval of and awe at the mysterious Chuck, and the subsequent friendship they embark on, cruising around New York in Chuck's Cadillac, is the key point of entry into the perspective of this marginalized group who are "invisible" to the city, which is just as significant as his alignment to the perspective of his wife and position among the Wall Street elite. This is the first gesture of a wider cultural inclusion by any of the 9/11 texts, and it clearly informs the balance of the novel in exploring this notion of post-9/11 anxieties. Also, though, the clear suggestion that cricket can serve as a metaphor for civility, and that these ethnically diverse New York cricketers can be held up as an example for the possibilities of civil conduct and harmony between different cultural groups, informs the exploration of the public and private split. The fundamental idea of individuals of different race, class or religious background united in the collective appreciation of the game and observance of its principles is loaded with suggestion, and this forms the novel's defining metaphor of multiculturalism. Unity among diversity is referred to frequently. Early on, Hans states that "my own teammates variously originated from Trinidad, Guyana, Jamaica, India, Pakistan and Sri Lanka" (O'Neil 2008: 8). On the next page he delineates their religious difference: "We huddled with arms round one another's shoulders—nominally, three Hindus, three Christians, a Sikh and four Muslims" (O'Neil 2008: 9). Both of these lists of difference are used in describing his cricket team—a group or collective. Hans' role as the only white man on the team is symbolically important and resonates with his own feeling of marginalization, and catalyzes his own readiness to try and see a different New York.

Netherland's use of cricket is a metaphor for civil conduct, plurality and unity, and, ultimately, an evocation of a classical vision of melting-pot American-ness, also reveals a more general literary reflexivity. Indeed, the quotes above seem to be directly referencing C.L.R. James' *Beyond a Boundary* (1963). James described one of his early teams as follows: "We were a motley crew. The children of some white officials and white business men, middle class blacks and mulattos, Chinese boys, some of whose parents spoke broken English, Indian boys" (James 2000: 25). O'Neil had written an article in *The Atlantic* magazine in 2007 in praise of *Beyond a Boundary* which articulates the importance of cricket as a reflection of society and politics in colonial Trinidad, and, indeed, globally, and it becomes an important point of reference in *Netherland*. In his article, O'Neil repeatedly advocates the way James' book "regard[s] games and politics as equal vessels of ethical and social values" (O'Neil 2007: n.p.). *Beyond a Boundary* underpins *Netherland* most succinctly, though, in the way it depicts politics surreptitiously invading the author's conscious. James writes, "Cricket had plunged me into politics before I was aware of it," and what happens to Hans is not unlike this; at a crucial point his renewed involvement in cricket gives him a perspective that he has been missing (James 2000: 65). In the way this occurs, though, O'Neil seems to be referencing another, seminal sociological study of cricket, Mike Marqusee's *Anyone but England* (1994). Marqusee's book is also autobiographical and describes his American "outsider" perspective of "English Cricket." To an important extent, *Netherland* inverts this basic premise by using cricket as an unusual and fresh way of evoking a vision of Americanness. Ultimately, the novel synthesizes fundamental ideas from both texts into its unique premise, which is able to interrogate and explore Hans' fraught identity issues that center on a tension between frequent allusions to a more traditionally European perspective and an emergent part of his identity as a "naturalised American." Through cricket and his experience with the Staten Island cricketers it is able to create a perspective that is both American and other.

The novel articulates this in two ways. Firstly, O'Neil very conspicuously characterizes Hans' purist perspective on cricket in a way that is exactly aligned with the traditional "colonist" perspective he cites in

"Bowling Alone," as he details the reason cricket is only played by a certain type of immigrant:

> Englishmen and Australians and South Africans don't bother to unpack their bats and whites, on account (I'm guessing) of the small, scruffy, thickly grassed and weedy fields that we play on, most of which are situated in public parks in downscale neighborhoods and come as a shock to a newcomer used to better things. He sees a playing track made not of turf but of coconut matting stretched over clay, and he sees a rough, overgrown outfield that undermines his notion of what batting is all about: hitting the ball along the ground, over beautifully mowed grass [O'Neil 2007: n.p.].

At first Hans takes exactly this perspective, and while he is happy to play, he is unable to adjust his batting game to the style of cricket his teammates play:

> It was, I felt, different for them. They had grown up playing the game in floodlit Lahore car parks or in rough clearings in some West Indian countryside. They could, and did, modify their batting without spiritual upheaval. I could not ... self transformation has its limits; and my limit was reached in the peculiar matter of batting. I would stubbornly continue to bat as I always had even if it meant the end of making runs [O'Neil 2008: 46].

Here, Hans delineates his traditionalist perspective, differentiating himself from his teammates and crucially relating this to his integration into America. Despite eagerly taking to "new customs and mannerisms at the expense of old ones," and generally not missing the "ancient clotted continent," he cannot, in the early stages of the novel, adapt to his new country in the way that his fellow émigrés have (O'Neil 2008: 46). As James Wood states, "Hans is not a 'colonial' like his fellow cricketers but a colonist, part of the history of Dutch imperialism that has marked places as different as Java and America" (Wood 2008: n.p.). However, Hans finds a way to bridge this gap between colonist and colonial. In a powerful scene late in the cricket season of 2003, Hans is batting while Chuck watches from the boundary. Hans is faced with the familiar dilemma of his batting style: "once again confronted by the seemingly irresolvable conflict between, on the one hand, my sense of an innings as a chanceless progression of orthodox shots—impossible under local conditions—and, on the other hand, the indigenous notion of batting as a gamble of hitting out" (O'Neil 2008: 169). In a passage that once again evokes James' ideas regarding cricket's relationship with the world, Hans continues: "There was the issue of self measurement. For what was an innings if not a singular opportunity to face down, by dint of effort and skill and self-mastery, the variable world?" (O'Neil 2008: 169). With Chuck and all that he represents urging him on from the boundary, Hans decides to acquiesce, to discard his traditionalist pretenses and bat in the American style:

> When the third ball came looping down towards my legs, something unprecedented happened. Following the spin, I executed an unsightly, crooked heave: the ball flew high into the trees, for six. A huge cheer went up. The next ball, I repeated the stroke with a still freer swing. The ball flew even higher.... I'd hit the ball in the air like an American cricketer; and I'd done so without injury to my sense of myself. On the contrary, I felt great. And Chuck had seen it happen and as much as he could have, had prompted it [O'Neil 2008: 170].

Not only does this increase Hans' affinity to Chuck and his immigrant teammates, but it makes him feel more American. He describes the incident as evoking a dream where Chuck's radical plan to build a cricket stadium in New York, Bald Eagle Field, is realized. The milieu of his dream is the packed stadium where he and Chuck enjoy the cricket as a truly American game. "There is a roar as the cricket stars trot down the pavilion steps onto this impossible grass field in America, and everything is suddenly clear, and I am at last naturalized" (O'Neil 2008: 170).

The importance of the device of cricket in *Netherland* is clear. Not only does it provide a model of pluralism and community in the larger immigrant community in New York, but it is able to formulate this marginalized group as American, and moreover as an embodiment of the "melting pot" origins of the United States. Ironically, it is able to articulate Hans' position as an outsider but also a genuine "naturalized American." Hans' immersion in this group is therefore significant in the way it illustrates a transformation, pitting his new perspective against his traditional European views and certainly against his wife's. Furthermore, this episode is emblematic of a genuine acceptance among this immigrant community; it is the culmination of a long section describing the growing importance of his relationship to the group. Hans describes helping a teammate, Shiv, whose wife of ten years had left him, and accepting the revelation that it was this group, and this group only, that he could rely on in his own time of need: "They happened to be the ones, should anything happen to me, whom I could prevail on to look after me as Shiv had been looked after" (O'Neil 2008: 168). Of course, Chuck is the most prominent figure within this community, and it is his dream of Bald Eagle Field that provides a symbolic site for the novel's evocation of this alternative American community. The name in itself is, of course, significant in emphasizing Americanness, but it is Chuck's blue sky entrepreneurialism that characterizes him as quintessentially American. His complex identity is brought out in a powerful scene during Hans' first visit to Bald Eagle Field. As Hans and Chuck sit and admire the perfect, newly cut grass on a hot summer night, Chuck tells Hans the story of his childhood in Trinidad over cold Cokes, describing his childhood in detail, including the experience of listening to the success of the same West Indies team, captained by Frank Worrell, that C.L.R James champions in *Beyond a Boundary*. At once he is at his most American, showing off his incredible business project, his entrepreneurial spirit and complete immersion in the American dream, and yet also, for Hans, he is at his most Trinidadian, talking for the first time about his childhood and homeland. The suggestion that emerges is that immigrant realities underpin classic American ideals; and in some ways, to be American is to be other.

Chuck's monologue on civility and tolerance at the cricket match is echoed in his account of his experience of 9/11, with its emphasis on community and difference. Chuck's story of 9/11 is also conspicuous in its emphasis on describing an alternative experience of the attacks:

> "After the attacks," Chuck said, "this was where the Humane Society of New York started up an emergency triage, practically from day one." We quickened away. "My God, what a scene. Cats, dogs, guinea pigs, rabbits, pigs, lizards, you name it, they were all here. Cockatoos. Monkeys. I saw a lemur with a corneal inflammation." Chuck volunteered his services and was put to work "rehoming" the pets. "It was a wonderful experience," Chuck said. "I made friends with people from Idaho, Wisconsin, New Jersey, New Hampshire, North Carolina, Ireland, Portugal, South Africa. People from out of state came for a couple days and ended up staying weeks." ... Chuck said simply, "I think for many of us it was one of the happiest times of our life."
>
> I believed him. The catastrophe had instilled in many—though not in

me—a state of elation. From the beginning, for example, I'd suspected that, beneath all the tears and the misery Rachel's leaving had basically been a function of euphoria [O'Neil 2008: 74].

This passage is clearly designed to provide as unusual or atypical an experience of 9/11 as possible in its description of the Humane Society's activities over the crisis days following the attacks. The notion of it being a very happy time is striking, though other 9/11 novels also depict positive or euphoric reactions. *A Disorder Peculiar to the Country*, for example, describes the mutually antagonistic central couple's joy as they both presume the other has perished in the attacks. Another example of this is, of course, Changez in *The Reluctant Fundamentalist*. Watching 9/11 unfold, he is surprised by his own sense of happiness: "I *smiled*. Yes, despicable as it may sound, my initial reaction was to be remarkably pleased" (Hamid 2007: 72). Changez's reasons are very different, but these two passages have the commonality of ostensibly providing alternative or unusual accounts of 9/11. While the responses dramatized in *The Reluctant Fundamentalist* and *A Disorder Peculiar to the Country* are potentially more provocative, the scene Chuck describes in *Netherland* is a more palpable vision of a shared response characterized by good will and, again, community and pluralism. This particular notion of positivity is perhaps more germane to the way many commentators have described a country united in collective grief and mourning in the early aftermath of the attacks. Similarly, many commentators have, like Chuck, lamented the quick passing of a time characterized by hope and promise. In the unpaginated introduction to *In the Shadow of No Towers*, Art Spiegelman describes how at first "Ground Zero marked a year zero as well," and "idealistic peace signs and flower shrines briefly flourished at Union square" (Spiegelman 2007: n.p.). Orly Lubin describes the way "people began to reminisce nostalgically about both the shock and the sense of togetherness; the terrible sense of vulnerability and the birth of new friendships; the feeling of isolation and the ability to rely on others for company and help" (Lubin 2003: 125). This is another way that *Netherland* reveals a clear self-reflexivity: it is aware of these precedents. In Hans' recollection of Chuck's story about the attacks, the sense of hope and community that is described is clearly present, though the untold aspect of the Humane Society retains the important notion of Chuck as an embodiment of an alternative New York.

Private and Public Traumas

It is important to note that this alternative experience of 9/11 is again marked by Hans' referring back to the intersections of personal and public, recalling his feelings about Rachel's leaving, his idea of her reaction being a "function of euphoria," and attempting to fit that in to a larger speculation about public reaction (something that related to "many—though not me"). Another one of the novel's more reflexive functions is precisely its ongoing discussion of individual and collective experience and consciousness, and, indeed, trauma. Hans' post-9/11 condition is in constant dialogue with the wider public response, and this invites questions: Is this individual psychic trauma? Is Hans participating in a larger collective mourning? Moreover, what emerges in this exploration of the intersection of personal and public is closely related to the larger question of what the post-9/11 condition is and, again, whether it must be understood on a continuum or as an epochal moment. Hans' "bachelor years" in New York are described in various terms; as Hollinghurst states, it is a condition "he never describes as depression, but rather 'a descent into disorder,' a fatalistic submission to a shrunken life, a state of unbroachable loneliness" (Hollinghurst 2008: 54). Perhaps more precisely and simply, Hans sees himself as lost:

> My life had shrunk to very small proportions—too small, certainly, for New York's pickier and more plausible agents of sympathy. To put it another way: I was, to anyone who could be bothered to pay attention, noticeably lost [O'Neil 2008: 68].

Hans' condition is something that the novel actively interrogates, and this is an interrogation of the "netherland," or world, that Hans is lost in. What is this netherland? It is largely existential, involving his personal losses and epistemological crisis, replete with a succession of flashbacks to childhood and internal monologues. Also, largely because of its repeated references to 9/11 (but also through Hans' friendship with Chuck and subsequent movements through some of the more marginalized circles of New York), it seems to invoke ideas of a shared or communal post-9/11 condition. As Andrew Anthony writes, "Hans' attempt to grasp common bonds amid his emotional desolation is resonant of the wider search for community and identity that marked the anxious aftermath of the attacks on the World Trade Center" (Anthony 2008: n.p.).

The novel is filled with instances of and references to Hans attempting to locate himself in a group or in the world—episodes which, as demonstrated, emphasize both togetherness and individuality within a group. From the very beginning he ponders his personal identity or place in the groups within which he circulates. As stated, this is embodied by the cricket team, "huddled with arms round one another's shoulders—nominally, three Hindus, three Christians, a Sikh and four Muslims" (O'Neil 2008: 9). Hans identifies himself as part of this group of Staten Island cricketers but also as the "only white player" on the team (O'Neil 2008: 9). On a larger scale there are several episodes that find Hans navigating the globe from his bedroom, trying to find his relocated family using Google Earth:

> Flying on Google's satellite function, night after night I surreptitiously travelled to England. Starting with a hybrid map of the United States, I moved the navigation box across the North Atlantic and began my fall from the stratosphere: successively, into a brown and beige and greenish Europe [O'Neil 2008: 119].

This repeated exercise is underpinned by the implicit metaphor of the internet: alone at your desk yet connected to millions. This recurring scene seems to embody the dialectical notion of Hans' occupation of a netherland and the preoccupation of locating individuality within a group. Hans' forlorn travels on Google Earth's satellite are ironic acts of connectedness, as they are characterized by loneliness, distance and melancholy. These scenes also engage explicitly with an underlying uncertainty over the nature and possibility of collective experience. Is this, they seem to ask, a unique, individual experience, or is it in some abstract way collective? This question is perhaps never satisfactorily answered, but the grappling with it is explicitly identified as a definitive part of what we may call "post-9/11 anxiety," and a dialogue between these two strands does begin to emerge. This self-reflexivity again contributes to the general self-conscious quality of the novel and evokes a question Michael Rothberg asks in an early essay response to 9/11 published in *Trauma at Home*. Rothberg believes that while trauma theory provides "essential therapeutic resources for individuals stricken with loss," he highlights questions about "whether and how trauma theory can provide intellectual resources for more large-scale historical and political tasks" (Rothberg 2003: 150). These questions are latent in *Netherland* when Hans describes his Google Earth perspective: "aloft at a few hundred meters, the scene was depthless. My son's dormer was visible, and the blue inflated pool and the red BMW; but there was no way to see more, or deeper. I was stuck" (O'Neil 2008: 119). This notion, in reference to trauma, that in a shared or collective position "there was no way to see more, or deeper," resonates in the suggestion that in this sphere of "connection" there is no way to get "deeper." And while trauma is inevitably shared in instances like 9/11, there is an individuality of experience for which notions of collective trauma cannot account.

Nevertheless, the novel continues to sustain its dialectic between individual and collective. One of the final passages seems to make a definitive statement about the relationship between Hans' existential emotional dislocation and the collective conscious of post-9/11 New York. In another flashback scene, where Hans turns to memories of his mother, he remembers a joyful moment a few years previous, sailing back into New York with her on a crowded Staten Island Ferry in the glow of a spectacular sunset:

> To speculate about the meaning of such a moment would be stained, suspect business but there is, I think no need to speculate. Factual assertions can be made. I can state that I wasn't the only person on that ferry who'd seen a pink watery sunset in his time, and I can state that I wasn't the only one of us to make out and accept an extraordinary promise in what we saw—the tall approaching cape, a people risen in light. You only had to look at our faces [O'Neil 2008: 247].

This concluding sentiment shows Hans emerging from the "haze" that he occupies through most of the novel, but the positive notion of a multitude united by their own individual version of this "promise" emerges (though qualified by the assertion that it is "stained business" to ascribe too much meaning to collective conscious). Furthermore, while failing to make a definitive statement about the dangers of any particular formulation of "collective trauma" or the limitations of personal trauma, it extends a satisfying sense of balance in the careful delineation of the importance of understanding the possibility of both collective and individual experience.

Six. 9/11 Meta-Fiction

Continuity and Discontinuity

This chapter has so far worked through three prominent strands of the self-consciousness of *Netherland*, analyzing their dialectical aspects: the marriage narrative, the "deterritorialized" New York narrative, and this running exploration of private and public. Before examining one final characteristic of the novel's self-awareness, it is useful to discuss another, alternative interpretation of "meta-fiction" in *Netherland*. Zadie Smith in the *New York Review of Books* extends her reading of uncertainty and anxiety in *Netherland* to the formal aspects of the novel, suggesting its awareness of its own "lyrical realist" form reveals a meta-fictional perspective that, rather than opening up new space, compromises its impact: "It certainly is about anxiety, but its worries are formal and revolve obsessively around the question of authenticity" (Smith 2008: n.p.). Smith cites *Netherland* as being a formal exemplar of a dominant literary strand of realism, "lyrical realism," and suggests that the self-aware aspect is detrimental to its sincerity. However, the criticism has mixed messages; at one point, after endorsing a certain kind of meta-fiction in lamenting the disappearance of "the American meta-fiction that stood in opposition to Realism," she states that "*Netherland* is a novel that wants you to know that it knows you know it knows." The critical tone here emphasizes the novel's meta qualities as the pivot in her reading of the way this "lyrical realism" is incompatible with the novel's self-awareness (Smith 2008: n.p.). Smith concludes her account, though, by somewhat reneging on this assertion, claiming that "*Netherland* is a novel only partially aware of the ideas that underpin it," which is somewhat closer to this interpretation of a self-consciousness that opens up new space for a more multi-cultural milieu and political engagement.

There is no doubt that the novel's self-awareness extends to its formal strategies, but this is also dialectical and not finite. Uncertainty and anxiety characterizes the novel's formal aspect in the way it is narrated retrospectively; this clearly relates to its awareness of the criticisms leveled at the canon of 9/11 fiction and gives it an aura of timeliness (in the sense that it is coming after and responding to the first waves of 9/11 fiction). The manifestations of this awareness have been discussed in depth, and O'Neil acknowledges this timeliness and awareness in the way the novel arrived at a readership ready for an alternative or more balanced account—though he does remind us that the novel was conceived of years before it was published: "It may be in tune with the zeitgeist but you don't know that seven years before. One year earlier or later? If this book comes out after Obama, probably nobody cares" (O'Neil 2008: n.p.). However, *Netherland* has evidently to some degree satisfied a "need" for a more multi-dimensional 9/11 novel and, along with *The Reluctant Fundamentalist*, marks a reflexive, international turn in 9/11 fiction. *New York Times* critic Dwight Gardner described "scanning the horizon for something else—the bracing, wide-screen, many angled novel that will leave a larger, more definitive intellectual and moral footprint on the new age of terror," citing *Netherland* as filling this gap: "On a macro level it's about everything: family, politics, identity. I devoured it in three thirsty gulps, gulps that satisfied a craving I didn't know I had" (Gardner 2008: n.p.). It is precisely this "wide screen, many angled" approach that Smith reads as a preoccupation with formal "authenticity." Smith states about the narrative:

> The stage is set, then, for a "meditation" on identities both personal and national, immigrant relations, terror, anxiety ... in other words it's the September 11th novel we hoped for.... It's as if, by an act of collective prayer, we have willed it into existence [Smith 2008: n.p.].

Smith furthers her argument that *Netherland* is formally anxious via the fact that it is full of self-consciously literary, poetic flourishes, and the view that Chuck's role is as an "authenticity fetish" for Hans. Crucial to this argument is her assertion that "everything must be made literary," though one of the most powerful and frequently evoked passages in the book is a simple swath of dialogue that contains none of the literary flourishes Smith discusses (which O'Neil is indeed prone to). This passage not only stands in opposition to Smith's criticism of the novel, but it ironically attests to the final way in which this novel does indeed operate on a self-conscious plain. It directly broaches the question that ripples under the surface of much of this dialectical novel, a question that, in terms of explicit engagement, is conspicuously absent from texts such as *Extremely Loud and Incredibly Close* or *The Emperor's Children*: what is the lasting significance of the attacks, and historically do they mark an epochal moment? It is worth remembering here that while this novel begins with the protagonists in a position of recovery (in terms of their marriage), it also begins with a death—the death of Chuck Ramkissoon, and this opposition of continuity and discontinuity underpins the whole novel.

Near the end of the novel Hans recalls a dinner party given by one of Rachel's friends after he had relocated to London and reestablished the marital home with Rachel. This passage is worth quoting at length, as it embodies the dialectical aspect of the text in several key ways and also directly engages with the questions mentioned above:

> ... then the conversation strays in a direction that's rare these days, to the events synonymous with September 11th, 2001. "Not such a big deal," Matt suggests, "when you think of everything that's happened since." He is referring to the numbers of Iraqi dead, and as a matter of arithmetic I understand his argument, indeed must admit it. He refers also to the dark amazement with which he and, if my impression is correct, most of the rest of the world have followed the various doings of this American administration, and on this score I again have not the slightest urge to contradict him. I speak up nonetheless. "I think it was a big deal," I say, interrupting whatever somebody was saying. Matt looks at me for the first time that evening. It's an awkward moment, because I look right back at him. Rachel says unexpectedly, "He was there, Matt." Out of the best of intentions and acting as my loyal wife and Englisher, she wants to accord me a privileged standing—that of survivor and witness. I'd feel dishonest to accept it. I've heard it said that the indiscriminate nature of the attack transformed all of us on that island into victims of attempted murder, but I'm not at all sure that geographic proximity to the catastrophe confers this status on me or anybody else.... I say, "That's not my point. I'm just saying, it was a big deal." "Well, of course," Matt says, his tone marking me out as a nitpicker. "I'm not arguing with that." "Good," I say, with as much abruptness as the situation allows. "So we're in agreement." Matt makes a pleasantly concessionary face. Someone else picks up the chatter and everything goes back to normal. However, I notice Matt leaning over and muttering out of the corner of his mouth to his neighbour, who mutters back. There is a secretive exchange of smiles. For some reason I'm filled with rage. I lean over to Rachel. I gesture with my eyes, Let's go. Rachel has not followed what's happened. She looks surprised when I stand up and put on my jacket. It's a surprise for all, since we have not finished our roast chicken. "Come on, Hans, sit down," Matt says. "Rachel, talk to him." Rachel looks at her old friend and then at me. She stands up. "Oh, piss off, Matt," she says, and waves goodbye to everyone. It is quite a shocking moment, in the scheme of things, and of course exhilarating. When we step out together into the wet street, holding hands,

there is a tang of glory in the air. Gratifyingly, Rachel doesn't ask me what exactly transpired. But in the taxi home, there's an epilogue of sorts: my wife mooning out of the window at rainy Regent's Park, says, "God, do you remember those sirens?" and, still looking away, she reaches for my hand and squeezes it [O'Neil 2008: 176–7].

This passage is rich in meaning and entirely free from the self-consciously literary prose that Smith draws attention to, which *Netherland* does contain a certain amount of. Firstly, it draws direct attention to a debate about whether or not 9/11 was a "big deal," with Matt positing the now routine comparative argument of death tolls and the devastation caused by the subsequent War on Terror, and wars in Afghanistan and Iraq, as far outweighing the damage of 9/11. Hans, of course, acknowledges the truth in this historical continuity argument, though the possible counter-arguments to this are many. Unstated, but perhaps implied, are ideas of the symbolic importance of 9/11 and that 9/11 was, in fact, the catalyst for the wars Matt is talking about—thus making it a "big deal." However, it is not this that Hans takes objection to. Hans isn't even certain why he is so "filled with rage," but we know that his personal experience of 9/11 has been defined by uncertainty, possibly trauma, and certainly years of feeling "lost." When he takes objection to Matt's comment, Hans is inevitably thinking of the personal episode in his life that coincided with 9/11. Also, though, his severe reaction, his "taking it personally," is ironically suggestive of the idea that such highly visible public events are experienced by different people in different ways. Hans takes offense because he feels his own post–9/11 experience is being degraded. Not insignificantly, this episode is important in the novel for marking the reconciliation of Hans and Rachel's marriage; however, unlike the majority of the 9/11 domestic dramas, this restoration of equilibrium doesn't amount to a surreptitious and opaque gesture toward continuity, but rather features the opposite: the flagrant insistence that 9/11 was "a big deal." The tensions between ideas of personal and public emerge here entangled in the question of 9/11 as history, and what comes across is a palatable reconciliation of the two narratives. There is the acknowledgment by Hans (the witness) that, in certain contexts, 9/11 was a moment on a historical continuum, though the recuperation of the feeling that in other contexts it was an epochal moment, an absolute. The implied rhetoric, then, is that perspective must be multilateral or multidirectional, which, of course, endorses one of the key projects of the novel as a whole, the inclusion of voices from the margins in the story, and views of Chuck Ramkissoon and the Staten Island Cricket Club—the underground or alternative New York. Lastly, but equally important in the passage above, is simply its explicitness. It directly asks a question that the novels discussed above have avoided engaging with directly and again reveals its meta-fictional quality in this respect.

Richard Gray has posited the idea of "deterritorialization" as a key way for authors to engage with post–9/11 realities; again, Gray describes "the obligation to insert themselves into the space between conflicting interests and practices and then dramatize the contradictions that conflict engenders" (Gray 2009: 147). Michael Rothberg, in his response to Gray's essay, endorses this call and also states that, in addition, "we need a fiction of international relations and extraterritorial citizenship," briefly highlighting *Netherland* as a novel that begins to do this (Rothberg 153). However, as we have seen, it is through *Netherland*'s self-consciousness that these gaps are identified. The significance of this is illuminated by looking back to Alex Houen's important essay of 2004, "Novel Spaces and Taking Place(s) in the Wake of September 11," which was published just before the first two waves of 9/11 fiction. Houen begins this essay by using Ulrich Baer's description of the need for and task of "literature" that addresses 9/11, in the introduction to *110 Stories* (2002). Houen identifies three "divergent strands": a "transformative realism—it honors the 'shocking singularity' of the event while turning it into a story"; a "seismographic registering of the events, in which writing is subject to them as a form of unconscious, historical symptom"; and, lastly, "a departure from the real to the extent that it poses other possible worlds" (Houen 2004: 421). In Chapter Three we have seen how many of the "domestic" novels of 9/11 have utilized combinations of the first two modes and in particular employed this "seismographic" element, which allows, at best, an oblique acknowledgment of continuity in narrating 9/11, lying beneath the decidedly micro-domestic stories. Houen, however, is interested in the third mode, which he identifies as meta-fiction. He argues that this "departure from the real" is the mode which is most capable of functioning in a politically engaged way. Houen uses a selection of pre–9/11 meta-fictional texts to illustrate the way they operate as social critique. He states, discussing DeLillo's *Mao II* (1991), "The text's power of critique is thus retained by self-consciously bringing the status of its fictionality into question" (Houen 2008: 421). But Houen also points out that a "novel that is playfully aware of itself presents a meta-fictional suspension of its own status in relation to the world while keeping the world in focus." Indeed, the task of self-reflexivity is only one part of the project Houen is advocating, the other being the idea of exploring "alternative forms of 'outer space' for us as subjects and other worlds of possibility" (Houen 2004: 424). This is where Houen's vision of meta-fiction diverges from the meta-fiction that Smith sees in *Netherland*. Where Smith sees only a very self-aware and contrived "lyrical realism," Houen identifies the possibility for meta-fiction to open up new space for political engagement. Houen goes on to describe how novels by Burroughs and Acker have demonstrated how "a novel's other world of possibility" might present a meaningful engagement with the world, while at the same time being "experientially affective." This is precisely what *Netherland* does and what Smith misses in her review. It must be said that Houen's discussion of meta-fiction and alternative worlds is focused on novels that deal directly with terrorism, and his examples pre-date 9/11 (because his essay pre-dates most 9/11 fiction). However, the meta-fictional or self-conscious aspects of *Netherland*, and their ability to coexist with and indeed facilitate this "alternative space," are a clear manifestation of Houen's formulation, and are vital in understanding the novel. Not only does O'Neil's novel continually react self-reflexively to the idea of 9/11 fiction, but it creates an alternative world on account of this. Furthermore, even when its self-consciousness does border on what Smith describes as the way it "wants you to know that it knows you know it knows," it is able to remain "experientially affective" in the alternative space it opens up. This alternative world that the novel creates provides the counter-narrative and the crux of its multifaceted narrative.

SEVEN

The Multidirectional Memorialization of 9/11 in Amy Waldman's *The Submission*

Amy Waldman's *The Submission* (2011) was released to mostly celebratory reviews, and, much more than *The Reluctant Fundamentalist* or *Netherland*, it was immediately identified as a new kind of 9/11 novel. By deploying the simple premise that an anonymous competition to design the 9/11 memorial is won by a secular Muslim man, which causes various degrees of outrage, confusion and defiance, Waldman's novel directly engages with the racism and fraught identity politics of post–9/11 America. Additionally, given the controversy surrounding the development of the Park51 Islamic Community Center, which gained national media attention in 2010 when several anti–Islam groups labeled it the "Ground Zero Mosque," the subject of the novel (which is actually mostly set in 2003) was firmly linked to this public debate. *The Submission* is directly political in a way that even the politically charged novels by Hamid and O'Neil are not. Kamila Shamsie (who, along with Claire Messud, was among several high-profile reviewers of the novel) begins her reading in *The Guardian* by noting a departure specifically from the domestic fiction of 9/11 and highlights what she sees as the incorporation of features of some of the non-fiction narratives of the attacks (which, incidentally, Shamsie sees as the more valuable accounts of 9/11 to date):

> Perhaps the representatives of fiction writing and non-fiction writing in America didn't gather in a smoke-filled room at the end of 2001 and divide territory. Perhaps the fiction writers didn't claim for themselves the indi-

vidual tales of trauma around the day itself (signatories include Jonathan Safron [sic] Foer, Don DeLillo, Claire Messud) while the non-fiction writers held on to History and Politics leading up to and on from 9/11 (Lawrence Wright, Jane Meyer, Rajiv Chandrasekaran). If it did happen, then Amy Waldman—former Bureau chief for the *New York Times*—simply decided to tear up the contract" [Shamsie 2011: n.p.].

The presence of a journalistic tone or elements of reportage-style writing are easy observations to make of *The Submission*, given Waldman's history as a *New York Times* reporter (which included three years as co-chief of the South Asia Bureau), and we will return to this aspect of the text. What is interesting about Shamsie's review, though, is that it immediately suggests one of the ways in which Waldman's novel deals with the kinds of post-9/11 conflictedness central to our concerns here, and particularly the multifaceted conflict or dynamic between trauma and politics. Shamsie states, alluding to the much maligned domestic novels of 9/11, "How do you take the trauma and grief of 9/11 as the starting point of a novel and move on to a tale of suspended civil liberties and prejudice without the former entirely overshadowing the latter? Waldman takes hold of this potential stumbling block and turns it into the bedrock of her novel" (Shamsie 2011: n.p.). While Shamsie suggests that the achievement of *The Submission* lies in the way it successfully transcends the paradigms of domestic trauma and mourning to portray the "suspended civil liberties and prejudice" of post–9/11 America, this chapter will argue that the real significance of Waldman's novel lies in what becomes its central theme, post-9/11 conflictedness: a portrayal of conflictedness that has the dialectical opposition between trauma and politics at its heart. While there are undoubtedly journalistic elements to the novel, such as its panoramic cast of characters (who represent a considerable range of demographics, given the length of the novel), it is its willingness to examine the internal conflicts and debates characters experience (even the ones that they repress in acquiescence to the unilateral rhetoric of the Bush administration, the conservative mainstream media and popular opinion) that makes it such an impactful portrayal of post–9/11 disorientation.

In mapping this post–9/11 conflictedness, *The Submission* provides a clear counter-narrative to the Manichean and unilateral rhetoric of the "Bush Doctrine." Noam Chomsky traces the origins of the Bush Doctrine back to the American National Security Strategy of September 2002 (Chomsky 2004: n.p.). The American National Security Strategy document has nine chapters, but the most notable, perhaps, were the third, "Strengthen Alliances to Defeat Global Terrorism and Work to Prevent Attacks Against Us and Our Friends," and the fifth, "Prevent our Enemies from Threatening Us, Our Allies, and Our Friends with Weapons of Mass Destruction" (Various authors, U.S. Department of State 2002: vii). The aims and targets outlined in this strategy document formed the basis for the War on Terror, Patriot Act, wars in Afghanistan and Iraq, and other key post–9/11 policies. Chomsky is mostly interested in identifying the inherent breaches of international laws, which, he argues, characterize the Bush Doctrine's aggressive and unilateral policies. More generally, David Holloway refers to the objectives of the Bush Doctrine as "preemptive war, unilateral policy-making and 'regime change' in 'rogue states'" (Holloway 2008: 4). The policies, wars and other legacies of the Bush Doctrine aside, it is the simplistic and carefully managed rhetoric of the Bush White House during this period that Waldman's novel challenges directly—the rhetoric of "us and them," of good and evil, and good guys and bad guys—rhetoric which we can actually see in the chapter titles above. In *The War on Terror Narrative: Discourse and Intertextuality in the Construction and Contestation of Sociopolitical Reality* (2011), Adam Hodges charts the patterns of conflation and repetition deployed by the Bush administration in creating what he describes as the War on Terror narrative. Hodges shows how through "narrative accrual," President Bush's official speeches "accumulate into a larger cultural narrative shared by many within the nation" (Hodges 2011: 4). Hodges details the way the "characterization of 9/11 as an act of war (rather than, as others have argued, a criminal act) and the response to terrorism as a 'war on terror' (rather than an investigation into terrorist crimes) is a discursive achievement" (Hodges 2011: 23). While the Bush administration went to great lengths to respond to the complex array of national and international issues that 9/11 brought to the surface or created by generating clear objectives and targets, creating heroes and protagonists, and identifying enemies to defeat, Waldman is interested in remembering both the emotional and socio-political complexities that were buried beneath this rhetoric. Waldman carries this out by first re-animating the myriad of nuance and complexity in intercultural relationships that was quashed by simplistic formulations of cultural conflict; and second by challenging one-dimensional images of trauma and grief by giving voice to the unspoken inner-conflicts of her traumatized characters. Waldman repeatedly shows how intellectual debate and discussion was suppressed by the mass media, usually through the character Alyssa Spier, a fictional *New York Post* reporter. In one revealing scene, considering what to report on from the public hearing on the memorial design, Spier immediately categorizes certain speakers' assessments or testimonies as too complicated or unpalatable, particularly for her editor, Chaz, even when they may offer interesting insight into the discussion: "Even Alyssa wasn't sure what to make of Stanton's comments: she was saying that this element of Khan's design was Islamic—but only if the buildings were Islamic too. Way too complicated for Chaz" (Waldman 2001: 286). As in *Netherland*, Waldman builds this narrative by utilizing a unique meta-fictional conceit. In *The Submission*, the meta-fiction comes from the simple fact that like the subject of the novel, the disputed process of memorializing 9/11, the novel itself is invested in the questions of how to remember and represent 9/11.

One of the strongest rhetorical strands of the novel harnesses some of the key ideas of Michael Rotherberg's *Multidirectional Memory* (2009), and even more so than in *The Reluctant Fundamentalist*, the rhetoric of multidirectionality becomes a key tenet of *The Submission*'s counter-narrative. Rothberg's theoretical text focuses on the intersections of collective memories of genocide and decolonization (with a focus on the Holocaust), and argues generally for more productive articulations of collective memory from "marginalized and oppositional groups." As in Hamid's novel, at the center of *The Submission* is Rothberg's staunch argument against "competitive memory" and the imperative to "think about the relationship between different social groups' histories of victimization" (Rothberg 2009: 2). The real relevance to my argument here, of the presence of some strands of Rothberg's *Multidirectional Memory* in Waldman's novel, is the way *The Submission* is particularly focused on "reject[ing] the notion that identities and memories are pure and authentic—that there is a we and a you that would definitively differentiate, say black and Jewish identities and black Jewish relations to the past" (Rothberg 2009: 3). The meta-fictional pretext of Waldman's novel opens it up for what this chapter will locate as a multidirectional memorialization of 9/11, which cuts against the unilateral rhetoric of the Bush Doctrine in its image of the tensions and conflictedness that shape the way all of the key characters deal with the aftermath of the attacks, as well as the clearly implied possibilities of less competitive modes of memory that the novel provides.

As stated, a final consideration of this chapter will be *The Submission*'s formal qualities. In Chapter Four we identified the way the formal qualities of Dave Eggers' work of narrative non-fiction, *Zeitoun*, particularly the balance between the documentary-style presentation of historical events and an array of conspicuously literary conceits heighten the emphasis of its response to the domestic fictions of 9/11. With this in mind we will examine the ways the much vaunted journalistic qualities of *The Submission* have contributed to its reception as a new kind of 9/11 novel. It is important to note here, briefly, that the novel was not unanimously celebrated. Christian Lorentzen, writing in the *London Review of Books*, has in fact been heavily critical of the novel precisely because of what he perceives as a particular kind of journalistic tone. Lorentzen argues that the novel betrays Waldman's background as a *New York Times* staff reporter in unproductive ways, stating that *The Submission*'s "prose suggests the earnest fact-gatherer trying to figure out what fiction ought to sound like" (Lorentzen 2011: 28). Betraying a certain bias, Lorentzen goes on to describe his

> feeling that the novel was written by the *New York Times* itself; that Waldman has so thoroughly internalized the paper's worldview that she can't see things any other way. The *Times* tends to flatter its readers in the way it writes about their educations, their ambitions and what they spend their money on, while gently stoking their anxieties—about surly Islamophobes from New Jersey, their children's safety, or cancer. In newsprint these tropes tend to be submerged under the weight of actual events but they are all too conspicuous in the long march of a novel [Lorentzen 2011: 29].

This may be a heavy-handed assessment, but there is an interesting suggestion here in the way Lorentzen bluntly argues that the novel has wholly adopted a *New York Times* or liberal middle-class perspective, that the formal aspects of the novel might also reinforce the way it operates as a counter-narrative. This is problematized by the fact that the novel condemns the hypocrisies of the character who is an embodiment of liberal middle-class values, Claire Burwell, but there is no doubt that there is some truth to Lorentzen's assertions. While many, if not most, of the authors of 9/11 novels might have similarly liberal middle-class identities or perspectives, the fact that *The Submission* is inherently critical of the conservative American mass media makes this perspective even more visible here and certainly becomes part of its counter-narrative. After all, if the unilateral rhetoric of the Bush Doctrine was supported by and delivered through mass media outlets such as Fox News, then Waldman's *New York Times*–style tone would certainly represent a counterpoint (at least in terms of mainstream news media).

The Submission's *Clash of Cultures*

The Submission begins its examination of post–9/11 cultural division and racial prejudice by evoking the Clash of Civilizations or "Islam versus the West" discourse, re-calibrated to also evoke one of the other popular War on Terror conceits—the "enemy within." When Mohammad Khan is revealed as the anonymous architect or designer behind the winning design, the mass media begins describing his entry, "The Garden," as an "Islamic Garden," a "Martyrs Garden," or a "Victory Garden." But while the public debate over the suitability of a Muslim architect to design the 9/11 memorial drives the narrative, the reductive clash of civilizations dynamic, discussed earlier in Chapter Four, immediately gives way to a more complex portrayal of the internal divisions within each "side" of this crude polarization and indeed within the inner worlds of the individuals involved. Waldman unpacks tensions that characterize different stratospheres and sections of society, revealing their nuances and webbed connections. On the surface, the post–9/11 New York of *The Submission* is again very similar to that of *The Reluctant Fundamentalist*—particularly the descriptions of patriotic bombast and the ubiquity of flag iconography. In many instances, though, Waldman also highlights the divisiveness within this patriotism; in this case between those representing both sides of the public debate: "both sides had begun wearing American flag pins to prove their patriotism, and arguments were breaking out on subways and in the streets between the beribboned and the stickered" (Waldman 2011: 161). The idea that dissent can be patriotic, and plurality and tolerance fundamentally American, was a popular rebuke to the Bush Doctrine, which, as Hodges notes, relied on repetition and exposure to retain prominence and hegemony. This, however, still pertains to the larger public debate at the center of the text, and the real complexity of the novel rests in its ability to move beyond simplistic two-sided debates and explore its characters' internal conflicts. A key starting point and context for our examination of the ways in which *The Submission* addresses these debates and articulates the inner struggles of characters (who again represent a real panorama of American society) is the novel's representation of Islam. As we have seen, this has been a deeply problematic area for previous narratives of 9/11, and this issue is engaged with directly by *The Submission*. Creating multidimensional Muslim characters was clearly an imperative in representing the complexities and conflicts of America's national response to 9/11.

The Submission is almost schematically panoramic in its cast of characters, and, again, this is one of the clear journalistic aspects the novel. Within its range of major and minor Muslim characters, several "types" are established or suggested, and then subverted to the extent that every cliché is challenged. The two most prominent female Muslims, for example, Asma Anwar and Laila Fathi, are set up as antithetical types or stereotypes. Asma is an illegal Bangladeshi immigrant whose husband, who was working illegally as a janitor in the World Trade Center, died in the 9/11 attacks. She lives in an insular Muslim community in Brooklyn called "Little Dhaka," wears traditional Muslim dress, and, before her husband's death, stayed at home to look after the couple's son Abdul. However, despite the stereotypical surface image, the characterization of Asma that emerges is of a strong and impassioned woman who won't accept her husband being written out of history (he is not recognized as a victim, initially, on account of his lack of citizenship). Her inner world is clearly conceived of to challenge stereotypes; and in one scene that breaks with the conventional Western portrayal of Muslim women, she is characterized as sexually liberal: "She lied when she told Inam that it didn't hurt the first time they made love, but after that the pain had become pleasure, so deep that she couldn't find words so it wasn't a bad lie" (Waldman 2011: 170). Asma's inner world is frequently depicted through her insightful and critical musings on her immediate community, and she is portrayed as a distinctly independent thinker. Asma is ultimately revealed to be antithetical to the submissive, deferent and Burka-clad Muslim woman common in Western cultural representation, and in one of the most dramatic scenes in the novel, in a great show of strength and courage, Asma tells her emotional story in front of the national media at the public hearing.

Laila is an equally complex character; she is a highly politicized lawyer who wears expensive suits and works exhaustive hours as an elite Manhattan professional. But cutting against this cold professionalism and ambition is an image of a passion for life: "Her suits were vividly colored and her passions ... many: food of all kinds; Persian poetry and Iranian films; her large extended family" (Waldman 2011 144).

While these characters are explicitly drawn to counter stereotypes and clichés, Khan himself exists as an example of how these stereotypes originate. In one important way, the characterization of Khan does rest against the stereotypes, and this is the deceptively simplistic trope that the competition-winning architect, despite being identified as a Muslim, is actually completely secular (which makes the demonization of him even more perverse). As stated, however, with Khan it is not simply a case of characterization against the stereotypes of Muslims, but a demonstration of how stereotypes are projected and perpetuated, and to some extent he is a cipher. Superficially, his defining characteristics are his career ambitions (his entry into the competition to design the memorial was purely motivated by career aspirations), which is accompanied by a complete immersion in multi-national capitalism; commensurate with this is his yuppie style and sensibility. He does certainly have a passion for architecture and tends to process his thoughts through this idiom. For example, meditating on the loss of the World Trade Center, he muses: "A skyline was a collaboration, if an inadvertent one, between generations, seeming no less natural than a mountain range that had shuddered up from the earth" (Waldman 2011: 36). Khan is also certainly antithetical to the all too common stereotypes of sexually repressed, angry young Muslim men, such as Hammad in *Falling Man* or Ahmad in John Updike's *Terrorist*. He is successful, stylish and presented as a stereotypical New York bachelor whose many ex-girlfriends of multiple ethnicities are frequently mentioned, and who wouldn't be out of place in the HBO television series *Sex in the City* (1998–2004)—if, of course, he were not a Muslim.

To the other characters, and to the reader, Khan becomes an enigma, and his behavior contributes to and to some extent invites this. This is not because he is sinisterly mysterious or because of any gestures toward violence or fundamentalism, but because he is undergoing his own identity crisis (quite understandably) on account of the media hyperbole and public outrage surrounding his anointment as the winning designer. This identity crisis and increasing sense of uncertainty is explicitly stated when a beleaguered Khan decides to observe Ramadan for the first time in his adult life amidst the rancor and spite of the 9/11 memorial debate:

> The truth was he didn't know why his first act each day now was abstention, and this uncertainty harbored so many others, even as it was born from them: uncertainty about whether he was right to pursue his memorial, whatever the cost, or right to refuse to explain [Waldman 2011: 236].

Khan's initial refusal to discuss or explain his design, or to thank the 9/11 widow Claire Burwell for her public support of him and his design, or to declare his own motivations for entering the competition in the first place, is partly down to the uncertainty he describes and partly out of a defiance that grows quickly in response to the identity the media creates for him and projects onto him.

In many ways this again echoes the way Changez responds to the post–9/11 racism, xenophobia and military aggression in *The Reluctant Fundamentalist*—by taking on aspects of the identity that is created for him by a biased conservative media. Khan's behavior is also closely linked to the phenomenon of dialogical stereotyping, which is well-described in Amina Yaqin and Peter Morey's *Framing Muslims: Stereotyping and Representation After 9/11* (2011). Morey and Yaqin, discussing group identities, state that "when Muslims see themselves constantly portrayed as having some indefinable propensity to barbarism ... it is unsurprising if, in the face of such vilification, particular embattled and defensive types of group identity emerge" (Yaqin and Morey 2011: 31). Khan does not enter into any particularly violent or outspoken groups, but as a secular man it is telling that he begins observing Ramadan amidst the hysterical criticism of his "Islamic Garden," and also, like Changez in *The Reluctant Fundamentalist*, grows a beard and begins to invite suspicion: "He had grown a beard on his return from Kabul merely to assert his right to wear a beard, to play with the assumptions about his religiosity it might create" (Waldman 2011: 146). As the novel progresses, Khan's troubled identity is repeatedly emphasized as a kind of defiance in response to the racism and vilification he suffers because of media outlets like *The New York Post*: "It was exactly because they had nothing to worry about from him that he wanted to let them worry" (Waldman 2011: 99–100). One of the examples of dialogic stereotyping that Yaqin and Morey use to illustrate the cycle of hatred and intolerance initiated by the American Christian Right is a useful context here:

> An extreme right-wing Christian, previously only noted for making homophobic statements about local political candidates, asserts that it is time for America to "stand up to Islam," which he sees as irrational and satanically inspired; he does so in the most provocative way possible (but one that mimics the book and effigy-burning antics of Muslim protesters in other parts of the world); and, in his turn, he provokes the kind of violent backlash that seems to prove his argument. Seen from the other "side," of course, the gesture of Koran burning acts as damning evidence of the godlessness and anti-Muslim attitude prevalent in the West and leads to the kind of frenzied, violent response that "proves" such societies' irrationality to Western onlookers [Yaqin and Morey 2011: 211–212].

What Khan experiences and expresses as an individual doesn't equate to the ever-proliferating cycle described by Yaqin and Morey, but there is no doubt that his defiance is expressed or articulated in the way he begins fulfilling or feigning to fulfill the role he is assigned by the conservative mass media and a society paralyzed by the culture of fear it creates. Essentially, though, what is dramatized is the experience of a man whose identity is thrown into crisis after being vilified by his own nation. Crucially, Khan's sense of self begins to fracture during this period:

> Mo began to put psychological distance between himself and the Mohammad Khan who was written and talked about as if that were another man altogether. It often was. Facts were not found but made, and once made, alive, defying anyone to tell them from truth. Strangers analyzed, judged, and invented him [Waldman 2011: 161].

Again, as with Changez in *The Reluctant Fundamentalist*, Khan is immersed in the American Dream, which he is successfully achieving as an elite New York architect, so his experience as an archetypal success story is thrown into crisis when he is portrayed as an enemy of everything that he is, and ultimately, it is his nationality that is at the heart of his increasingly troubled sense of identity.

Khan struggles with the repeatedly posited notion that he should defend his design and reassure the American public that he is a good Muslim, a fellow American and "one of them," or whether he should demand the benefit of the doubt from his country of birth. In a flashback episode that takes place in the immediate weeks after 9/11, which describes Khan discussing the "threat" of Islam with his then girlfriend, he actually argues the case for racial profiling at airports: "'So be it—I have nothing to hide. I'm not going to pretend that all Muslims can be trusted. If Muslims are the reason they're doing searches in the first place, why shouldn't Muslims be searched?'" (Waldman 2011: 51). But when he becomes the target and focal point of serious racial prejudice, and when he ceases to be judged on the merits of his work, his sense of identity as an American becomes deeply problematic. This reaches its nadir when he is confronted by previously mentioned Alyssa Spier. When Khan accuses her and her newspaper of making it "open season on Muslims" she retorts:

> "No, you did, by entering the competition, by insisting on your right to win, even though it offended so many Americans, hurt so many of the families' feelings. So are you going to withdraw?"
> "Offended so many Americans? Was that what you said?" Khan said. He was moving toward her. They were only a couple of feet apart, giving her no choice but to walk backward. "I am an American, too," he said, contingent to advance on her. "Put that in your paper. I, Mohammad Khan, am an American, and I have the same rights as every other American." She peddled backward; he moved toward her. "I am an American. That's the only quote I'm going to give you. I am an American" [Waldman 2011: 334–335].

Khan here asserts his identity as strongly as possible, but in the final chapter of the book, which takes place twenty years in the future, we learn that Khan left the United States shortly after the memorial hearing and has been working in "the Middle East, India, or China," and is currently living in Mumbai: "For nearly two decades now, he had been a global citizen, American only in name" (Waldman 2011: 369). As vociferous as he is in asserting his nationality, Khan's sense of national identity is clearly, permanently, altered.

Juries, Coalitions, and "Representatives"

Another tactic *The Submission* employs in dramatizing the suppressed complexities of America's national response to 9/11, as well as the heightened racism and xenophobia that characterized the immediate years after the attacks, is to focus on the various interest groups and "representatives" that vie for attention and media space during the memorial debate. The jury members chosen to select the winning memorial design are ostensibly, of course, the most prominent of these, but just as important are the many groups that become visible or form in the wake of the announcement of the identity of the winning design and designer. There are groups in support of Khan ("The Committee to Defend Mohammad Khan," "The Mohammad Khan Defense Fund," "The Mohammad Khan Protection League") and against Khan ("The Memorial Defense Committee"), against Islam ("Save America from Islam"), and in advocacy of Islam (the "Muslim American Coordinating Council"), and each group, even the ones that share the same fundamental interests, are shown to differ greatly in their aims and motivations (which often are revealed to be self-serving and unrelated to the alleged core cause). This focus on groups and representatives functions to firstly illustrate how they fail to adequately represent the larger sections of society they claim to be acting or advocating on behalf of, as well as the individuals within those groups; and secondly, how their existence demonstrates the complexities and fractures within inter-cultural relationships that were and are erased by clash of civilizations rhetoric. Yaqin and Morey remind us that "clash of civilizations discourse begins from the assumption that cultures and nations are fixed, finished, and stable"; and the depiction of interest groups in *The Submission* certainly works as an example of just how simplistic and retrograde this discourse is.

Yaqin and Morey discuss the phenomenon of representatives and interest groups extensively in *Framing Muslims*, particularly in reference to the way they figure in post–9/11 and post–7/7 formulations of multiculturalism. Yaqin and Morey argue convincingly that, particularly in Britain, what they describe as "professional Muslims" were cultivated and relied upon to reassure the public by both staying "on message" as moderate and peaceful Muslims, and by being evidence that the fundamental tenets of a "tolerant" society that embraces "multiculturalism" are intact. Crucially, though, these representatives are arbitrarily installed and frequently unrepresentative:

> Liberal multiculturalism invests much in the notion of "authenticity"; imbuing certain spokespeople and organizations with the right to speak on behalf of wider communities. In the case of Muslim representatives, the nature and scope of their "representations" has been severely curtailed in the current climate ... particular voices representing certain recognized and accommodated strands within Islam have been cultivated and brought to the fore, while others have been downplayed and marginalized, treated as "less representative" [Yaqin and Morey 2011: 80].

While British and American notions of multiculturalism are very different, the power dynamic that Yaqin and Morey discuss in relation to "representatives" has much bearing on *The Submission*. Indeed, while Waldman's depiction of the hugely diverse MACC (Muslim American Coordinating Council) emphasizes the enormous range of interpretations of Islam, the leader of the group, Issam Malik, is clearly invested in the kind of power available to a figurehead or representative, and is an archetypal "professional Muslim." Yaqin and Morey describe the way in which "the fascination with representativeness and authenticity has led to a situation in which what one might almost call 'professional Muslims' are touring the circuits of think tanks, select committees, and talk shows" (Yaqin and Morey 2011: 94). Malik certainly fits this description well, and it is notable that during Khan's first meeting with the MACC, Malik focuses on power or "capital," as he calls it. As the group debates about whether the MACC should support Khan, Malik states, "This is about amassing capital, not squandering it" (Waldman 2011: 103). Malik is described by Khan as "the slick front man for a special interest," and his focus on power is repeatedly reiterated.

Malik is one of several figureheads or representatives who are shown to have other vested interests. In one scene late on, he is even reproached by a fellow MACC member about his motivations for advocating for Khan, suggesting that his own status and power are a priority: "We seem to be sending out a lot of emails soliciting donations on the back of this controversy. A lot of emails noting how many times MACC—you—are in the press" (Waldman 2011: 250). Khan is particularly adverse to Malik and characterizes him as an "unctuous phony" for the way he uses him to gain publicity and leverage power (Waldman 2011: 221). Another figurehead who is revealed to be deeply self-serving is Debbie Dawson, the self-appointed leader of SAFI (Save America from Islam). Debbie's interest group is also her profession, her main source of income, and she is shown to thrive on the celebrity status it affords her. At the "Rally to Protect Sacred Ground" event she even hires bodyguards as emblems of her status or importance:

> Debbie Dawson was kitted out in tight black pants and yet another T-shirt she had designed, this one reading "Kafir and Proud." Two buff men in Ray-Bans, blue blazers, and khaki pants trailed her through the crowd. When she stopped to give interviews or greet supporters, they positioned themselves on either side of her, facing out, feet planted in a wide stance, arms never fully relaxed ... she looked like she was having the time of her life [Waldman 2001: 191].

Debbie lives in New York City with her three teenage children, who are provided for by donations to "the cause," and we are frequently reminded of her personal financial gains as the main figurehead of SAFI. When Sean Gallagher, another important opponent of Khan's memorial, stays with Debbie for a few days, Debbie posts a blog that describes how Sean "has been threatened for being brave enough to speak up against the Islamist threat and against Mohammad Khan. Now he has had to flee his home. We are feeding and housing him. DONATE NOW!" (Waldman 2011: 211). Both Debbie Dawson and Issam Malik are high-profile representatives who are characterized as self-absorbed and shown to make important personal gains through their campaigning.

The unrepresentative quality of these representatives is foregrounded in the opening scenes of the novel, which describe the final deliberations of the memorial jury. The jury chairman, Paul Rubin, takes the position purely for professional reasons (or the belief that "this chairmanship would lead to others"), bowing to the pressure of his wife, who imagines him in other "prestigious positions" (Waldman 2011: 7). The jury's final deliberations are mostly defined as a rivalry between the 9/11 widow Claire Burwell and a preeminent sculptor, Ariana, who is "the jury's most famous figure" and "dominant personality" within the group (Waldman 2011: 1). As the thirteen-person jury reduces the competition to the final two entries, Claire and Ariana are fiercely adversarial, each working feverishly to convince the other jurors to choose their preferred design. The process is quickly shown to take on the characteristics of a personal rivalry, and when Claire's choice, Khan's "The Garden," finally wins, at first it is described as a victory for Claire rather than the design itself. After the winning entry is finally decided, Paul reflects, "the dark horse had won—he hadn't thought Claire could trump Ariana—and this seemed appropriately American" (Waldman 2011: 15). Again, this image of jurors, who are meant to represent the greater American public, entrenched in personal combat and rivalry foregrounds the later characterizations of characters such as Malik, Debbie and Sean Gallagher, all of whom are shown to be deeply influenced by private issues or personal aspirations rather than the groups they are representing.

Despite this negative portrayal of certain key representatives, the other key function of the series of coalitions and groups that vie for power and attention during the memorial debate is to reveal and unpack the diversity of belief, opinion and emotion behind each "side" of the clash of civilizations polarization. This is particularly the case with the MACC, which is repeatedly characterized as diverse and rife with internal conflict:

> The council was an umbrella organization for assorted Muslim groups, some political, some theological, others legal. The group was striking in its diversity: South Asians, African Americans, Arabs; bearded men and clean-shaven, in suits and in djellabas; two women in headscarves and one—striking and black-haired in an aubergine suit—without" [Waldman 2011: 101].

The fact that the distinction between "bearded men and clean-shaven men is cited as a mark of diversity is perhaps an indicator of the sense of mystery projected onto the "Muslim World" by the West, or the fear of bearded Islamists generated by the Western media. Nevertheless, the MACC is shown to include disparate ethnicities, interpretations of Islam, and political orientations, and this is brought out at several stages in the novel. It first surfaces in their initial discussion over whether or not to publicly support Khan, which divides the group (only after lengthy debate does a two-thirds majority vote prove decisive and initiate the MACC's role in helping Khan). In a later scene, the debate over whether the MACC should be supporting Khan becomes even more intense. One member states, "We've got people yanking headscarves off our women, and our young people being radicalized in return, and who can blame them? This is going to end in a bad place" (Waldman 2011: 250). Crucially, this diversity and range of opinion and belief does not simply exist to counter the simplistic, one-dimensional image of Islam that clash of civilizations discourse relies upon. It also uses this range of Muslim voices to make several allusions to the possibility of a multidirectional memory of 9/11. This is powerfully evoked by a member of the MACC called Ansar:

> Since we're talking about memorials, where is the memorial to the half-million Iraqi children killed by U.S. sanctions? To the thousands of innocent Afghans killed in response to this attack, or the Iraqis killed on the pretext of responding to this attack? Or to all the Muslims slaughtered in Chechnya, or Kashmir, or Palestine, while the U.S. stood by.... The attack here becomes no less tragic if we acknowledge these other tragedies and demand equal time, equal care for them [Waldman 2011: 101].

This clearly evokes the deeply problematic dynamic of "competitive memory" here, but latent in Ansar's comment is the obvious notion that many American Muslims will have family or relatives in the countries he lists, and to remember 9/11, for these individuals, will also involve remembering the conflicts that were launched in its aftermath. While Ansar is clearly being adversarial, his notion that the tragedies be given "equal time, equal care" certainly evokes Rothberg's condemnation of competitive memory in favor of multidirectionality: "Those who understand memory as a form of competition see only winners and losers in the struggle for collective articulation and recognition. But attention to memory's multidirectionality suggests a more supple social logic" (Rothberg 2009: 5).

Ansar's rhetoric of multidirectionality doesn't stop here, as he makes reference to another violent clash of cultures in American history, the Native American genocide: "They say that when you watch the movies, you root for the cowboys, but when you read the history you root for the Indians. Americans are locked in a movie theater watching Westerns right now, and we've got to break down the walls" (Waldman 2011: 102). This is a powerful suggestion in the way it reminds us of some of the key premises of Susan Faludi's *The Terror Dream: What 9/11 Revealed About America* (2007). As we have seen in previous chapters, particularly in Chapter Four, *The Terror Dream* demonstrates how the American government and mass media relied on retrograde tropes of "Western" or "frontier" masculinity, heroism and leadership—what Faludi memorably describes as "Long Ranger leaders and Davy Crockett candidates and John Wayne 'manly men'"—to mitigate a pervasive national mood of vulnerability (Faludi 2007: 199). Ansar's evocation of a more multidirectional understanding of 9/11 is made even more powerful through his evoking the Bush Doctrine's characterization of the good guys and bad guys.

Trauma and Identity in The Submission

While the unrepresentativeness of representatives, and the internal divisions of the MACC, including Ansar's rhetoric of multidirectionality, go some ways toward illuminating the complexities and divergences of the Muslim-American response to 9/11, it is the two central non–Muslim characters, Sean Gallagher and Claire Burwell, both of whom lost loved ones in the attacks, that are most revealing in terms of the internal debates and conflicts they undergo and experience. These two characters seem to also represent both class division and political orientation, as Claire is clearly a liberal middle-class woman—a *New York Times* reader—and Sean is a blue-collar Republican. As we have seen, one of the features of the novel's journalistic quality, and one of the ironies in its criticism of "representatives," is that the characters are all designed to be representative. As Shamsie states, "The characters are wholly realized and believable as individuals, but they also stand in for stories and conflicts that go beyond their own lives" (Shamsie 2011: n.p.). However, while Shamsie admires the "mirroring of Khan's growing self-righteousness with Burwell's crumbling liberal attitudes," in terms of inner struggle, a comparison between Claire and Sean is much more productive. For the purposes of this chapter, a consideration of the representation of Sean is particularly important, as he represents the average American who in 2003 was fully invested in the Bush Doctrine. *The Submission* characterizes him as deeply troubled and conflicted in his private or internal world, but, driven by anger and fear, uncompromising and aggressive in his actions. Claire, similarly, is tormented by the conflicting realities of her liberal political orientation and suspicion of Khan. Claire's inner struggle is encapsulated by a phenomenon that Khan reads about in a magazine: "Manhattanites who had always prided themselves on their liberalism confessed that they were talking to their therapists about their discomfort with Mohammad Khan as the memorial's designer" (Waldman 2011: 160). Both characters are shown to be deeply conflicted and, crucially, to have other external pressures influencing their emotions.

Sean is introduced as an obviously volatile and angry character, and his narrative essentially consists of a sequence of incidents where he demonstrates a capacity for complex understanding and sensitivity but ends up acting singularly on anger and fear. The first of these incidents occurs at the "Rally to Protect Sacred Ground," where Sean is giving a speech as leader of the Memorial Defense Committee. Sean becomes wary of the belligerence of the crowd and begins doubting that he is actually honoring his lost brother by fueling this hysteria. As Sean looks out at the crowd, he sees the way the

> ... overfed, overeager faces listening to him hungered for what couldn't be bought, and he pitied them for the desire to go somewhere deeper, be part of something larger. Horrible as the attack was, everyone wanted a little of its ash on their hands [Waldman 2011: 192].

Because of his muted and ineffective speech, and some logistical problems, the rally doesn't go as planned for Sean, and he reflects that his "original vision had been constricted by a series of compromises" (Waldman 2011: 192). As the rally fails to have the impact he had hoped, the circumstances become "enfeebling," and he focuses on a group of counter-protesters holding placards, one of which reads "BIGOTS=IDIOTS" (Waldman 2011: 193–4). This ignites Sean's anger, and his earlier reflections on whether or not the rally was honorable quickly gives way to blind rage. He approaches one of the counter-protesters and accuses her of calling him and his parents "bigots." When she coolly and respectfully responds, he acts out in violence: "Her placidity, so provoking, made him want to provoke her in return, to get a rise, and the most provocative act he could think of was to tug back her headscarf..." (Waldman 2011: 195). After Sean is cheered by the protesters, arrested, and eventually praised by Debbie Dawson, he reflects on his action: "He'd out–Debbied Debbie, and it didn't feel that great" (Waldman 2011: 196). The next incident occurs when Sean decides to officially apologize for his violent act at the MACC headquarters. After meeting with the woman he attacked, Zahira Hussein, and speaking one to one, he apologizes in what seems like a sincere manner, and Zahira subsequently urges him to apologize publicly to stop a growing spate of headscarf-pullings. When placed in front of an eager media, Sean repeats his apology, but, again overcome with humiliation and emotionally charged after hearing his brother's name, he adds, "We will never apologize for not wanting anything Islamic connected to this memorial—not a person, not a design" (Waldman 2011: 235). This completely compromises what was intended to be a conciliatory gesture. However, when Sean returns home, he sees "the anguish on Zahira Hussain's face," and again the text portrays Sean as possessing a private sensitivity and empathy but choosing a unilateral and belligerent way of acting. The suggestion is that, in order to cope with his traumatic loss and disorienting emotions, Sean gravitates toward a clear narrative and set of objectives.

Sean's empathy rises to the surface again at the public hearing, and his identity, once so invested in anti–Islam, begins to completely fracture. After rushing out of the hearing following Ansa's emotional testimony, he is reeling and desperately trying to curtail his sympathy for her plight. "Sean had to stamp out these glimmerings of sympathy. To lend his heart to the other side would weaken his own" (Waldman 2011: 299). But this inner turmoil overcomes him, and he is thrown into crisis in a manner not dissimilar to that of Khan:

> Some scramble of images had beset him up there: Debbie serving him eggs at home, then hurling insults outside MACC; Zahira warming behind that desk, then aghast; Eileen, cold fierceness one minute, childlike grief the next. All these doubles. He couldn't get a fix on anyone, least of all himself, the brother left behind and the striving son, the shabby handyman and the suited man on the make, the guy pulling the headscarf and the one apologizing and somehow meaning both.

Sean's disorientation again evokes what Kristiaan Versluys describes as "the mental crisis 9/11 provoked and ... the moral confusion left in its wake" (Verluys 2009: 148). It is also, however, clearly depicted as a disorientation that is fundamentally related to the conflictedness that Sean feels and the polarized "doubles" that seem to pull him in opposite directions. But while Sean is shown here to be divided and stretched in opposite directions, and to feel sympathy for Zahira and Ansa, he remains desperate to "choose a side." It is almost as if he needs a clear enemy— just as the Bush administration was so eager to identify clear enemies.

Just as Sean is sinking into crisis, he sees Claire, and when Claire tells Sean that "people like me, who can see both sides, are needed," he again becomes angry and nearly violent: "Cowardice is what it's called! You can see all the sides you want, but you can only be on one. You have to choose, Claire. Choose!" (Waldman 2001: 301).

Sean is easily identifiable as an allegorical character, one who is shown to be capable of a deeper understanding and response, but who desperately needs objectives, enemies and someone to blame. It is impossible not to read this as an account of America under the influence of the rhetoric of the Bush Doctrine. But if Sean Gallagher is an allegorical character, so is Claire Burwell. As we have seen, Claire is the liberal American whose beliefs in tolerance, plurality and multiculturalism are tested to the limit when she too is working through the trauma of losing a loved one. Claire continually repeats the refrain that there are "two sides to everything, including this ... more than two sides." But as her own certainty wavers, this becomes more and more a way to justify her own increasing doubts about Khan as she gives more and more credence to the "side" that she initially, staunchly opposed. Claire's own conflictedness is actually very similar to Sean's; and just three pages after Sean's breakdown, Claire's inner struggle reaches its nadir. This comes in the recollection of a series of dolls that her deceased husband had commissioned—a personalized representation of their whole family. The first version of the dolls featured the four family members as matryoshkas where Cal (Claire's husband) was the biggest, Claire the second biggest and so on. Realizing the political incorrectness of this, Cal had four versions made so that each of the family members were represented four times in four different sizes so that they could all contain each other, and there could be four distinct matryoshkas where each member of the family could be the biggest. For Claire, though, now without Cal, the four different representations of herself provides a metaphor for her unstable identity:

> Claire now could create a matryoshka of just herself—Claire within Claire within Claire within Claire. During the hearing, all these different Claires, who just happened to look alike, seemed to rest inside her, so that every argument, no matter how contradictory, found sympathy. Each time she thought she had reached the last Claire, the true and solid one, she was proved wrong. She couldn't find her own core [Waldman 2011: 302].

Ultimately, of course, Claire gives in under the pressure of her own trauma and decides to turn against Khan's design—even though she had been its most vocal supporter through most of the novel. The crucial moment comes when, during an intense one-to-one discussion, Khan evokes the death of her husband and, while not meaning to offend Claire, compares his own victimization with her husband's tragic death. The personal, emotional strain is too much for Claire, who finally decides to reverse her alliance and campaign for Khan to retract his submission. Therefore, while Sean and Claire are clearly drawn as antithetical, they acquiesce to fear, under the pressure of personal trauma, in similar ways, and ultimately even Claire is seeking a clear agenda and purpose.

Waldman is eager to dramatize the complexity of both characters' actions and emotions, and another key trait that they share is that they are both subject to myriad external pressures which effect their experiences of trauma and grief. This becomes another key strategy in building in the internal complexities of a response that, on the surface is or becomes unilateral. It also relates closely to the phenomenon of aggregated trauma, as theorized by Irene Kacandes and discussed earlier in relation to *In the Shadow of No Towers* and *The Reluctant Fundamentalist*. Here, the aggregation of trauma is refashioned as an aggregation of frustration, fear, anger and helplessness. Sean is characterized as the less successful younger brother who has struggled with alcohol and been unable to emulate his brother or father's success as a fireman. Claire is wealthy and independent, thanks to her inheritance, but without direction; her "future was gilded blankness," and her fear of a rudderless existence increases her personal investment in the memorial and memorial debate. In both cases, the identity crises the characters experience at the height of the memorial dispute are not solely down to issues raised by this alone, and the novel continually stresses that these external pressures, unique to the individuals, complicate their responses.

Conclusion

The meta-fictionality of *The Submission* allows us to reflect back on some of the previous texts that we've examined. Indeed, one of the most obvious suggestions the novel makes is that the fictional memorial design is being judged much less than the designer himself, and that this is fundamentally wrong. The implication of this is that we, as readers, are to judge the novel and not the novelist, and this is, perhaps, a luxury that many of the novelists we've discussed in previous chapters have not been afforded. Writers such as Don DeLillo, Cormac McCarthy, Jay McInerney and Art Spiegelman are among the most celebrated American literary authors, and their previous work and profiles will have inevitably played a role in the way their 9/11 novels have been interpreted. Ironically, in spite of Waldman's rhetoric, and despite the fact that *The Submission* is her first novel, critics have relied on biographical details in interpreting the novel. As we have seen, the fact that Waldman was a staff reporter for the *New York Times* was certainly jumped on by reviewers who have been positive and negative about the novel. Lorentzen's *London Review of Books* review criticizes Waldman for the way she has "so thoroughly internalized the paper's worldview that she can't see things any other way"; and while it at least tries to locate its criticism in the text itself, it remains ironic that it is so preoccupied with biographical details in its assessment of the novel—this is, after all, what the novel warns against. Whatever merit we see or do not see in the style of the novel, its journalistic aspects are obvious, and clearly its schematic panorama of American society allows it to bring out the complexities and differences that have been excluded from the narratives of private trauma and that were sublimated by the Bush Doctrine and clash of civilizations discourse. It certainly also shares some of the documentary-style techniques and attention to detail that enable Eggers' *Zeitoun* to respond to the limitations of the early 9/11 novels.

In its representation of Islam, its representation of the conflicted inner worlds of key characters and its rhetoric of multidirectionality, *The Submission* goes to great lengths to dramatize the post–9/11 conflictedness that affected all spheres of society. Waldman's novel also ultimately suggests that the conflictedness remains unresolved, as each of the key narrative strands ends negatively. Khan is disillusioned with his own country, Asma is killed, Claire gives in to intolerance, and Sean is on the brink of being disowned by his family. However, while the conflictedness that *The Submission* dramatizes remains unresolved, we can see an evolution in *The Reluctant Fundamentalist*, *Netherland* and

Waldman's novel that amounts to a growing awareness or consciousness of it, and an increasing politicization. Additionally, despite the negative conclusions of these key narrative strands, as noted previously, the novel's underlying rhetorical drive advocates a multidirectional memory of 9/11.

Conclusion

I began by discussing what I have described as post–9/11 conflictedness and disorientation by discussing a current television program, *Homeland*, and I will conclude here by returning to television and to a program that provided the very first narrative response to 9/11. Indeed, one of the most notable and revealing cultural responses of the immediate post–9/11 era came from NBC's prime-time political drama *The West Wing* (1999–2007). As an established, well-loved dramatic imagining of an alternative liberal, democratic White House, the program and its creator/writer Aaron Sorkin perhaps felt obliged to respond. They did so with remarkable efficiency, rushing "Isaac and Ishmael" into production for airing on October 3, 2001, just three weeks after the attacks. But as the fictional President Bartlett and his staff were conceived of as completely antithetical to the G.W. Bush White House, the rubric they might use to engage with 9/11 became the subject of much speculation as soon as the episode was announced. Would *The West Wing* deviate from the rhetoric of the real White House? How would it handle such a difficult task? The episode begins with the cast addressing the audience out of character, and they make it clear that this is a special episode which does not fit with the continuity of the award-winning series; it is referred to by Bradley Whitford (who plays Deputy Chief of Staff Josh Lyman) as a "storytelling aberration." They also make it clear that the purpose and function of the episode will be didactic. The premise is that the White House staffers are stuck in the canteen with a group of "Presidential Classroom" high school students because the White House is experiencing a lock down or "crash" due to an unspecified security threat. As the students begin to ask questions, such as "Why do they want to kill us?" echoing the same question that President Bush had addressed just days before to a joint session of Congress, the members of the White House staff begin giving lessons to the students on terrorism and "Islamic extremism" in turn. There has been much discussion, debate and criticism of the lessons that the fictional White House staff members give and the statements they make; for example, Josh Lyman's formulation that "Islamic extremism is to Islam as the KKK is to Christianity," or President Bartlett's declaration to the school group: "We don't need martyrs right now. We need heroes. A hero would die for his country, but he'd much rather live for it." Essentially, though, America is repeatedly applauded for its policy of "freedom" while a brief history of the evils of "Islamic extremism" (containing many of the base truisms of the time) is constructed over the course of the episode. Lynn Spigel summarizes much of the retrospective criticism of the episode, stating that in "Isaac and Ishmael, *The West Wing* performs some of the fundamental precepts of contemporary Orientalism." Indeed, while the staffers are ostensibly trying to promote "pluralism" and go to great pains to make a distinction between "Islam" and "Islamic extremism," they certainly work through some sweeping generalizations about Islam and construct a very one-dimensional history of it. Furthermore, while it is undoubtedly the case that the liberal or democratic ideological base that the show is built upon collapses, and the episode fails, as Spigel states, to open any "real engagement with Islam, the ethics of U.S. international policy or the consequences of the then-impending bomb strikes," it is perhaps useful to also consider the "conflictedness" that pervades this episode.

To a certain extent, this may surreptitiously emanate from the ideological difficulty the show had in ultimately upholding the position of the Bush White House, but ultimately it is an embodiment of the paradigm of continuity and discontinuity. As Spigel points out, the episode is flagrant in "signalling its utter discontinuity from the now routinely serialized/cumulative narrative structure of contemporary prime-time 'quality genres.'" Every aspect of this episode marks it as being separate from the ordinary—the direct address from the cast out of character, the "public service announcement" aesthetics (at one point a phone number is provided for viewers to call to make donations for rescue workers), the premise of a locked down White House, and, most obviously, the overtly didactic function which signals an acknowledgment that an epochal moment has occurred and we must attempt to come to terms with a new world order. This is, again, explicitly reinforced by the specific designation of the episode as a "storytelling aberration." However, the performance of the lessons pulls in precisely the opposite direction, groping for historical references and contexts at every turn, almost desperate to find points of meaningful reference, and repeatedly relying on the conceit of America as an unbreakable embodiment of freedom and democracy. Toby Ziegler states at one point, "When you think of Afghanistan think of Poland, when you think of the Taliban think of the Nazis, when you think of the citizens of Afghanistan think of Jews in concentration camps." When asked to assert his claim that terrorism has "100 percent fail rate," Rob Lowe's Sam Seaborne states, "What about the IRA? The Brits are still there, the Protestants are still there; the Basque extremists have been staging terrorist attacks in Spain for decades with no results; from the Red Brigade left wing of the sixties and seventies, the Bader Meinhoff gang to the Weathermen." When asked to locate the "first act of terrorism, Zeigler points to the history of "Islamic Extremism": "What was the first act of terrorism? In the 11th century secret followers of Hasan ibn-al-Sabbah, who were taught to believe in nothing and dare all, carried out very swift and treacherous murders of fellow Muslims in a state of religious ecstasy." The point here, though, is that the impulse is to provide context, narrative and history to the current crisis, and this impulse is completely at odds with the formal signifiers of the episode. Furthermore, when asked "what should we do now," the staffers emphatically echo the "return to normal life" strand of President Bush's own conflicted rhetoric.

Returning now to *Homeland*, thirteen years later, we can see that in the conflictedness that characterizes the key protagonists, Carrie and Brody, there is an evident line of continuity from the conflicted rhetoric of *The West Wing*'s "Isaac and Ishmael." This gives us a clear idea of how prevalent and enduring this post–9/11 condition is. The difference, of course, is that "Isaac and Ishmael" reveals its fundamental conflictedness in its underlying rhetoric—its urgent need to declare epoch and rupture while simultaneously groping for context and historical antecedents— while *Homeland* is, to a large extent, a story about this conflictedness. The program's creators have developed two characters who embody this condition, so while *Homeland* is still working through the complexities of this issue, it is doing it self-consciously and with a much more politicized lens.

This jump from *The West Wing* to *Homeland* provides a snapshot of the evolution we get in detail in these key instances of the 9/11 novel that the previous chapters have worked through. It has been my contention that this body of 9/11 novels, when examined as documents or artifacts, unravel this conflictedness in key ways, providing a reflection of the ways in which society (in particular, American society) has negotiated this struggle over the last decade. In the opening two chapters we have seen the ways in which the early representations, *In the Shadow of No Towers*, *Extremely Loud and Incredibly Close* and *Windows on the World*, were characterized by an unresolvable conflict between the imperatives to honor and find appropriate stylistic registers for private traumas, and to build in historical and transnational narratives. Simultaneously, these texts also negotiate the conflicted rhetoric of the Bush administration: the declaration of a new world order, presented in the aesthetics and language of nostalgia. We have seen how, in what have been identified as the "domestic novels" of 9/11, *Falling Man*, *The Good Life* and *The Emperor's Children*, the emphasis on trauma finds a real locus in the American domestic sphere; but while these novels move away from any kind of meaningful political or transnational gesturing, they share a suggestive or "seismographic" restoration of narrative equilibrium that evokes a return to "normal life." This again marks a real narrative conflict in the thematic emphasis on trauma and rupture coexisting with plots that suggest this restoration of equilibrium. We have seen how Cormac McCarthy's *The Road* marks the culmination of this trend of indirect or symbolic discussions of 9/11—which was also found in the 2006 cinematic representations of the attacks, *United 93* and *World Trade Center*—while also simultaneously exhausting this possibility, signaling a shift in the cultural representation of 9/11. Indeed, *The Road*'s poetic resonance with Hurricane Katrina both strengthens the character of its stark aesthetic and reinforces the suggestion that a new, directly politicized approach to 9/11 is necessary. In the third section we turned to the first of these politicized, post–Katrina novels, *The Reluctant Fundamentalist*, and examined the way this novel's unique first world national allegory suggests that preexisting issues are latent in America's national response to 9/11. I have argued that this narrative of continuity converges with the traumatic narrative of the text, reaching some points of narrative reconciliation in the way that the emphasis on trauma does not obscure the politics of the novel. The penultimate chapter, which examined Joseph O'Neil's *Netherland*, argued that this text is the first self-conscious 9/11 novel in that it is meta-fictionally aware of the existing tropes and trends in 9/11 fiction. While *Netherland* responds to the preoccupation with "marriage and relationships," the lack of convincing representations of otherness, and inability of early 9/11 fiction to directly confront the attacks, it also maintains a conspicuous balance in its dynamic between the trauma that characters experience and the politics of the novel, and, as in *The Reluctant Fundamentalist*, to a certain extent this narrative and thematic tension is reconciled. In the final chapter I have argued that Amy Waldman's highly politicized novel directly confronts American society's condition of post–9/11 conflictedness and re-animates the complex and nuanced binaries that the Bush Doctrine and clash of civilizations rhetoric sublimated, but which, hopefully, have been brought out in my readings of this group of novels. Waldman's novel, I argue, is a counter-narrative to the Bush Doctrine and, like this group of novels as a whole, constructs a more accurate reflection of the fraught American national mood after 9/11.

Waldman's novel is also notable for including a final chapter set roughly 20 years in the future and has a strange point of convergence with Jennifer Egan's celebrated novel from the same year, *A Visit from the Goon Squad* (2011). Egan's novel also features a final chapter set in the future (Egan's final chapter is set in 2020, so not quite as distant as Waldman's) and which also has an important reference to the memorialization of 9/11 in its conception of a site called "The Footprint," where Ground Zero used to be. The driving theme of *A Visit from the Goon Squad* is decline, and while this is generally in relation to the collection of connected individual characters that populate the novel, it has also been identified as a wider, national decline. Pankaj Mishra writes that "Egan commemorates not only the fading of a cultural glory but also of the economic and political supremacy that underpinned it," and that an "almost mystical conviction of individual and collective failure pervades" the novel (Mishra 2011: 30). This description of Egan's novel also seems appropriate for Waldman's final chapter, set in the future. Khan has been failed by his country—America; Claire has failed to live up to her pretenses of liberalism and tolerance; Ansa has been killed during the poisonous memorial hysteria; and Sean has failed to act with the sensitivity and empathy of which he is clearly capable. The key characters' failures equate to the "collective failure" that Mishra locates in *A Visit from the Goon Squad*. Does this indicate that a new facet to the way we will remember 9/11 might be as a moment that initiated or accelerated American national decline? This, perhaps, will be the subject of another study, but the post–9/11 conflictedness charted here certainly may be a vital element of this thesis—even if the later 9/11 novels offer points of convergence between the binaries of 9/11. Indeed, one division in American society that pre-dates 9/11 has certainly been unprecedented in its post–9/11 polarization of the nation: the divide between Republican and Democrat, red and blue, liberal and conservative. As we have seen, this is one of the underlying tensions in the 9/11 novel, and the extent to which 9/11 will be remembered as the moment when this division was made untenable may be another key point of enquiry in the future.

Notes

1. The *New York Times* "Portraits of Grief" ran from September to December 2001 and included over 1800 short glimpses into the lives of the victims of the 9/11 attacks. Editor Janny Scott described them as "informal and impressionistic, often centered on a single story or idiosyncratic detail. They were not intended to recount a person's résumé, but rather to give a snapshot of each victim's personality, of a life lived. And they were democratic; executive vice presidents and battalion chiefs appeared alongside food handlers and janitors."
2. One of the clearest examples of this came at the September 20 State of the Union Address when President Bush asked the nation for its "continued participation and confidence in the American economy." This full speech is available at http://www.washingtonpost.com/wp-srv/nation/specials/attacked/transcripts/bush_092701.html.
3. The National Security Strategy of September 2002 features chapters such as "Strengthen Alliances to Defeat Global Terrorism and Work to Prevent Attacks Against Us and Our Friends" and "Prevent Our Enemies from Threatening Us, Our Allies, and Our Friends with Weapons of Mass Destruction." The full document is available at the United States Department of State website: http://www.state.gov/documents/organization/63562.pdf.
4. Art Speigelman's statement "Go out and shop" refers to an infamous and mythological statement that actually has its origins in a speech he made in Chicago on September 27, 2001: "Get on board. Do your business around the country. Fly and enjoy America's great destination spots. Go down to Disney World in Florida, take your families and enjoy life the way we want it to be enjoyed." Full transcript available at http://www.washingtonpost.com/wp-srv/nation/specials/attacked/transcripts/bushaddress_092001.html.
5. Susan Sontag was widely criticized for her *New Yorker* article, composed two weeks after the attacks. Sontag wrote, "The disconnect between last Tuesday's monstrous dose of reality and self-righteous drivel and outrageous deceptions being peddled by public figures and TV commentators is startling, depressing. The voices licensed to follow the event seem to have joined together in a campaign to infantilize the public. Where is the acknowledgment that this was not a 'cowardly' attack on 'civilization' or 'liberty' or 'humanity' or 'the free world,' but an attack on the world's self-proclaimed superpower, undertaken as a consequence of specific American alliances and actions." Sontag's article is available here: http://www.newyorker.com/archive/2001/09/24/010924ta_talk_wtc.
6. Chalmers Johnson's *Blowback*, originally published before 9/11, argues that there are and will be significant consequences for American imperialism. Johnson's preface to the post–9/11 second edition of *Blowback* (2002) suggests that President Bush's claim that the attacks were out of the blue was a way of evading responsibility for the "blowback that America's imperial projects have generated." Chalmers Johnson, *Blowback* (London: Time Warner, 2002).

7. The book jacket sleeves for the paperback version of *A Disorder Peculiar to the Country* and the hardcover release of *The Good Life* both feature images of the World Trade Center towers casting shadows of a man and woman.

8. Susan Faludi's account of George Bush and John Kerry's posturing as cowboys and "guardians of the homestead" is most focused in her chapter "President of the Wild Frontier" (pp. 146–164) in *The Terror Dream: What 9/11 Revealed About America* (2008). In this chapter she details the frequent appearances during the 2004 presidential campaign of the candidates dressed as cowboys or sporting the camouflage of hunters, carrying guns.

Bibliography

Abel, Marco. "Don DeLillo's 'In the Ruins of the Future': Literature, Images and the Rhetoric of Seeing 9/11." *PMLA* 118.5 (October 2003): 1236–1250.
Abel, Stephen. "Moments of Truth." *Times Literary Supplement* (May 18, 2007): 21–22.
Agamben, Georgio, trans., and Kevin Attell. *State of Exception*. Chicago: University of Chicago Press, 2005.
Ahmad, Aijaz. "Jameson's Rhetoric of Otherness and the 'National Allegory.'" *Social Text* 17 (Autumn 1987): 3–25.
Ahmed, Kamal Vulliamy, Peter Beaumont, Gabby Hinsliff. "Worlds Apart in War." *The Observer*, February 16, 2003, "Focus" section.
Amis, Martin. *The Second Plane*. London: Jonathan Cape, 2008.
Anthony, Andrew. "Perfect Delivery." *The Observer*, September 7, 2008, available at http://www.guardian.co.uk/books/2008/sep/07/celebrity (accessed 05/09/12).
Atchison, S. Todd. "'Why I Am Writing from Where You Are Not': Absence and Presence in Jonathan Safran Foer's *Extremely Loud and Incredibly Close*." *Journal of Postcolonial Writing Summer* 46.4 (2010): 360–368.
Auster, Paul. *Man in the Dark*. London: Faber, 2009.
Baer, Ulrich, ed. *110 Stories: New York Writes After September 11*. New York: New York University Press, 2002.
Baudrillard, Jean. *The Spirit of Terrorism*. New York: Verso, 2002.
Billias, Nancy, ed. *Territories of Evil*. Amsterdam: Rodopi, 2008.
Bradley, Arthur, and Andrew Tate. *The New Atheist Novel: Fiction, Philosophy and Polemic After 9/11*. London: Continuum, 2010.
Bradshaw, Peter. "Review of *United 93*." *The Guardian*, June 2, 2006, available at http://www.guardian.co.uk/culture/2006/jun/02/1 (accessed 05/09/01).
Bragard, Veronique, Chris Dony, Warren Rosenberg. *Portraying 9/11: Essays on Representations in Comics, Literature, Film and Theater*. Jefferson, NC: McFarland, 2011.
Brigand, Alain. "Producer *11'09'01*." Artificial Eye, 2002 (DVD).
Cañadas, Ivan. "Spike Lee's 'Uniquely American [Di]vision': Race and Class in *25th Hour*." *Bright Lights Film Journal* 63 (February 2009), available at http://www.brightlightsfilm.com/63/63spikelee.php (accessed 05/09/01).
Cant, John. In *Bloom's Modern Critical Views: Cormac McCarthy*, edited by Harold Bloom. New York: Infobase, 2009.
Carlsten, Jenny. "Containing Their Rage: Anger and the Liberal Cinema." *Cinephile* 3.1 (Spring/Summer 2007): 5–11.
Caruth, Cathy. *Unclaimed Experience: Trauma, Narrative, and History*. London: Johns Hopkins University Press, 1996.
———, ed. *Trauma: Explorations in Memory*. Baltimore: Johns Hopkins University Press, 1995.

Bibliography

Chabon, Michael. "After the Apocalypse." *The New York Review of Books* (February 15, 2007): 26-27.
Chaudhuri, Amit. "Not Entirely Like Me." *London Review of Books* (October 4, 2007): 25-26.
Chomsky, Noam. "Understanding the Bush Doctrine." *Information Clearing House*, October 2, 2004, available at http://www.chomsky.info/articles.htm.
Claybaugh, Amanda. "Life and Death Stuff." *London Review of Books* (October 19, 2006): 15-16.
Conrad, Peter. "The Presumption of Art." *The Observer*, September 8, 2010, available at http://www.guardian.co.uk/world/2002/sep/08/september11.georgebush (accessed 05/09/01).
Cooper, Lydia. "Cormac McCarthy's *The Road* as Apocalyptic Grail Narrative." *Studies in the Novel* 43.2 (2011): 218-236.
Craps, Stef. "Conjuring Trauma: The Naudet Brothers' 9/11 Documentary." *Canadian Review of American Studies* 37.2 (Summer 2007): 183-199.
Crownshaw, Richard. "Deterritorializing the 'Homeland' in American Studies and American Fiction After 9/11." *Journal of American Studies* 45.4 (2011): 757-776.
Culverwell, Ezekiel. Quoted in Eifion Evans, "The Puritan Use of Imagination." *A Quarterly Journal for Church Leadership* 10 (2001): 46-84.
Däwes, Birgit. "Celluloid Recoveries: Cinematic Transformations of 'Ground Zero.'" In *Transnational American Memories*, edited by Udo J. Hebel, 285-309. New York: Walter de Gruyter.
———. "On Contested Ground (Zero): Literature and the Transnational Challenge of Remembering 9/11." *American Studies* 52.4 (2007): 517-543.
DeLillo, Don. "In the Ruins of the Future." *Harpers*, December 2001, pp. 33-40.
———. Interview in *Guernica*, July 2007, available at www.guernicamag.com/interviews/373/intensity_of_a_plot/ (accessed 05/09/01).
———. Interview in *Die Zeit*, October 11, 2007, available at http://www.zeit.de/2007/42/Don-DeLillo-Interview (accessed 05/09/01).
———. "Looking at Meinhoff." *The Guardian*, August 17, 2002, available at http://www.guardian.co.uk/books/2002/aug/17/fiction.originalwriting (accessed 05/09/01).
———. *Mao II*. London: Vintage, 1991.
Durand, Alain-Philippe. "Beyond the Extreme: Frédéric Beigbeder's *Windows on the World*." In *Novels of the Contemporary Extreme*, edited by Naomi Mandel and Alain-Philippe Durand, 109-120. London: Continuum, 2006.
Duvall, John, and Robert Marzec. "Narrating 9/11." *Modern Fiction Studies* 57.3 (2011): 381-400.
Edkins, Jenny. "Forget Trauma? Responses to September 11." *International Relations* 16.2 (Summer 2002): 244-256.
Eggers, Dave. *Zeitoun*. New York: Vintage, 2009.
Erikson, Kai. "Notes on Trauma and Community." In *Trauma: Explorations in Memory*, edited by Cathy Caruth, 183-199. Baltimore: Johns Hopkins University Press, 1995.
Esperitu, Karen. "'Putting Grief into Boxes': Trauma and the Crisis of Democracy in Art Spiegelman's *In the Shadow of No Towers*." *The Review of Education, Pedagogy, and Cultural Studies* 28.2 (Spring 2006): 179-201.
Faludi, Susan. *The Terror Dream: What 9/11 Revealed About America*. London: Atlantic, 2007.
French, Phillip. "United 93." *The Observer*, June 4, 2006, available at http://www.guardian.co.uk/film/2006/jun/04/philipfrench (accessed 05/09/01).
Frost, Laura. "*Falling Man*'s Precious Balance." *The American Prospect* online, available at http://www.prospect.org/cs/articles?article=falling_mans_precarious_balance (accessed 05/09/01).
———. "Still Life: 9/11's Falling Bodies." In *Literature After 9/11*, edited by Ann Keniston and Jeanne Follansbee Quinn, 181-20. London: Routledge, 2007.

Frye, Steven. *Understanding Cormac McCarthy*. Columbia: University of South Carolina Press, 2009.
Garner, Dwight. "The Ashes." *The New York Times*, May 18, 2008, available at http://www.nytimes.com/2008/05//books/review/Garner-t.html?scp=4&sq=The+Ashes&st=nyt (accessed 05/09/01).
Gauthier, Tim. "9/11, Image Control, and the Graphic Narrative: Spiegelman, Rehr, Torres." *Journal of Postcolonial Writing* Summer 46.4 (2010): 370–379.
Gessen, Keith. "Horror Tour." *The New York Review of Books* (September 22, 2005): 68–72.
Gilbey, Ryan. "*25th Hour*." *Sight and Sound* (March 2003): 58.
Glejzer, Richard. "Art Spiegelman and the Persistence of Trauma." In *Literature After 9/11*, edited by Ann Keniston and Jeanne Follansbee Quinn, 98–119. London: Routledge, 2007.
Goldman, Derek. "What Was That Unforgettable Line? Remembrances from the Rubbleheap." *South Atlantic Quarterly* 103.4 (Winter 2004): 46–55.
Grandin, Greg. "Review of *Zeitoun*." *London Review of Books* (January 6, 2011).
Gray, Richard. *After the Fall: American Literature Since 9/11*. Chichester: Wiley-Blackwell, 2011.
———. "Open Doors, Closed Minds: American Prose Writing at a Time of Crisis." *American Literary History* 21.1 (Spring 2009): 129–150.
Greenberg, Judith. "Wounded New York." In *Trauma at Home: After 9/11*, edited by Judith Greenberg, 21–38. Lincoln: University of Nebraska Press, 2003.
———, ed. *Trauma at Home: After 9/11*. Lincoln: University of Nebraska Press, 2003.
Greif, Mark. "Alzheimer's America." *London Review of Books* (July 5, 2007): 19–20.
Gupta, Suman. *Globalization and Literature*. Cambridge: Polity, 2009.
Hardt, Michael, and Antonio Negri. *Multitude*. London: Penguin, 2004.
Hartnell, Anna. "Moving Through America: Race, Place and Resistance in Mohsin Hamid's *The Reluctant Fundamentalist*." *Journal of Postcolonial Writing* Summer 46.4 (2010): 337–348.
Hauerwas, Stanley, and Frank Lentricchia, eds. *Dissent from the Homeland: Essays After 9/11*. Durham: Duke University Press, 2003.
Hebel, Udo J., ed. *Transnational American Memories*. New York: Walter de Gruyter, 2009.
Herman, Judith Lewis. *Trauma and Recovery*. New York: Basic Books, 1992.
Hirsch, Marianne. "I Took Pictures: September 2001 and Beyond." In *Trauma at Home: After 9/11*, edited by Judith Greenberg, 69–86. London: University of Nebraska Press, 2003.
Hoberman, J. "Unquiet Americans." *Sight and Sound* (October 2006): 21–23.
Hodges, Adam. *The War on Terror Narrative: Discourse and Intertextuality in the Construction and Contestation of Sociopolitical Reality*. Oxford: Oxford University Press, 2011.
Hollinghurst, Alan. "Underground Men." *The New York Review of Books* (September 25, 2008): 54–56.
Holloway, David. *9/11 and the War on Terror*. Edinburgh: Edinburgh University Press, 2008.
Hornung, Alfred. "Terrorist Violence and Transnational Memory: Jonathan Safran Foer and Don DeLillo." *Transnational American Memories*, edited by Eudo J. Hebel, 171–183. New York: Walter de Gruyter.
Houen, Alex. "Novel Spaces and Taking Place(s) in the Wake of September 11." *Studies in the Novel* 36.3 (Fall 2004): 419–437.
———. *Terrorism in Modern Literature*. Oxford: Oxford University Press, 2002.
Huehls, Mitchum. "Foer, Spiegelman, and 9/11's Timely Traumas." In *Literature After 9/11*, edited by Ann Kenniston and Jeanne Follansbee Quinn, 43–59. London: Routledge, 2007.

———. *Qualified Hope: A Postmodern Politics of Time*. Columbus: Ohio State University Press, 2009.
Huntington, Samuel P. *The Clash of Civilizations and the Remaking of World Order*. London: Free, 2002.
James, C.L.R. *Beyond a Boundary*. London: Serpent's Tail, 1994.
Jameson, Frederic. "The Dialectics of Disaster." In *Dissent from the Homeland: Essays After 9/11*, edited Stanley Hauerwas and Farnk Lentricchia, 55–62. Durham: Duke University Press, 2003.
———. "Third-World Literature in the Era of Multinational Capitalism." *Social Text* 15 (Autumn 1986): 65–88.
Johnson, Chalmers. *Blowback*. London: Time Warner, 2002.
Kacandes, Irene. "9/11/01=1/27/01: The Changed Posttraumatic Self." In *Trauma at Home: After 9/11*, edited by Judith Greenberg, 168–183. Lincoln: University of Nebraska Press, 2003.
Kakutani, Michiko. "A Boy's Epic Quest, Borough by Borough." *The New York Times*, March 22, 2005, available at http://www.nytimes.com/2005/03/22/books/22kaku.html?scp=31&sq=jonathan+safran+foer&st=nyt (accessed 05/09/01).
Kalfus, Ken. *A Disorder Peculiar to the Country*. New York: Ecco, 2006.
Kaplan, E. Ann. "A Camera and a Catastrophe: Reflections on Trauma and the Twin Towers." In *Trauma at Home: After 9/11*, edited by Judith Greenberg, 95–106. Lincoln: University of Nebraska Press, 2003.
———. *Trauma Culture*. New Brunswick: Rutgers University Press, 2005.
Kauffman, Linda S. "The Wake of Terror: Don DeLillo's 'In the Ruins of the Future,' 'Baader Meinhoff' and *Falling Man*." *Modern Fiction Studies* 54.2 (Summer 2008): 353–377.
Kazdin, Cole. "Remember Terror Sex." *Salon*, September 11, 2002, available at http://www.salon.com/sex/feature/2002/09/11/terror_2 (accessed 05/09/01).
———. "Sex in a Time of Terror." *Salon*, September 21, 2001, available at http://www.salon.com/sex/feature/2001/09/21/terror (accessed 05/09/01).
Kellner, Douglas. *Cinema Wars: Hollywood Film and Politics in the Bush-Cheney Era*. Chichester: Wiley-Blackwell, 2010.
Kelly, Alison. "Words Fail Me: Literary Reaction to 9/11." *21: A Journal of Contemporary and Innovative Fiction* 1 (Autumn/Winter 2008–09): 49–81.
Kendrick, James. "Representing the Unrepresentable: 9/11 on Film and Television." In *Why We Fought: America's Wars in Film and History*, edited by Peter C. Rollins and John E. O'Connor, 511–527. Lexington: University of Kentucky Press, 2008.
Keniston, Ann, and Jeanne Follansbee Quinn, eds. *Literature After 9/11*. London: Routledge, 2007.
Kerr, Sarah. "In the Terror House of Mirrors." *The New York Review of Books* (October 11, 2007): 22–24.
Kirn, Walter. "*Extremely Loud and Incredibly Close*: Everything Is Included." *The New York Times*, April 3, 2005, available at http://www.nytimes.com/2005/04/03/books/review/0403cover-kirn.html?scp=36&sq=jonathan+safran+foer&st=nyt (accessed 05/09/01).
Kunkel, Benjamin. "Men in White." *London Review of Books* (July 17, 2008): 20–22.
Kunsa, Ashley. "'Maps of the World in Its Becoming': Post-Apocalyptic Naming in Cormac McCarthy's *The Road*." *Journal of Modern Literature* 33.1 (2009): 57–74.
Lasdun, James. "The Empire Strikes Back." *The Guardian*, March 3, 2007, available at http://www.guardian.co.uk/books/2007/mar/03/featuresreviews.guardianreview20.
LeSalle, Mark. "Best Movies of the Decade." *The San Francisco Chronicle*, April 3, 2009.
Lorentzen, Christian. "Shave for Them." *London Review of Books* (September 22, 2011): 28–29.
Lubin, Orly. "Masked Power: An Encounter with the Social Body in the Flesh." In *Trauma*

at Home: After 9/11, edited by Judith Greenberg, 124–131. Lincoln: University of Nebraska Press, 2003.
Marqusee, Mike. *Anyone but England*. London: Verso, 1994.
Mason, Wyatt. "Like Beavers." *London Review of Books* (June 2, 2005).
McCarthy, Cormac. *The Road*. London: Picador, 2006.
McCrum, Robert. "The Need for Novelists." *The Observer*, September 23, 2001.
McEwan, Ian. "Only Love and Then Oblivion." *The Guardian*, September 15, 2001, available at http://www.guardian.co.uk/world/2001/sep/15/september11.politicsphilosophy andsociety2 (accessed 05/09/01).
———. *Saturday*. London: Vintage, 2005.
McGrath, Patrick. *Ghost Town*. London: Bloomsbury, 2005.
———. "Pen in One Hand, Cricket Bat in the Other." *The New York Times*, May 17, 2008, available at http://www.nytimes.com/2008/05/17/books/17cric.html?scp=1&sq=pen+ in+one+hand+cricket+bat+in+the+other&st=nyt (accessed 05/09/01).
McGuire, Kelly. "The Art of Disorientation." *Enculturation* online journal available at http://enculturation.gmu.edu/6.2/mcguire (accessed 05/09/01).
McInerney, Jay. "Brightness Falls." *The Guardian*, September 15, 2001, available at http://www.guardian.co.uk/books/2001/sep/15/september11.usa1 (accessed 05/09/01).
———. Interview with author, available at Random House at http://www.randomhouse.com/catalog/display.pperl?isbn=9780375725456&view=auqa (accessed 05/09/01).
———. "The Uses of Invention." *The Guardian*, September 17, 2005, available at http://www.guardian.co.uk/books/2005/sep/17/fiction.vsnaipaul last accessed 22/07/2010 (accessed 05/09/01).
Melnick, Jeffrey. *9/11 Culture*. Oxford: Wiley-Blackwell, 2009.
Menand, Louis. "The Earthquake: A Manhattan Affair." *The New Yorker*, February 6, 2006, available at http://www.newyorker.com/archive/2006/02/06/060206crbo_ books1 (accessed 07/22/10).
Millard, Kenneth. *Contemporary American Fiction*. Oxford: Oxford University Press, 2000.
Millbank, John. "Sovereignty." In *Dissent from the Homeland: Essays After 9/11*, edited by Stanley Hauerwas and Frank Lentricchia, 63–82. Durham: Duke University Press, 2003.
Miller, Cheryl. "9/11 and the Novelists." *Commentary* (December 2008): 32–35.
Mishra, Pankaj. "The End of Innocence." *The Guardian*, May 19, 2007, Saturday Review, pp. 4–8.
———. "Modernity's Undoing." *London Review of Books* (March 31, 2011): 27–30.
Morley, Catherine. "'How Do We Write About This?' The Domestic and the Global in the Post-9/11 Novel." *Journal of American Studies* 45.4 (2011): 717–731.
Moss, Stephen. "Not Just Cricket." *Times Literary Supplement*, May 23, 2008.
Mullins, Mathew. "Boroughs and Neighbours: Traumatic Solidarity in Jonathan Safran Foer's *Extremely Loud and Incredibly Close*." *Papers on Language and Literature* 45.3 (Summer 2009): 298–323.
Nidday, Jackson, A. "A Rhetoric of Trauma in 9/11 Stories: A Critical Reading of Ulrich Baer's *110 Stories*." *War, Literature and the Arts* 16.1 (2004): 59–76.
Oates, Joyce Carol. "Dimming the Lights." *The New York Review of Books* (April 6, 2006): 33–36.
———. "Men Without Qualities." *The New York Review of Books* (October 5, 2006): 29–31.
O'Brien, Geoffrey. "Is It All Just a Dream." *The New York Review of Books* (August 12, 2004): 17–19.
O'Hagan, Andrew. "Racing Against Reality." *The New York Review of Books* (June 28, 2007): 4–8.
O'Neil, Joseph. "Bowling Alone." *The Atlantic*, October 2007, available at http://www.the atlantic.com/magazine/archive/2007/10/bowling-alone/6185 (accessed 05/09/01).

Bibliography

Özcan, Ceylan. "Oliver Stone's *World Trade Center* as a Representation of the Collective Trauma of 9/11." *Journal of Faculty of Letters* 25.2 (December 2008): 205-221.
Penner, D'ann R. "Assault Rifles, Separated Families, and Murder in Their Eyes: Unasked Questions After Hurricane Katrina." *Journal of American Studies* 44.3 (2010): 573-599.
Powers, Scott M. "Post-Modern Narratives of Evil and 9/11: The Case of Frédéric Beigbeder." In *Territories of Evil*, edited by Nancy Billias, 133-150. Amsterdam: Rodopi, 2008.
Rajagopal, Arvind. "America and Its Others." *Interventions* 6.3 (Autumn 2004): 317-329.
Rich, B. Ruby. "Out of the Rubble." *Sight and Sound* (October 2006): 14-18.
Rothberg, Michael. "A Failure of the Imagination: Diagnosing the Post-9/11 Novel: A Response to Richard Gray." *American Literary History* 21.1 (Spring 2009): 129-150.
———. *Multidirectional Memory: Remembering the Holocaust in the Age of Decolonization.* Stanford: Stanford University Press, 2009.
———. "Seeing Terror, Feeling Art: Public and Private in Post-9/11 Literature." In *Literature After 9/11*, edited by Ann Kenniston and Jeanne Follansbee Quinn, 123-141. London: Routledge, 2007.
———. "'There Is No Poetry in This': Writing, Trauma, and Home." *Trauma at Home: After 9/11*, edited by Judith Greenberg, 147-157. Lincoln: University of Nebraska Press, 2003.
Shamsie, Kamila. "Review of *The Submission*." *The Guardian*, August 24, 2011, available at http://www.theguardian.com/books/2011/aug/24/the-submission-amy-waldman-review.
Shulan, Michael, Gilles Peress, Alice Rose George, and Charles Taub, eds. *Here Is New York: A Democracy of Photographs*. New York: Scalo, 2002.
Simpson, David. *9/11: The Culture of Commemoration*. Chicago: University of Chicago Press, 2006.
———. "Telling It Like It Isn't." In *Literature After 9/11*, edited by Ann Kenniston and Jeanne Follansbee Quinn, 209-223. London: Routledge, 2007.
Smith, Jordan Rendall. "9/11 TragiComix: Allegories of National Trauma in Art Spiegelman's *In the Shadow of No Towers*." *Shift* 1 (2009), available at http://www.shiftjournal.org/archives.htm Accessed 05/09/01.
Smith, Zadie. "Two Paths for the Novel." *The New York Review of Books* (November 20, 2008).
Sontag, Susan. *Regarding the Pain of Others*. New York: Farrar, Straus and Giroux, 2003.
———. "Talk of the Town." *The New Yorker*, September 22, 2001, available at http://www.newyorker.com/archive/2001/09/24/010924ta_talk_wtc. Accessed 06/06/2013.
Spiegelman, Art. *In the Shadow of No Towers*. London: Pantheon, 2004.
———. *Maus: A Survivors Tale: And Here My Troubles Began*. New York: Pantheon, 1992.
———. *Maus: A Survivors Tale: My Father Bleeds History*. New York: Pantheon, 1986.
Spigel, Lynn. "Entertainment Wars: Television Culture After 9/11." *American Quarterly* 56.2 (June 2004): 235-268.
Stamelman, Richard. "Between Memory and History." *Trauma at Home: After 9/11*, edited by Judith Greenberg, 11-20. Lincoln: University of Nebraska Press, 2003.
Stone, Oliver. "Interviewed by Ali Jaafar: 'I'm Not a Political Filmmaker Goddamit!'" *Sight and Sound* online, available at http://www.bfi.org.uk/sightandsound/feature/49325/ (accessed 05/09/01).
Strong, Benjamin. "Last Night." *Village Voice*, January 26, 2006, available at: http://www.villagevoice.com/2006-01-24/books/last-night/ (accessed 05/09/01).
Szeman, Imre. "Who's Afraid of National Allegory? Jameson, Literary Criticism and Globalization." *South Atlantic Quarterly* 100.3 (Summer 2001): 804-827.
Taylor, Helen. "After the Deluge: The Post-Katrina Cultural Revival of New Orleans." *Journal of American Studies* 44.3 (2010): 483-501.

Bibliography

Thomas, Cal. "Review of *World Trade Center*." Townhallwww, available at http://townhall.com/columnists/CalThoas/2006/07/20/world_trade_center_is_a_world_class_movie (accessed 05/09/01).
Thurschwell, Adam. "Writing and Terror: Don DeLillo on the Task of Literature After 9/11." *Law and Literature* 19.2 (Spring 2007): 277–302.
Tsoilkas, Christos. "11'09'01—September 11: The Rest Is Silence." *Senses of Cinema* 24 (January 2003), available at http://archive.sensesofcinema.com/contents/03/24/sept_11.html (accessed 05/09/01).
Updike, John. Contribution to "Talk of the Town" section in *The New Yorker*, September 24, 2001, available at http://www.newyorker.com/archive/2001/09/24/010924ta_talk_wtc (accessed 05/09/01).
———. "Mixed Messages." *The New Yorker*, March 14, 2005, available at http://www.newyorker.com/archive/2005/03/14/050314crbo_books1 (accessed 05/09/01).
———. *Terrorist*. London: Penguin, 2006.
Various Authors. *911 Commission Report*. London: W.W. Norton, 2003. Available at http://www.9-11commission.gov/ (accessed 05/09/01).
Various Authors, United States Department of State. "National Security Strategy September 2002." Available at http://www.state.gov/documents/organization/63562.pdf.
Versluys, Kristiaan. "Art Spiegelman's *In the Shadow of No Towers*: 9/11 and the Representation of Trauma." *Modern Fiction Studies* 52.4 (Winter 2006): 980–1003.
———. "9/11 as a European Event: The Novels." *European Review* (February 2007): 65–79.
———. *Out of the Blue*. New York: Columbia University Press, 2009.
Virilio, Paul. *Ground Zero*. New York: Verso, 2002.
Waldman, Amy. *The Submission*. London: Windmill, 2011.
Wall, Irwin M. "The French American War Over Iraq." *Brown Journal of World Affairs* X.2 (2004).
Whitehead, Anne. *Trauma Fiction*. Edinburgh: Edinburgh University Press, 2004.
Wood, James. "Beyond a Boundary." *The New Yorker*, May 26, 2008, available at http://www.newyorker.com/arts/critics/books/2008/05/26/080526crbo_books_wood (accessed 05/09/01).
———. "Tell Me How Does It Feel?" *The Guardian*, available at http://www.guardian.co.uk/books/2001/oct/06/fiction (accessed 05/09/01).
Wyatt, Edward. "Literary Novelists Address 9/11, Finally." *The New York Times*, March 7, 2005, available at http://www.nytimes.com/2005/03/07/books/07novel.html?_r=1&scp=2&sq=9%2F11+novelists&st=nyt (accessed 05/09/01).
Yaqin, Amina. "Mohsin Hamid in Conversation." *Wasafiri* 23 (June 2008): 44–49.
———, and Peter Morey. *Framing Muslims: Stereotyping and Representation After 9/11*. New Haven: Harvard University Press, 2011.
Young, Alison. "Documenting September 11: Trauma and the (Im)possibility of Sincerity." In *The Rhetoric of Sincerity*, edited by Ernst Van Alphen, Miede Bal, and Carel Smith, 231–246. Stanford: Stanford University Press, 2009.
Žižek, Slavoj. *Welcome to the Desert of the Real*. New York: Verso, 2002.

Index

Al-Qaeda 3, 32, 38, 132
allegory 15, 103–107, 113–114, 116–138
American Beauty 47
Amis, Martin 99

Baer, Ulrich 7, 70, 163
Beigbeder, Frédéric: *Windows on the World* 7, 14, 41–56, 67–6
Bin Laden, Osama 32, 130
Bush, George 9, 10, 24, 25, 28–34, 51, 59, 68, 73, 85, 92, 96, 102–103, 106–107, 113, 116, 136, 145, 167, 184, 191–193

capitalism 20
Christianity 28, 99, 103–109, 150, 157
Clash of Civilizations 16, 54, 96–99, 170, 178
Cold War 72, 132, 142

DeLillo, Don: *Falling Man*, 7, 12, 14, 69–71, 74–83, 90–91, 115, 139, 172; "In the Ruins of the Future" 6–7, 47–48; *Mao II* 42–43, 163
Dresden 33, 42, 61, 63–65
Drone Program 3–4

Egan, Jennifer: *A Visit from the Goon Squad* 192–193
Eggers, Dave: *Zeitoun* 14, 107, 114, 169
The Emperor's Children 14, 69, 83–92, 115, 139
Extremely Loud and Incredibly Close 8, 41–46, 56–6, 93, 139

Falling Man 7, 12, 14, 69–71, 74–83, 90–91, 115, 139, 172
Fanon, Frantz: *The Wretched of the Earth* 53

globalization 50–54
The Good Life 7, 12, 14, 69–76, 78–83, 90–91, 115, 139
Greengrass, Paul: *United 93* 6, 47, 93, 96–99
Ground Zero 30, 34
Guantanamo Bay 108, 110

Hamid, Mohsin: *The Reluctant Fundamentalist* 14, 114–127, 135–139, 154, 174
Hiroshima 33, 61, 64–65
Homeland 3–6, 188, 190
Huntington, Samuel P. 14, 97–99
Hurricane Katrina 13–15, 93, 107–14

In the Shadow of No Towers 8, 14, 17–39
Islam 54–56, 96–99, 115, 125, 127, 138, 150–151, 157, 165–190

James, C.L.R. 151, 154
Johnson, Chalmers 53, 91

Kalfus, Ken: *A Disorder Peculiar to the Country* 12, 93, 148, 154

Lee, Spike 112; *Do the Right Thing* 131; *25th Hour* 6, 31, 127–137

Marquesee, Mike 151
masculinity 54–56, 72, 100–103, 134–135
McCarthy, Cormac: *The Road* 14, 92–96, 110–115
McEwan, Ian: *Saturday* 92, 95
McInerney, Jay: *The Good Life* 7, 12, 14, 69–76, 78–83, 90–91, 115, 139
media 30, 57
Messud, Claire 12, 14, 69, 83–92, 115, 139
meta-fiction 15, 40–42, 139–164, 185–186

Index

Moore, Michael: *Fahrenheit 9/11* 25, 28–31

National Security Strategy 2002 167
Netherland 15, 139–164
9/11 Commission Report 59

110 Stories 7, 70, 163
O'Neil, Joseph: *Netherland* 15, 139–164
Otherness 139, 148–155

Park 51 Islamic Community Centre 165
"Portraits of Grief" 6, 21
postmodernism 40–42, 45–46, 63

racism 20, 31, 107–110, 118, 121–132, 138, 165–187
realism 48–50, 159–162
The Reluctant Fundamentalist 14, 114–127, 135–139, 154, 174
The Road 14, 92–96, 110–115

Safran Foer, Jonathan: *Extremely Loud and Incredibly Close* 8, 41–46, 56–6, 93, 139
Said, Edward 97–99
Saturday 92, 95
Spiegelman, Art: *In the Shadow of No Towers* 14, 17–39, 41; *Maus* 19, 20, 32
Stone, Oliver 6, 29; *World Trade Center* 6, 29, 95, 99–100
The Submission 8, 14, 16, 114, 165–187

Terrorist 54, 92, 95, 172
transnationalism 41, 52, 61
trauma 10, 11, 13, 14, 17–23, 26–27, 36, 38, 43, 57–58, 74, 76–81, 83, 86–87, 94, 100, 112, 119–12, 143, 145, 156–158, 166, 183; PTSD 17, 20, 22, 23, 143
25th Hour 6, 31

United 93 6, 47, 93, 96–99
Updike, John 7: *Terrorist* 54, 92, 95, 172

A Visit from the Goon Squad 192–193

Waldman, Amy: *The Submission* 8, 14, 16, 114, 165–187
War in Afghanistan 33
War in Iraq 33, 52–53, 145–146, 163
War on Terror 10, 11, 28–31, 33, 34, 108–114, 121–124, 166–168
The West Wing 188–191
Windows on the World 7, 14, 41–56, 67–6
World Trade Center 6, 29, 95, 99–100
World War II: Dresden 33, 42, 44; Hiroshima 33, 44, 64–65; Holocaust 20–22, 24, 28–29, 33; nostalgia 10–11, 72, 75, 123; Pearl Harbor 64; trauma 23
The Wretched of the Earth 53

Zeitoun 14, 107, 114, 169

www.ingramcontent.com/pod-product-compliance
Lightning Source LLC
Chambersburg PA
CBHW032057300426
44116CB00007B/778